UNITED STATES POLICY TOWARD EGYPT
1830–1914

UNITED STATES POLICY
TOWARD EGYPT
1830-1914

L. C. Wright

EXPOSITION PRESS INC.

An Exposition-University Book

EXPOSITION PRESS · NEW YORK

E X P O S I T I O N   P R E S S   I N C.

50 Jericho Turnpike   Jericho, New York 11753

FIRST EDITION

LIBRARY OF CONGRESS CATALOGUE CARD NUMBER: 78–83503

EP 46945

TO MY MOTHER

Preface

The emergence of the United States into a position of world leadership and responsibility in the post–World War II era has brought with it increased interest in Egypt and in the Suez Canal. It would be difficult to overestimate the importance of the Nile Valley and the Canal in United States strategic planning for the whole of the Middle East. The Department of State, the Defense Department and other responsible agencies in Washington, therefore, must make the most careful analysis and study of Egyptian affairs. But our present-day American policy regarding Egypt is not made in a vacuum; one of the factors conditioning it is the background of the previous relationship between the two countries.

The primary source material for this book has been the largely unexplored United States Department of State files to be found in the National Archives, Washington, D.C. A careful examination was made, not only of the despatches from and instructions to the United States consuls at Alexandria and Cairo but also of the correspondence of American diplomatic representatives in Turkey, England and France, as affecting the Egyptian scene. Reports of the American missionaries and Egyptologists, and a variety of secondary materials, were likewise consulted. Since, however, the orientation of this work is United States policy toward Egypt, no attempt was made to use or analyze Egyptian or Turkish sources.

Chapter I sketches in general terms the situation in Egypt at the time of the official arrival of the United States in 1830. Egypt's relations with the Ottoman Sultan, the background of Anglo-French rivalry over Egypt and the significance of the capitulatory regime are discussed briefly. Succeeding chapters deal with United States interests in Egypt. The British occupation of 1882 provides the dividing line between the two main sections of this book. In order to give a complete and rounded picture of American policy in Egypt, political, economic and cultural matters are considered separately in each section. Because none of these three factors operated independently in practice, of course, an attempt has been made to suggest points of interaction; nevertheless, the primary emphasis has been placed upon the political side. The work of the American missionaries in Egypt, for instance, undoubtedly has intrinsic value, but it is the political implications of their activities that are stressed here.

Although certain isolated aspects of pre–World War I United States–Egyptian relations have been carefully treated, there exists no work, at least in a Western language, in which the exact nature and extent of all facets of American interests in Egypt are considered. And in point of fact there was a much wider range of American activity than one might normally have supposed. Parenthetically, it may be added that the pattern of United States conduct in Egypt was being duplicated (with some local differences) in other parts of the Near East in this period. But the crucial question raised by this study is why the United States did not pursue an even more active role in Egypt particularly in view of the frequent invitations from the Egyptian and Turkish governments to do so. This question is examined in the Conclusion.

This study is based substantially on my Ph.D. dissertation submitted to and approved by Columbia University, New York City, in 1953. The material has been revised in order to incorporate subsequent research by myself and other scholars in the field down through the spring of 1967. My basic conclusions, however, have not been fundamentally altered.

L. C. W.

Acknowledgments

Like every other worker in the scholarly vineyards, I am deeply indebted to a number of people for kind and valuable assistance. I wish to thank particularly Professor J. C. Hurewitz of Columbia University, who directed the doctoral dissertation upon which this work is based. He gave of himself patiently and unstintingly in my behalf, and his wise counsel and great knowledge have saved me from many grievous errors. He has not, however, been exposed to the errors I may have committed in this revision.

Dr. E. Taylor Parks, Chief, Research Guidance and Review Division, Department of State, and the late Dr. Carl L. Lokke, formerly Chief, Foreign Affairs Section, National Archives, Washington, and their staffs, were exceedingly helpful and smoothed the path of my research by many remembered acts of kindness and courtesy.

I wish also to thank Mrs. Marie Ann Seabury for valuable advice and editorial assistance in connection with the original draft of this study. My wife, Dorothea, has performed the same most helpful service with the present draft. Miss Susan Griswold has earned my gratitude for her cheerful and efficient typing of the final version.

Finally, I wish to express my appreciation to the Faculty Research Council of the University of North Carolina at Greensboro for grants that have in part made this publication possible.

As is only proper, I fully absolve all the above-named persons from any blame accruing from the errors and shortcomings of this book.

1967   L. C. WRIGHT

Abbreviations

Ann. Repts., Am. Bib. Soc. American Bible Society, Annual Reports

Ann. Repts., U.P. Ch. Board of Foreign Missions, United Presbyterian Church of North America, Annual Reports

B.P. Barbary Powers

B.F.S.P. British and Foreign State Papers

C.D. United States, Department of State, Consular Despatches

C.I. United States, Department of State, Consular Instructions

Cmd. Great Britain, Command Paper

Comm. Rels. United States, Department of Commerce, Commercial Relations of the United States with Foreign Countries

Con. Regs. United States, Department of State, Consular Regulations

D.C.T.R. United States, Department of Commerce and Labor, Daily Consular and Trade Reports

D.D. United States, Department of State, Diplomatic Despatches

D.F. United States, Department of State, Decimal Files

D.I. United States, Department of State, Diplomatic Instructions

Dip. Diplomatic

Eg. Egypt

Ex. Agr. Ser. United States, Department of State, Executive Agreement Series

For. Comm. and Navig. United States, Department of Commerce, Foreign Commerce and Navigation of the United States

For. Rels. United States, Department of State, Papers Relating to the Foreign Relations of the United States

G.B., A.P. Great Britain, Accounts and Papers

H. House of Representatives

Ltrs. from Adm. Nicholson United States, Navy Department, European Squadron, Letters from Admiral J. W. A. Nicholson

M.C.R. United States, Department of Commerce and Labor, Monthly Consular Reports

M.C.T.R. United States, Department of Commerce and Labor, Monthly Consular and Trade Reports

N.F. United States, Department of State, Numerical File

Ops. At. Gen.   Opinions of the United States Attorney General
S.   Senate
Spec. Con. Repts.   United States, Department of State, Special Consular Reports
U.S.A.C.G.   United States (Diplomatic) Agents and Consul-General
U.S.C.G.   United States Consul-General
U.S.V.C.G.   United States Vice Consul-General

Contents

PART TWO

THE BRITISH OCCUPATION PERIOD: 1882–1914

Tables

PART ONE

The United States and the Powers in Egypt, 1830—82

PART ONE

The United States and the Powers in Egypt, 1830–82

CHAPTER I

The International Position of Egypt

THE IMPORTANCE OF EGYPT

The ribbon-like oasis that is habitable Egypt has been significant since the dawn of history. A warm climate and the annual blessing of the Nile flood, felicitously combined, made this area one of the cradles of civilization. Today, although deficient in coal, iron, timber and other vital resources, Egypt still possesses in her rich soil an economic asset of tremendous value. Under the customary system of rotation, three crops, including cotton, can be produced every two years. Despite the antiquated agricultural methods of the *fallahin,* or peasants, some 8 million *feddans*[1] were under cultivation in 1937, supporting some 16 million people in a country where the population density is the highest in the world and furnishing crops, such as cotton, maize and wheat, worth about $180 million, primarily for export.[2] The attractiveness of Egypt as a potential market for the industrialized nations of the West should be apparent. But Egypt has not been content to remain solely an agricultural nation. In the post–World War II era especially, she has become one of the leaders in the Middle East in developing her own industries.

Egypt's strategic role is further enhanced by her geographic location. Since Pharaonic days she has been a bridge between Asia and Africa over which conquerors, commerce and culture have passed. Of even greater contemporary significance is

---

[1] A *feddan* is approximately an acre.

[2] C. P. Issawi, *Egypt: An Economic and Social Analysis* (London, 1947), pp. 43-81.

Egypt's position astride the vital Suez route to India. In limited use for centuries, this artery, especially since the opening of the Suez Canal in 1869, has been of grave concern and interest to military strategists and to businessmen in all parts of the world.

No less notable among Egypt's assets is her long-standing prestige and influence as a fountainhead of religions, cultural ideas and political ideas in the Middle East. The entire Muslim world respects Cairo's ancient Al Azhar as the most important training and study center in Islamic theology and law. The Egyptian press, led by *Al-Ahram,* "the *Times*" of Egypt, is read throughout the Arab world, where it has been instrumental in molding public opinion. The production of Arabic movies, an increasingly popular medium in the Middle East, is also centered in Egypt. The headquarters of the Arab League—a new political force in the Near East—is in Cairo, and its first two secretaries-general have been Egyptians.

Warlords from Darius to Hitler, therefore, have been attracted to Egypt. The rivalry of Great Britain and France in the nineteenth and twentieth centuries for control of the Suez Canal and the Nile Valley played a crucial part in the background of United States–Egyptian relations.

ANGLO-FRENCH RIVALRY IN EGYPT

British and French rivalry in Egypt, as in other parts of the Ottoman Empire, originated with commercial competition. English merchants established themselves in the Near East—but outside Egypt—in the face of strong opposition from the French and also from Spanish and Venetians; with the development of the all-sea route via the Cape of Good Hope, however, their primary energies were concentrated on the more exciting prospect of direct trade with India. French traders, meanwhile, gained the ascendancy in the Near East. Not until the mid-eighteenth century did England redirect attention to Egypt, British merchants finding incentive at this time in the quicker communications route via the Red Sea and Suez. In the last third of the eighteenth century the British and French conducted sporadic and eventually ineffectual negotiations with the Mamluk Beys of Egypt to secure exclusive rights to use the "overland" Suez route.[3]

As early as the 1760's French political writers began to suggest that in the event of the collapse of the Ottoman Empire, France might profitably occupy Egypt. This move, they argued, not only would be productive of commercial advantage but would provide an excellent base from which the British in India might be attacked. This theory was kept alive in French thought; indeed, it formed the basis of Napoleon's ill-fated expedition to Egypt in 1798. The English, though able to deal decisively with the French threat, found it impossible thereafter to adopt a complacent attitude toward Egyptian affairs. Bonaparte's Near Eastern adventures therefore introduced a new factor into Anglo-French rivalry. No longer was the competition to be confined to commerce. Egypt itself became an object of contention because of political and strategic considerations involving the integrity of the Ottoman Empire and the defense of India.[4]

Events now led directly to the British occupation of Egypt in 1882. But this is to anticipate. More immediate problems for Egypt, and for the British and French, followed the rise to power in Egypt of that extraordinary personage, Mehmed 'Ali.

MEHMED 'ALI AND THE SETTLEMENT OF 1841

Mehmed 'Ali, a Turkish subject from Kavalla in Macedonia, had participated in the Anglo-Turkish campaign of 1799–1801 against Napoleon in Egypt, as commander of a contingent of Albanian troops. When the French were finally defeated and driven out in 1801, Egypt, a province of the Turkish Empire since 1517, was restored to the Sultan. Mehmed 'Ali stayed on, and by skillfully playing off competing factions, was soon able to take over power from the Turkish governor. He then secured

---

[3] See H. L. Hoskins, *British Routes to India* (Phila., 1928), chaps. i, ii.

[4] *Ibid.*, chap. iii; see also J. A. R. Marriott, *The Eastern Question* (3rd ed.; London, 1924), pp. 148-59.

from the Sultan a reluctant confirmation of his status as Viceroy of Egypt. In the years immediately following, the new Viceroy consolidated his position internally by liquidating the decadent Mamluk oligarchy, and assisted by French advisers, began to build his armed power.[5]

The ambitious Egyptian Pasha was now ready for greater adventures. Rebuffed in his initial peaceful efforts to secure independence, he concealed his disappointment and became the Sultan's staunchest lieutenant. At the Sultan's behest, in 1818, for example, the Wahhabi "Puritans" of Arabia were finally crushed by Mehmed 'Ali's son, Ibrahim. The Sudan was then subdued. But intervention in the Greek War of Independence in 1823 on behalf of the Sultan brought a halt to the Pasha's successes. Not only was his fleet decimated at Navarino, and Ibrahim's army ignominiously forced to evacuate the Morea, but the Sultan's promise of the four Syrian provinces remained unfulfilled. Mehmed 'Ali had had his first encounter with Britain, France and Russia, all of whom for diverse reasons had actively supported the Greek cause.

But Mehmed 'Ali, driven by insatiable ambition and by contempt for the Ottoman military machine, was determined to secure at least his promised Syrian provinces. The French gave him secret aid and encouragement in this endeavor. However, the Pasha's failure to judge accurately the temper of the other European Powers was to lead him to his eventual destruction. In particular the Viceroy underestimated the determination of the British to preserve the Ottoman Empire, rotten as it might be, and to prevent the establishment of an "independent Egypt" under French tutelage. Subsequent events may be summarized as follows: In 1831 the Egyptian Army, led by the gifted Ibrahim, moved into Syria and advanced northward in a series of decisive

---

[5] H. H. Dodwell, *The Founder of Modern Egypt: A Study of Muhammad 'Ali* (Cambridge, Eng., 1931), pp. 1-38; S. Ghorbal, *The Beginnings of the Egyptian Question and the Rise of Mehmed Ali* (London, 1928), *passim*; H. A. B. Rivlin, *The Agricultural Policy of Muhammad 'Ali in Egypt* (Cambridge, Mass., 1961), chap. i; Marriott, *op. cit.*, chap. ix.

victories. The Turkish opposition of 1832 was easily smashed. By December of 1832, Ibrahim was in Anatolia, unopposed and within striking distance of Constantinople itself. At this juncture the Russians, alone of the European Powers, intervened and saved the Ottoman capital, but at a price extracted in the famous secret clause of the Treaty of Hunkyar Iskelesi of 1833. A renewal of hostilities between the Egyptians and the Turks in June, 1839, shattered an uneasy peace. Again, Ibrahim routed the Sultan's army in Syria. The deflection of the Turkish fleet in July further strengthened Mehmed 'Ali's position, and the French, while never in formal alliance, were openly sympathetic to his cause. Thoroughly alarmed, Lord Palmerston took the lead in negotiating an agreement for "the pacification of the Levant," dated July 15, 1840, and signed by Great Britain, Russia, Prussia and Austria. The four European Powers quickly forced Mehmed 'Ali to capitulate, and the "Egyptian Question" was resolved as a part of the over-all Near Eastern settlement of 1841, with France finally participating. Arabia, Syria and Crete were returned to Turkey. Mehmed 'Ali's governorship was limited to Egypt, which was to remain a province of the Ottoman Empire. Under pressure from the Powers the Sultan had issued a *firman,* or decree, on June 1, 1841, making Mehmed 'Ali hereditary pasha or governor of Egypt, the title to pass by seniority to his direct male descendants. His administrative authority was subject, however, to certain limitations. The *firman* of June 1 fixed a yearly tribute. The size of the Egyptian Army was restricted. The Pasha could make no treaties and all agreements, existing or to be concluded, between the Porte and friendly countries were to apply in Egypt.[6]

Subject to the above restrictions, Mehmed 'Ali was permitted considerable autonomy. Furthermore, his successors, by various means such as bribery and increase of tribute, were able to

---

[6] For text of the *firman* of June 1, 1841, in English, see *For. Rels.* (1879), pp. 1031-32; also J. C. Hurewitz (ed.), *Documents of Near East Diplomatic History* (New York, 1950), pp. 51-53; on this topic generally see Dodwell, *op. cit.,* chaps. ii-vi.

secure *firmans* enlarging the scope of their power. But until
World War I, Egypt remained nominally attached to the Ottoman Sultan.[7]

The authority of the rulers of Egypt was further circum-
scribed by the capitulations.

THE CAPITULATORY REGIME

It is impossible adequately to understand the relationship
between the Western Powers and the Turkish Empire without
first knowing something about the complicated superstructure
upon which it all rested—the system of capitulations that Nasim
Sousa has explained as follows:

> The first time that the term officially used to denote an
> agreement dates back to 1275 when the Greek Emperor issued
> a declaration concerning the Genoese referring to the articles
> therein as "capitula," and it is possible that shortly thereafter
> the term "capitulation" came to be used in this sense. The term
> is thus derived from the Medieval Latin, and signifies a treaty
> the terms of which are specified under articles (capitula) or
> minor heads of several stipulations. The term "capitulation,"
> therefore, may be explained as designating a treaty by the terms
> of which foreigners resident in Turkey are entitled to special
> immunities and rights and are more or less subject to the laws
> of their respective countries.[8]

However ancient its origin, the idea of the capitulation with
its basis of extraterritoriality appears to have been well established in the Near East prior to the fall of Byzantine Constantinople to the Turks in 1453. This system the Turks took over

---

[7] Marriott, *op cit.*

[8] N. Sousa, *The Capitulatory Régime in Turkey* (Baltimore, 1933), pp.
2-3; Sousa's book is the latest and probably the most satisfactory in English;
see also P. M. Brown, *Foreigners in Turkey* (Princeton, 1914); G B.
Ravndal, *The Origins of the Capitulations and the Consular Institution*, 67th
Cong., 1st Sess., S. Docs., Vol. 9, No. 34; E. A. Van Dyck, *Capitulations of
the Ottoman Empire,* in two parts: 46th Cong., Special Sess., S. Ex. Docs.,
Vol. 3, No. 3;and 47th Cong., 1st Sess., S. Ex. Docs., Vol. 4, No. 87.

and extended. It is generally agreed that the capitulations issued by the Turkish Sultan to the French in 1535, the first in the form of a treaty of amity and commerce, was the model from which the system of Western privilege in the Turkish Empire was later built. The European nations encouraged the custom of renewing these treaties with each succeeding Sultan, since this permitted the Powers to enlarge the scope of their prerogatives. Soon, by means of the most-favored-nation clause,[9] and through the operation of custom and usage, there was developed a substantial body of rights and privileges collectively referred to as the capitulatory regime.

The benefits conferred upon the Franks (Europeans) by the capitulatory system included personal privileges, such as freedom to trade, freedom of worship and inviolability of domicile; economic privileges, such as a fixed tariff and exemption from direct taxes; judicial privileges, such as the right, in general, of foreigners to be tried in their own consular courts; and additional privileges acquired by custom and usage, such as the right to operate foreign post offices within the Turkish Empire, and the right to appoint Ottoman subjects as "protégés," thus giving them the benefits of the capitulations.

Egypt, as an integral part of the Turkish Empire, was subject to the capitulatory regime. Indeed, according to Hinckley, "the privileges of extraterritoriality in Egypt have been considerably greater than elsewhere in the empire. . . ."[10] In Turkey there had been considerable modification of the original privileges.[11] This was not true in Egypt; there the basic capitulations had been greatly enlarged by customs originating from the time of

---

[9] This was a device in treaties dating from the Middle Ages by which one nation or state received rights granted, or to be granted, to other nations or states. See Arthur Nussbaum, *A Concise History of the Law of Nations* (New York, 1947), pp. 30-31.

[10] F. E. Hinckley, *American Consular Jurisdiction in the Orient* (Washington, 1906), p. 27.

[11] For instance, the Porte successfully imposed certain taxes and exercised jurisdiction in cases where Franks and Ottoman subjects were involved.

Mehmed 'Ali. Foreigners in that country, as a consequence, paid no taxes at all, and in general enjoyed complete immunity from local law. It should be borne in mind that no changes could be made in the capitulations without the consent of all the participating Western Powers. In Egypt such permission was rarely, if ever, granted until the latter part of the nineteenth century. The agreement of the Powers that permitted the establishment of the Mixed Courts of Egypt in 1876 will be discussed in a later chapter.[12]

---

[12] See J. H. Scott, *The Law Affecting Foreigners in Egypt* (Edinburgh, 1907), pp. 136-37, 196-99 and *passim; C. D., Eg.,* 3, desp. no. 21 from Charles Hale, U.S.A.C.G., Alexandria, Mar. 14, 1865; *ibid.,* 5, desp. no. 161, June 14, 1869.

CHAPTER II

First Steps in Egypt

THE TURKISH TREATY OF 1830

The American Continental Congress considered the desirability of negotiating a commercial treaty with the Ottoman Empire as early as 1774. But not until 1785 did American traders reach Turkey and inaugurate commercial relations on a small scale, primarily through the port of Smyrna (present-day Izmir).[1]

American merchants trading in Turkey were at a considerable disadvantage because of the absence of any treaty relations with the Ottoman Empire. True, they were allowed to share the privileges of the Levant Company, holders of a monopoly of English trade in the Near East (1581–1825), but only after paying the tariff applicable to the English plus a "protection" fee to the British consul. David Offley, however, an American merchant who arrived in Smyrna, in 1811, soon put an end to this lucrative British arrangement. After a dispute in which the English unsuccessfully tried to impose a double duty on United States goods, Offley finally was able to obtain permission from the Ottoman Government for American merchants to use the French tariff. And in 1818 when the French commercial agreement expired, he secured the right for Americans to continue trading on the basis of the old French tariff. The United States was the only nation not in treaty arrangement with the Sultan

---

[1] L. J. Gordon, *American Relations with Turkey* (Philadelphia, 1932), pp. 8, 41-44. Gordon's book, while not a definitive treatment, is the best general work on U.S.-Turkish relations for the period 1830–1930.

that was so favored. American consuls had been appointed for Smyrna in 1802 and again in 1808, but neither had been allowed to serve. In 1824, Offley, who had been acting semi-officially as consular agent at Smyrna since 1811, was named United States consul for that port and permitted by the Sultan to exercise his office.[2]

After the establishment of the American republic the Department of State despatched several secret agents to Turkey to explore the possibility of concluding a commercial treaty. Luther Bradish, one of these agents, reported in 1820 that United States trade, totaling $1.5 million annually, was suffering from the lack of government protection. Ottoman officials, Bradish advised, encouraged the prospect of an agreement with the United States but cautioned secrecy in the negotiations in view of anticipated opposition from the British:

> I am explicitly informed by the Porte itself that Great Britain under the idea that the United States contemplate negotiations with the Porte, has within a few days past presented to the latter a formal and solemn protest against such negotiations, in which she threatened in case the Porte should conclude a treaty with the United States to break off her present relations and declare war against the Porte.[3]

He added that the same reaction, though less severe, could be expected from Austria, France and Holland.[4] Bradish's apprehensions appear in hindsight to have been exaggerated, yet there is no doubt that the diplomatic representatives of the European Powers accredited to the Sublime Porte resented the prospect of American commercial competition, and intrigued against it.

Impressed by the favorable reports of its agents, and by con-

---

[2] *D. D., Turk.*, I, Pt. I, unnum. desp. from D. Offley, Smyrna, Jan. 24, 1824; Gordon, *op. cit.*

[3] *D. I., Turk.*, I (this volume contains both despatches and instructions), unnum. desp. from Luther Bradish, Constantinople, Dec. 20, 1820; the terms "Porte" and "Sublime Porte" as used in this book refer to the Turkish Govt.

[4] *Ibid.*

tinued encouragement from various Ottoman officials, the United States Government decided to initiate formal discussions for a commercial treaty with the Turkish Government. Unsuccessful efforts were made in 1825 and again in 1828. Finally, on September 12, 1829, a third attempt was undertaken with the appointment of Commodore James Biddle, David Offley and Charles Rhind as commissioners. Their endeavors were successful, Rhind alone signing for the United States on May 7, 1830.[5]

There is some evidence to show that the prospect of trade with Egypt at least partly figured in the conclusion of this treaty with the Ottoman Empire. In 1832, Representative H. A. S. Dearbon (Mass.), in a House debate on appropriations for the expenses of the mission to Turkey, said:

. . . The whole trade of the Greeks, before their late revolution, was in carrying the products of the Black Sea to Italy, France and Egypt. Here a market would be opened for all the manufactured articles of our own soil. Hence a triple and even quadruple voyage might be made from our own country to Constantinople; thence into the Black Sea, and thence to different ports in the Mediterranean; the whole trade of Egypt and Palestine would, in like manner, be free to our vessels, and a circuitous commerce would be carried on of immense advantage to the United States. It was indeed surprising that no greater amount of trade had before this time been carried on between Egypt and the United States. A most advantageous commerce had long been enjoyed by the French between the ports of Marseilles and Alexandria. From this we had been almost entirely foreclosed, because we were not known. Our Government had had no intercourse with theirs, and our merchants, in consequence of this state of things, had participated less in the new channels which were opening to the enterprise of commercial nations in that part of the world than those of any other flag. . . .[6]

By the terms of the Treaty of 1830, the United States ac-

[5] *Ibid.*, I, unnum. inst. to Biddle, Offley and Rhind, Sept. 12, 1829; Gordon, *op. cit.*, pp. 9-10; C. O. Paullin, *Diplomatic Negotiations of American Naval Officers, 1778-1883* (Baltimore, 1912), chap. v.

[6] Gales and Seaton, *Register of Debates in Congress*, 22nd Cong., 1st Sess., House, Mar. 16, 1832, Vol. 8 (2), p. 2190.

quired, in general, most-favored-nation treatment for her commerce throughout the Ottoman Empire, including Egypt; the right to establish consulates; access to the Black Sea; and participation in the benefits of the capitulatory regime.[7]

Capitulatory rights and privileges were conferred on the United States by Article IV of the treaty, the official American translation of which read as follows:

> If litigations and disputes should arise between Subjects of the Sublime Porte and Citizens of the United States, the parties shall not be heard, nor shall judgment be pronounced, unless the American Dragoman be present. Causes in which the sum may exceed 500 piastres, shall be submitted to the Sublime Porte, to be decided according to the laws of equity and justice. Citizens of the United States of America, quietly pursuing their Commerce, and not being charged or convicted of any crime or offence, shall not be molested; and even when they may have committed some offence, they shall not be arrested and put in prison by the Local Authorities, but they shall be tried by their Minister or Consul, and punished according to their offence; following in this respect, the usage observed towards other Franks.[8]

A storm of controversy, coming to a head first in 1868, raged over proper interpretation of this article. In 1868 the Department of State protested the arrest and trial of two United States citizens by the Turkish Government, alleging that the last sentence in the translation above gave the United States jurisdiction in all criminal cases, even those involving Ottoman subjects and American citizens. The Porte denied the American protests,

---

[7] For text in English see W. M. Malloy (ed.), *Treaties, Conventions, International Acts, Protocols and Agreements between the United States and Other Powers, 1776-1909* (Washington, 1910), II, 1318-20; see also Hurewitz, *op. cit.*, pp. 34-35. The Turkish treaty would seem to reflect the influence of 18th-century French radical thought on reform of foreign policy, that is, "no diplomacy other than the diplomacy of commerce" and freedom of trading opportunity for all nations. See F. Gilbert, "The 'New Diplomacy' of the Eighteenth Century," *World Politics*, X, No. 1 (Oct. 1951), 1-38.

[8] *Ibid.*

contending that the phrases "they shall not be arrested" and "they shall be tried by their Minister or Consul" were not to be found in the Turkish original of the 1830 Treaty, which, it was alleged, the United States had agreed to accept as binding.[9]

Another clash over Article IV occurred in Egypt in 1879. On July 17 of that year Stephen Mizram, a naturalized American citizen, shot and killed Dr. Alexander Dahan, a prominent lawyer and Turkish subject, following a quarrel on the streets of Alexandria. With Horace Maynard, American Minister to Turkey, presiding, Mizram was tried in the United States consular courts in Egypt and found guilty of murder. His sentence of death, however, was commuted to life imprisonment.[10] The Turkish Government protested the United States' assumption of jurisdiction in this case and refused to regard the Egyptian Government's failure to contest the trial as any sort of precedent.[11]

Since neither side would yield, the bitter argument over Article IV continued until 1930 when the new United States–Turkish Treaty of Ankara omitted the disputed article entirely. But by this time the matter had become academic; the whole capitulation system had been abandoned in the Turkish Republic by the European Powers under the Treaty of Lausanne (1923).

Soon after the successful negotiation of the Treaty of 1830 with Turkey the United States took steps domestically to implement American participation in the capitulatory regime. This was done by a series of Acts of Congress establishing and im-

------

[9] For a careful analysis of this problem, see D. H. Miller, *Treaties and other International Acts of the United States* (Washington, 1933), III, 541-98; see also J. B. Moore, *A Digest of International Law* (Washington, 1906), II, 668-722; Hinckley, *op. cit.*, pp. 23-30; Gordon, *op. cit.*, pp. 190-200.

[10] *C.D., Eg.*, 16, desp. no. 325 from N. D. Comanos, U.S.V.C.G., Cairo, July 30, 1879; *D. D., Turk.*, 36, desp. no. 397 from H. Maynard, U.S. Min. to Turkey, Cairo, June 21, 1880; *D. I., Turk.*, 3, tel. to G. H. Heap, Chargé, Constantinople, Sept. 7, 1880; see also New York *Times*, Aug. 12, 1879, and July 25 and Sept. 10, 1880.

[11] *Notes from Turk. Leg.*, 4, note no. 3874 from Aristarchi Bey, Turk. Min., Washington, D.C., Dec. 17, 1881; *D. D., Turk.*, 37, desp. no. 36 from G. H. Heap, Constantinople, July 26, 1881.

proving a system of consular courts throughout the Ottoman Empire. The earliest of these statutes (August 11, 1848) was entitled "An Act to Carry into Effect certain Provisions in the Treaties between the United States and China and the Ottoman Porte, giving certain judicial powers to Minister and Consuls of the United States in those Countries." For some curious reason this Act created a system of consular courts for China and then, almost as an afterthought, provided in section 22 that "the provisions of this Act, so far as the same relates to crimes committed by citizens of the United States, shall be extended to Turkey, under the treaty with the Sublime Porte of May seventh, eighteen hundred and thirty. . . ."[12]

Not until 1858 did the American Minister to Turkey call to the attention of the Department of State a fact previously overlooked: although the United States consular courts in the Turkish Empire exercised jurisdiction both in civil and in criminal cases, authority to do so was provided by the Act of 1848 only in the case of criminal actions. The Secretary of State asked for an opinion of the United States Attorney General on this point and was advised on March 16, 1859, that it was "clear that U.S. Consuls in Turkey have jurisdiction only in criminal cases."[13] This official pronouncement resulted in a natural embarrassment to American merchants currently doing business with the Ottoman Empire. But the situation was soon alleviated by passage of the Act of Congress of June 22, 1860, which amplified and expanded the Act of 1848. This time care was taken to extend consular jurisdiction in the Ottoman Empire to cover civil as well as criminal cases. Further, in accordance with Article 5 of the Act of 1860, the American Minister at Constantinople promulgated on December 18, 1862, rules and regulations for the consular courts in the Turkish Empire.[14]

---

12 *U.S. Stats. at Large*, Vol. 9, pp. 276, 279 (1851).

13 *Ops. At. Gen.*, IX (1869), 296.

14 *U. S. Stats. at Large*, Vol. 12, pp. 72-79 (1863); *D. D., Turk.*, 17, desp. no. 47 from E. J. Morris, U.S. Min., Constantinople, Jan. 29, 1863; the rules and regulations of 1862 are set out in Hinckley, *op. cit.*, pp. 255-66; also in Brown, *op. cit.*, pp. 119-34, incl. amends. of June 14, 1880.

There was one final development relevant to the consular courts in this period. By Act of Congress of July 28, 1866, the provisions of the law of 1860 were expressly extended to Egypt, and the consul-general at Alexandria was given the power of a consul or consul-general of a country where there is no minister.[15] Congressional debates on this extension of 1866 indicate that the act was passed solely to extend certain powers to the consul-general in Egypt that he had not enjoyed under the law of 1860.[16]

THE CONSULAR AGENCY IN EGYPT

The establishment of normal diplomatic and consular relations paralleled the development of the consular court system in the Ottoman Empire. On April 15, 1831, Commodore David Porter was appointed as "Chargé d'Affaires of the United States near the Government of the Sublime Porte." After exchanging ratifications of the new treaty, Porter was directed by the Department of State to secure a tariff based on the most-favored-nation clause and to work for an extension of commerce and for the protection of American citizens. Secretary of State Van Buren made explicit reference to Egypt in this instruction:

> Our actual treaty with Turkey gives us commercial advantages which we have not heretofore enjoyed and places them under the firm guarantee of its stipulations. Our vessels may now trade to the ports of Egypt and Asia Minor, to the Turkish islands of the Archipelago, and to the Ottoman ports of Europe and on the Asiatic shores of the Black Sea.[17]

The new American representative at Constantinople was authorized also to make provisional appointments of consular agents within the Ottoman Empire, with the caution that such

---

[15] *U. S. Stats. at Large*, Vol. 14, p. 322 (1868).

[16] *Cong. Globe*, 39th Cong., 1st Sess., Vol. 36(5), pp. 4128, 4258.

[17] *D. I., Turk.*, 1, inst. no. 2 to D. Porter, U.S. Chargé, Constantinople, Apr. 15, 1831.

appointees were not to receive any salary from the United States Government.

On January 12, 1832, Commodore Porter appointed John Gliddon, an English merchant resident at Alexandria, Egypt, as the first United States consular agent for that port. In accepting, Gliddon referred to his commission as "Consular Agent in the Dominions of the Bey of Egypt."[18]

Within several months after Gliddon's appointment, it will be recalled, Mehmed 'Ali, the Viceroy of Egypt, was engaged in his first war against the Turkish Sultan. This unsettled state of affairs, however, did not mar the reception of the new American consular agent in Egypt. He seems to have been warmly received, and the prospect of trade with the United States welcomed. Indeed, the Pasha's real complaint appears to have been that Gliddon was appointed by the American representative at Constantinople and not directly by Washington. For its part, the Sublime Porte refused to grant berats, or exequaturs, to American consular representatives in Egypt and Syria until peace was restored in 1833.[19] In the struggle that ensued between Mehmed 'Ali and the Sultan, the United States, in contrast to the European Powers, remained strictly neutral. Porter advised Gliddon to follow such a course in order that America should benefit were an independent government established in Egypt.[20] The Department of State itself gave no instruction on this point, and it is probable that although it was well informed on the course of events, this silence reflected the then almost complete absence of American political and economic interest in Egypt.

The new United States consular agent at Alexandria did not, however, enjoy the same good relations with his colleagues, the

---

[18] *D. D., Turk.*, 2, desp. no. 36 from Porter, Jan. 12, 1832; *ibid.*, desp. no. 44, Apr. 4, 1832, encl. desp. from Gliddon to Porter, Feb. 16, 1832.

[19] *Ibid.*, 2, desp. no. 46 from Porter, Apr. 9, 1832, encl. desp. from Gliddon to Porter, Mar. 14, 1832; *ibid.*, 4, desp. no. 235, Aug. 12, 1834, encl. desp. from Gliddon to Porter, July 4, 1834; *ibid.*, 3, desp. no. 120 from Porter, July 11, 1833.

[20] *Ibid.*, 2, desp. no 97 from Porter, Mar. 7, 1833, encl. inst. from Porter to Gliddon, Mar. 6, 1833.

British and French consuls-general, who apparently reflected a common disinclination to welcome a potential commercial rival in the area. They attempted to harass Gliddon on the theory that as a British citizen, he was subject to the English consul-general. But in the end firm opposition by Gliddon and support by Porter at Constantinople put an end to this annoyance.[21]

HODGSON'S MISSION TO EGYPT

In October, 1833, at a time when Mehmed 'Ali was at the peak of his spectacular military successes, having been stopped at the gates of Constantinople only by the intervention of Russia, the Department of State decided to send a confidential agent to explore fully the political and commercial situation in Egypt. William B. Hodgson, dragoman (interpreter) of the United States diplomatic service at Constantinople, was chosen for this mission. His basic instructions required him to ascertain the Pasha's power to make commercial treaties with foreign Powers and his disposition toward the United States; to report the status of foreign commercial agents in Egypt; and to determine the conditions of Egyptian trade and the best means of improving American commerce with that country.[22]

Hodgson arrived in Alexandria in August, 1834. In an interim despatch he furnished the Department with his interesting reaction to the state of Egyptian agriculture:

Egypt is a land of striking contrasts; the people, a soil fertile beyond all comparison, and agricultural wealth beyond measure; yet in no country are the *fellahs* or peasantry so wretched. They are miserably clothed, housed and fed. They cultivate the soil and the Pasha takes the fruit of their labor, leaving to the Arab, the least possible means of subsistence. This may be estimated at four cents per day. Egypt, with her 4,000,000 acres of arable

[21] *Ibid.*, 4, desp. no. 188 from Porter, Mar. 30, 1834, encl. corresp. between Porter and Gliddon, and Porter and the Fr. Amb. at Constantinople.

[22] *Special Missions, Insts.*, 1, inst. no. 1 to W. B. Hodgson, Oct. 10, 1833.

land, and 2,500,000 inhabitants, may be compared to a southern plantation at home. The Pasha is the lord, both of the land and the *fellah*. He is the sole great farmer and merchant; he collects the crops, transports them to Alexandria and there sells them to Frank merchants or ships them, on his own account, to Europe. This mal-administration does not probably affect the quantity of Egyptian produce offered to European commerce, which alone is of interest to the United States.[23]

It was not until his return to Washington in March, 1835, that Hodgson submitted his excellent and comprehensive report on political and economic conditions in Egypt to the Secretary of State. The first problem to which he addressed himself was whether Mehmed 'Ali had the power to make treaties and whether he had actually entered into such arrangements with the foreign Powers. His conclusion was in the negative. The Egyptian Viceroy, despite his successes, had not yet renounced his fealty to the Sultan for fear of European intervention and of offending Muslim religious sentiment, the Sultan being also the Caliph. With regard to the state of foreign consulates in Egypt, Hodgson advised that it was the custom of European nations to appoint consuls-general from their foreign offices but in deference to the Porte to request exequaturs for them directly from Constantinople, although this latter practice was complicated because of the prevailing conflict.

The final problem considered by Hodgson was an examination of the conditions of Egyptian trade and how commerce between the United States and Egypt could be established and expanded. Since this will be discussed in a later chapter, it is sufficient now to say that Hodgson, while admitting the dearth of existing trade between the two countries, was enthusiastic about its future prospects. He recommended the appointment of an American consul-general for "Egypt, Syria and the Dependencies of Mohammed Ali Pasha's Dominions." Such a step was justified, he argued, because of the vast extent and commercial importance of the Pasha's territory, which was now practically

---

[23] *D. D., Turk.,* 6, unnum. desp. from Hodgson, Malta, Dec. 2, 1834.

independent. In addition, Mehmed 'Ali himself had specifically requested such an appointment.[24]

There was nothing very startling or new in Hodgson's reports, but they did serve to point up the necessity for the United States to adopt a separate and more affirmative policy on Egypt. One immediate response by the American Government was the elevation in 1835 of its consular agent at Alexandria to the rank of consul. But it is not clear from the records of the Department of State whether Hodgson's recommendations directly influenced this action.

THE ALEXANDRIA CONSULATE, 1835–48

Commodore Porter, the American representative at Constantinople, had a high regard for John Gliddon and urged the Department to name him consul. Gliddon himself sought the promotion, which not only carried a salary but would strengthen his position vis-à-vis the British and French representatives in Egypt. Porter was quick, however, to reject his protégé's suggestion that United States consular agents in Syria report directly to Alexandria; since he, Porter, had appointed them, they were therefore responsible to him.[25]

Gliddon eagerly complied with an instruction from the Department of State concluding with a reference to "expected regularity of correspondence," securing afterwards Porter's willing consent. Porter, however, requested that he be kept advised of important events in Egypt.[26]

On March 3, 1835, John Gliddon was appointed United States consul at Alexandria, and in due course a berat or exequatur, was secured for him. In acknowledging receipt of his appoint-

---

24 *Ibid.*, unnum. desp. from Hodgson, Washington, Mar. 2, 1835.

25 *D. D., Turk.*, 4, desps. nos. 188, 235 and 244 from Porter, Constantinople, Mar. 30, Aug. 12 and Sept. 4, 1834, Porter himself felt humiliated for want of ministerial rank. *Ibid.*, desp. no. 190, Mar. 31, 1834.

26 *Post Records, Cairo*, desp. no. 1 from J. Gliddon, U.S. Con. Agt., Alexandria, Oct. 23, 1834; *D. D., Turk.*, 5, desp. no. 276 from Porter, Jan. 23, 1835, encl. corresp. with Gliddon.

ment, Gliddon referred to his commission as consul "for this Port [Alexandria] and its Dependencies."[27]

The extent of John Gliddon's jurisdiction outside Egypt proper varied, of course, with the fortunes of Mehmed 'Ali's expansionist policy. The new American consul complained to the Department in 1838 that, having been instructed "to secure all information of a general nature relative to the places under the Government of the Pasha of Egypt," the United States consuls at Beirut, Aleppo, and Candia and Canea (both on Crete) neglected or refused "to channel their reports through him but reported directly to the Department."[28] Very soon, however, such problems became theoretical. Mehmed 'Ali having launched his second attack on his suzerain, the Sultan in 1839 lost Crete, Syria and Arabia because of the intenvention of the European Powers, and was left in 1841 with only the Province of Egypt.

Upon Gliddon's death in 1844, his Scottish-born son-in-law, Alexander Tod, who had spent the previous fourteen years in Egypt, was appointed United States consul at Alexandria, a post he held until 1848.[29]

From all reports, both Gliddon and Tod were capable and honorable merchants. They operated, however, under two serious handicaps. Their status as British subjects, mentioned above, gave rise to the English consul-general's claim to jurisdiction over Gliddon. One may also presume that mere consuls would be at a considerable disadvantage generally by comparison with colleagues who were agents and consuls-general. At any rate, this was the view expressed by the Secretary of State in a letter

---

[27] *Post Records, Cairo,* desp. no. 8 from J. Gliddon, Alexandria, Dec. 3, 1835. A year later his son, Geo. R. Gliddon, who had been acting as vice consul in Cairo since May, 1832, was appointed consul for that city; this post, however, was abolished in Apr., 1840. *Insts. to Consuls,* 8, unnum. insts. to G. R. Gliddon, Cairo, Oct. 7, 1837 and Apr. 10, 1840.

[28] *Post Records, Cairo,* desp. no. 17 from J. Gliddon, Alexandria, July 13, 1838.

[29] *C. D., Cyprus, Alex., Stancho,* 1, unnum. desp. from Geo. R. Gliddon, Philadelphia, Aug. 3, 1844; *ibid.,* unnum. desp. from Alexander Tod, U.S. Con., Alexandria, Dec. 26, 1844; Appendix A—Consular Officers by Post: Egypt.

dated December 14, 1846, in answer to a resolution of the House of Representatives of August 10, 1846, calling for information on the United States consular system. In recommending the appointment of certain consuls-general, the Secretary stated:

> . . . In the latter countries [the Barbary States and some of the ports in the Levant] rank is often of great importance; and our simple consuls have not enjoyed the same privileges there, and for this reason have not had it in their power to serve their government and their countrymen to the same extent with the consuls-general of other nations. To refer to a single instance: our consul at Alexandria is deprived of the advantage of holding personal intercourse with the Viceroy of Egypt, simply because he does not bear the title of consul-general. . . .[30]

The accuracy of the Secretary of State's statement, so far as it applied to the United States consuls at Alexandria, was publicly denied by W. Lea Roberts, former partner of Alexander Tod, and by George R. Gliddon, son of John Gliddon.[31] Although the Secretary's specific argument relative to Egypt was questionable, his general position was sound; in 1848, Congress created a consulate-general at Alexandria, with an American citizen named to fill the post.

No developments of moment to the United States occurred during the thirteen years John Gliddon and Alexander Tod, served as American consuls in Egypt. Indeed, they were left practically uninstructed; their few reports touched only on the small beginnings of trade between the United States and Egypt or the possibilities thereof.

---

[30] U.S. 29th Cong., 1st Sess., H. Ex. Docs., Vol. 3, No. 12, p. 3; quoted in New York *Commercial Advertiser,* Jan. 23, 1847.

[31] Letter to Editors, signed "Alexandrinus" (W. Lea Roberts), New York *Commercial Advertiser,* Jan. 21, 1847; ltr. from Geo. R. Gliddon to W. Lea Roberts, pub. in *North American* (Philadelphia), Feb. 10, 1847.

CHAPTER III

The Early Consulate

CONSULS-GENERAL MACAULEY AND DE LEON

With the establishment of a consulate-general at Alexandria the United States entered into a more active phase in her relations with Egypt. The new emphasis was apparent in the general instructions issued by the Department of State to Daniel S. Macauley, first American consul-general:

. . . We have, heretofore, had no direct diplomatic relations with the Pasha of Egypt; and but little commercial intercourse with his dominions. But, nominally dependent upon the Porte, Egypt has become in point of fact, an independent power; and it is of great importance that we should cultivate the most friendly relations with the Pasha. . . .

Another principal object of your missions will be to extend and foster commercial intercourse between the United States and Egypt. For this purpose you will obtain all the commercial and statistical information concerning that country, which you can acquire, and communicate it to the Department . . . The subsisting relations between the Government of Egypt and the Porte is, also, a subject of much interest. . . .[1]

From 1848 to 1861 two able, aggressive Americans, Macauley and Edwin De Leon, who served four and and eight years respectively, occupied the post of United States consul-general at Alexandria.[2] Several factors combined to create a situation in which

---

[1] C. I., B. P., 14, inst. no. 2 to D. S. Macauley, U.S.C.G., Alexandria, Oct. 25, 1848.

[2] R. B. Jones was consul-general from Dec., 1852, to May, 1853. See Appendix A.

Macauley and De Leon could exert an influence in Egypt, in excess of the real power position of the United States in that country. The effectiveness of these early American consuls-general was increased because Macauley and his successors assumed the rank of (diplomatic) agents, in addition to their commissioned titles of consul-general. The Department of State consented to this as long as it was restricted to Egypt, and it continued until June 20, 1864, when, by Act of Congress, the American representative in Egypt was officially designated "Agent and Consul-General at Alexandria."[3] Macauley and De Leon thus acquired additional prestige, useful in dealing both with the Egyptian Government and with their Western colleagues.

The position of the American consuls-general in Egypt in this period was further exalted in that the great distance from Washington and inadequate communications often presented the United States representatives with both the opportunity and the necessity of making important decisions and taking action on their own initiative.[4]

It should be remembered, finally, that the over-all effect of the expanded capitulatory regime in Egypt was to create little islands of foreign control, ruled, as it were, by the respective consuls-general. David Serpell has aptly commented that under Mehmed 'Ali's successors the representatives of the smaller Western Powers "were able to exploit their positions on a scale

---

[3] *C. D., Eg.*, 1, desp. no. 3 from Macauley, Mar. 22, 1849; *C. I., B. P.*, 14, inst. no. 4 to Macauley, May 31, 1849; *U.S. Stats. at Large*, Vol. 13, pp. 137, 138 (1866). On June 11, 1874, following a change in the seat of the Egyptian Gov., the title of the U.S. representative was changed to "Agent and Consul-General at Cairo." *Ibid.*, Vol. 18 (3), pp. 66, 67 (1875).

[4] Communication difficulties are suggested by the fact that in 1840 mail service between Egypt and England by ship required three weeks or even a month, although the French did have a faster mail service between Alexandria and Marseilles that in 1847 operated three times a month. It was not until shortly after the Crimean War that France and Malta were connected by submarine cable; in 1861 this cable was extended to Alexandria via Tripoli and Bengazi, but no really effective direct service to Alexandria was achieved until 1869. Hoskins, *op. cit.*, pp. 248-390.

quite unwarranted by the economic and political status of the nations they represented. Much naturally depended on the character of the individual; a certain vigilance, for instance, might be inspired by national pride. . . ."[5]

Three incidents that occurred during Macauley's term illustrate not only the high degree of sensitivity of Western consuls in the Ottoman Empire in the mid-nineteenth century to affronts to their "national honor" but also the techniques used for dealing with such insults. The first of these, in 1849, involved an insult to one of the junior officers of the U.S.S. *Constitution* by a group of Egyptians. After advising the Department of State that full satisfaction and reparation had been obtained, Macauley reported that he had declined assistance offered by the captain of H.M.S. *Frolic.* "I must rely," he told the British captain, "solely upon the force and position of my own government for obtaining a satisfactory redress."[6] A second incident concerned an attack by Egyptians on a party of American tourists in their Nile boat in 1852. Satisfactory results in the form of indemnity and punishment of the culprits were obtained only after a threat to sever diplomatic relations.[7]

The last "insult" involved destruction by the Egyptian Government of a bakery owned by Francis Barthow, a former United States consul, in the course of Alexandria city improvements in 1852. When protests to the Egyptian authorities went unanswered, Macauley appealed to the United States Legation at Constantinople for assistance, but was informed that in view of the prevailing strained relations between the Porte and the Viceroy it was idle to expect redress through the Turkish Government. Macauley finally lowered the American flag and severed diplomatic relations. This had the desired effect, and the damages claimed were paid forthwith. The settlement of this incident

---

[5] D. R. Serpell, "American Consular Activities in Egypt, 1849–1863." *Journal of Modern History,* X (Sept., 1938), pp. 344-45. In this useful survey Serpell also discusses Macauley's and De Leon's activities in some detail. *Ibid.,* pp. 356-63.

[6] *C. D., Eg.,* 1, desp. no. 4 from Macauley, July 1, 1849.

[7] *Ibid.,* desps. nos. 32 and 34, Jan. 15 and Feb. 7, 1852.

was followed by a raising of the American flag "with full honors" —a twenty-one-gun salute by the Alexandria batteries and a display of flags by all the European Powers to express solidarity on matters of "national honor." The Department congratulated Macauley on the successful conclusion of the Barthow affair, but added a gentle reprimand:

> . . . The flag of the Consulate being now rehoisted and harmony restored, it is sincerely hoped that nothing will occur in future to render it necessary for you to resort again to so extreme a measure as that to which you have been impelled in striking the United States flag, and interrupting a friendly intercourse with a power which it is our interest and desire to cultivate good understanding.[8]

Edwin De Leon, a South Carolinian, who served as United States consul-general at Alexandria from 1853 to 1861, was perhaps even more active and influential than Macauley. He eventually became *doyen* (dean) of the "diplomatic corps" in Egypt, and in this capacity enjoyed increased prestige.[9]

De Leon had barely set foot in Egypt when he became involved in an exciting incident following the assassination of 'Abbas I. In his book *The Khedive's Egypt*, De Leon vividly describes how he and Sir Frederic Bruce, English agent and consul-general, with the greatest of difficulty dissuaded the Egyptian Governor of Cairo from making a rash and unlawful attempt, contrary to the "seniority" principle of the settlement of 1841, to proclaim El-Hami, a son of 'Abbas, as Viceroy in place of Sa'id Pasha, the lawful successor.[10]

An early problem of a relatively formal nature with which

---

[8] *C. I., B. P.*, 14, inst. no. 13 to Macauley, Apr. 20, 1852; see also *D. D., Turk.*, 11, desp. no. 25 from G. P. Marsh, U.S. Min., Constantinople, Dec. 25, 1851; *C.D., Eg.*, 1, desp. no. 35 from Macauley, Mar. 16, 1852.

[9] J. H. Brown (ed.), *Lamb's Biographical Dictionary of the United States* (Boston, 1900), II, 418; De Leon's activities while consul-general are described in E. De Leon, *The Khedive's Egypt* (London, 1879) and *Thirty Years of My Life on Three Continents* (London, 1890).

[10] De Leon, *Khedive's Egypt*, pp. 86-88.

De Leon had to deal concerned an instruction from the Department of State to negotiate a convention of neutral rights with the new Viceroy. Similar orders were sent to American representatives in other countries. In Egypt the real significance lay in the proposal to conclude a treaty of any sort with the Egyptian ruler independent of the Turkish Sultan. When first approached, Sa'id Pasha appeared considerably pleased but put off the decision. In the second interview, however, the Viceroy declined with thanks, fearing that the Porte would deem it a hostile measure if he entered into independent negotiations with a foreign country. The whole project of the series of bilateral treaties on neutral rights was ultimately abandoned because of the opposition of "certain powers," especially England. It is interesting to note that Sa'id had consulted the British agent and consul-general in the interval between the two interviews; as a result, the Department of State was queried by Her Majesty's Minister to Washington. From the point of view of Great Britain, chief supporter at this time of the integrity of the Ottoman Empire, the creation of an undesirable precedent had been prevented.[11]

The "Jaffa outrages" showed very clearly De Leon's capabilities in independent and forceful action. Briefly, the facts were as follows: On the night of January 11, 1858, an attack was made on the house of Walter Dickson, an American missionary living at Jaffa. Dickson was murdered, his wife raped, and the house pillaged. J. Warren Gorham, United States consul at Jerusalem, solicited De Leon's help. De Leon notified Captain Bell, commanding a United States Naval Squadron then at Alexandria, and himself immediately embarked for Jaffa "to vindicate the National Honor." As Jaffa was under the immediate jurisdiction of the consul at Jerusalem, who was responsible to the American minister at Constantinople, De Leon hastened to advise the Department that he was not attempting to assume jurisdiction where none existed but was acting only on Gorham's request.[12]

---

[11] *C. I., B. P.,* 14, inst. no. 8 to E. De Leon, Alexandria, Sept. 8, 1854; *C. D., Eg.,* 2, desp. no. 18 from De Leon, Nov. 30, 1854; *Notes from Br. Leg.* 32, note from J. F. Crampton, Br. Min., Washington, Jan. 12, 1855.

[12] *C. D., Eg.,* 2, desp. no. 45 from De Leon, Jan. 29, 1858.

Faced with the usual procrastination of the local Turkish officials in punishing the culprits, De Leon threatened to call in a naval squadron to bombard Jaffa, on the theory that this was the only language the Turks understood. There is a revealing report of one stormy interview De Leon had with the Turkish Governor:

> When asked further by the Governor whether our countries were not at peace, I promptly responded "no," we regard murder of men and violation of women permitted and screened by governors as a declaration of war. You have commenced it, not we. These with the threat of a war squadron, were the key notes of my proceedings. . . .[13]

The Department approved De Leon's action in this matter, though regretting the necessity for such peremptory language. In 1859 the American consul-general complained that Turkish officials continued to postpone settlement of the Dickson affair. His explanation was that the United States Government failed to make a show of force in support of his threat to do so.[14]

In assessing the achievements of Consuls-General Macauley and De Leon, two points must be stressed. Perhaps in emphasizing the forceful aspects of their activities, an erroneous impression may have been created that United States–Egyptian relations were seriously disrupted during this period. Undoubtedly both men reflected to some extent the nineteenth century imperialistic outlook of exaggerated concern with such matters as "national honor" and readiness to use force to secure favorable settlements; none of the incidents, however, was very serious. Even more important was the United States lack of ulterior motives in Egypt—a crucial factor in comparing American activities with those of the British and French at this time.

The incidents mentioned above do not by any means exhaust the full scope of diplomatic and consular activities in which

---

[13] *Ibid.*, desp. no. 47, Mar. 9, 1858.

[14] *C. I., B. P.*, 14, inst. no. 16 to De Leon, Apr. 16, 1858; *C. D., Eg.*, 2, desp. no. 50 from De Leon, Feb. 10, 1859.

Macauley and De Leon engaged. In addition to customary commercial duties, both were active in the early stages of many continuing problems, such as protection of Turkish subjects, which were to harass American consuls-general in Egypt for many years.

Macauley and De Leon gave able and effective service to their country. Their excesses only mirrored the times. Their successors included, of course, some capable and forceful men, but others, at least until the foreign-service reforms of 1906, showed that politics rather than merit was the primary criterion in their appointments.

CONTINUING PROBLEMS

A number of controversial issues in United States-Egyptian political relations emerged in the period preceding the end of the American Civil War. A few of these have been treated in the previous section. Several other problems of a more persistent nature will now be discussed: the United States agency and consulate-general and its relations with the American diplomatic representative in Turkey; "diplomacy by navy"; protection of Ottoman subjects; and consular agents. Questions dealing specifically with the American Civil War will be reserved for separate treatment.

The agent and consul-general is an anomaly in diplomatic practice and in international law. In Egypt the combination of normally separate consular and diplomatic functions in one individual stemmed from the semi-independent status of the Egyptian Viceroy.[15] The general situation existing in Egypt has been described by Sir Ernest Satow:

---

[15] Under other unique conditions there were also U.S. agents and consuls-general for a while in Morocco and Bulgaria, and from 1941 to 44, in Syria and Lebanon; one also represented the U.S. in Tangier. See G. H. Hackworth, *Digest of International Law* (Washington, 1940), IV, 415, and C. C. Hyde, *International Law Chiefly as Interpreted by the United States* (2nd ed.; Boston, 1945), II, 1230-31.

. . . In Egypt, a vassal State of Turkey until 1914 [sic], the representatives of the powers were "Agents and Consul-General." Legally they were consul-general with a *bérat* from the Porte. But for a long time the title of agent (or diplomatic agent) had been recognized. Most of the powers gave local diplomatic rank to their agents. Thus the Russian was envoy extraordinary and consul-general. Many others had also the honorary rank of envoy and minister, minister-resident or chargé d'affaires. But these titles did not affect precedence, which was regulated by seniority only, according to the date of arrival in Egypt. . . .

. . . The English Foreign Office list shows that an Agent and Consul-General is regarded as a diplomatic agent in the ordinary sense of the term.[16]

In conformity with Turkish wishes and procedure, representatives of foreign Powers in Egypt were designated consuls-general, since the Sultan emphatically denied the right of the Egyptian Viceroy to send or receive diplomatic representatives. The Western Powers were required to secure for these consuls-general exequaturs through their ministers or ambassadors in Constantinople. A *firman*, or decree, from the Sublime Porte addressed to the Egyptian Government ordering it to honor the terms of the exequatur was also customarily obtained. Having satisfied the requirements of the Sultan, the Powers at the same time recognized the *de facto* independence of the Pasha of Egypt by giving their consuls-general letters of credence, which are usually reserved for diplomatic, as opposed to consular, officials.[17]

The United States followed the procedure described above in regard to her agent and consul-general in Egypt, but with some limitations. As we have seen, the title itself was not officially

---

[16] E. Satow, *A Guide to Diplomatic Practice* (2nd rev. ed., London, 1922), I, 246-48.

[17] For an English translation of the Ottoman Regulations of Aug. 9, 1863, relating to foreign consulates see A. H. Feller and Manley O. Hudson (eds.), *A Collection of the Diplomatic and Consular Regulations of Various Countries* (Washington, 1933), I, 479-82. For an English translation of a *firman* and a Letter of Credence relative to E. E. Farman, U.S.A.C.G., see E. E. Farman, *Egypt and Its Betrayal* (New York, 1908), pp. 12-13.

conferred until 1864. Furthermore, the American Government did not follow the example of many European countries, who gave their representatives additional local or honorary rank. Supplementary evidence showing the lack of importance that the United States Government attached to its relations with Egypt in this period may be inferred from a comparison of the salaries received by the American agents and consuls-general with those paid to some of their European colleagues. In 1848, D. S. Macauley was given only $3,000, with an additional $500 for an interpreter and $500 more as a contingent fund. By 1874 this amount had been raised to $4,000, plus extras; it was still at this level in 1882 when Agent and Consul-General Simon Wolf resigned, claiming that a representative of the United States could not adequately live in Cairo on such a small amount. The English agent and consul-general, by contrast, received $8,000, with extras, in 1834, and his Russian colleague $6,000. By 1884 the British and French representatives were paid $12,500 and $10,000, respectively.[18]

American consuls at Alexandria were quite early faced with a touchy problem born of attempts by United States representatives at Constantinople to exercise jurisdictional control over consular activities in Egypt. This question was left unresolved for a long time by the Department of State, undoubtedly because at bottom a proper decision depended on the solution of the power conflict between the Egyptian Viceroy and the Turkish Sultan.

John Gliddon, first United States consular agent at Alexandria, it will be recalled, was definitely and willingly under the control of Commodore Porter, American chargé d'affaires at the Porte. All of his reports, for instance, were sent via Constantinople. In 1835 several new consulates were created in the

---

[18] *C. I., B. P.,* 14, inst. no. 2 to D. S. Macauley, Oct. 25, 1848; *ibid.,* 15, no. 101 to R. Beardsley, U.S.A.C.G., Jan. 9, 1874; *C. D., Eg.,* 19, unnum. desp. from S. Wolf, Washington, June 1, 1882; *D. D., Turk.,* 6, unnum. desp. from W. B. Hodgson, Washington, Mar. 2, 1835; E. Schuyler, *American Diplomacy and the Futherance of Commerce* (New York, 1886), p. 179.

Ottoman Empire, including one at Alexandria with Gliddon as its first consul. A despatch from Porter to the Department of October of that year furnishes evidence that he intended to continue his supervision even after 1835. "I shall," he wrote, "be watchful over their conduct and from time to time give them such advice, as the peculiar situation and character of the new consuls may call for."[19]

The appointment in 1848 of a consul-general in Egypt introduced a period of uncertain relations between American representatives in Alexandria and Constantinople. No definitive instruction was forthcoming from the Department. The only approach to it was a clause in an instruction dated February 8, 1851. After the appointment of consular agents in Egypt had been vested in him, Macauley was told: "Cases may and do arise, which it would be both expedient and proper to refer to the American Minister at Constantinople. His advice, under all circumstances, is important to you and may often be indispensably useful."[20] This directive was couched so generally as to leave American consuls in Egypt with considerable discretion. Perhaps this explains why, although the advice of the Minister to Turkey may have been sought informally, there is no record of any such requests in the official correspondence with the Department. There were, however, a number of instances where American representatives at these two points exchanged mutual recriminations on the subject of jurisdiction. "From motives unknown to this Legation," Chargé d'Affaires J. P. Brown at Constantinople complained in 1864, "the United States has not placed the Consulate-General of Egypt in the same relationship to it as other consulates in the Ottoman Empire."[21] In a despatch from Cairo the following year, Agent and Consul-General Charles Hale alleged that the American Minister to Turkey was blindly following the lead of the English

---

[19] *D. D., Turk.*, 7, desp. no. 351 from Porter, Oct. 8, 1835.

[20] *C. I., B. P.*, 14, inst. no. 11 to Macauley, Feb. 8, 1851.

[21] *D. D., Turk.*, 18, desp. no. 10 from J. P. Brown, Chargé, Constantinople, July 29, 1864.

in advocating a policy of bringing the Egyptian Pasha more tightly under the Sultan's control.[22]

Matters remained on this unsatisfactory basis until 1881, when Lewis Wallace, the able American Minister to Turkey, brought the issue to a head with a direct request to the Department of State for a ruling on the point. To this query the Secretary of State replied:

> This Department is unprepared without further consideration and for more urgent reasons than are now apparent to subordinate the Consul-General at Cairo to the Legation at Constantinople as to jurisdiction or official duties; but it views with favor your suggestion that you should be kept informed of political affairs as they transpire in Egypt. I have, therefore, instructed Mr. Comanos, now in charge in Mr. Wolf's absence, to send your Legation, for its information, copies of such despatches, on matters of political or international interest, as he may write to the Department.[23]

Even this arrangement as to "information copies" proved unsuccessful. In May, 1882, at a time when important negotiations preliminary to the British occupation were being conducted both in Cairo and in Constantinople, Wallace complained that he was receiving no news from Egypt. His plea went unanswered in the confusion of the 'Arabi revolt and the bombardment of Alexandria by the British. After 1882 the already apparent trend toward independence of the American agent and consul-general at Cairo from the control of the minister at Constantinople was acentuated. This matter will be explored in greater detail in a later chapter.

The problem of "diplomacy by navy" as it affected United States-Egyptian relations can be viewed in at least two aspects.

---

[22] *C. D., Eg.,* 3, desp. no. 21 from C. Hale, U.S.A.C.G., Cairo, Mar. 14, 1865. The previous October, Rev. G. Lansing, an American missionary at Alexandria, had written a vigorous letter to the Sec. of State on this same theme. See *ibid.,* pvt. ltr. from Lansing, Alexandria, Oct. 27, 1864.

[23] *D. I., Turk.,* 3, inst. no 30 to L. Wallace, Dec. 31, 1881.

There were a few instances in the 1830's and 1840's where American naval officers, acting without authority, undertook to meddle in their country's diplomatic relations with the Ottoman Empire. One example, found in a report in 1837, states that Commodore I. D. Elliott of the U.S. frigate *Constitution* had told the Egyptian Viceroy that in view of steps he, Elliott, had taken in the United States, a consul-general for Egypt would be appointed. Chargé d'Affairs Porter relayed this news to the Department of State, observing that the Porte would be offended at not hearing the news through the American diplomatic representative in Turkey. He suggested caustically that the Navy Department be advised to instruct its officers to confine themselves "to the sphere of their proper duties and leave those under the orders of the Department of State uninterruptedly in the exercise of their functions." Porter added that he had similar trouble with Elliott in the past.[24] Usually, however, the State and Navy departments worked harmoniously in the furtherance of national policy. For example, Commodore Biddle, as previously noted, was specifically selected as one of the commissioners for negotiating the United States–Turkish treaty of 1830.

A second facet of "diplomacy by navy" was the practice among all the Western Powers interested in the Eastern Mediterranean of using, on occasion, their respective fleets to put pressure on local governments or even on the Sultan to secure some desired end, and in periods of internal unrest in the Ottoman Empire, to offer a haven for their citizens in the area. The

[24] *D. D., Turk.*, 8, desp. no. 408 from Porter, Oct. 11, 1837. In this particular case it should be observed, however, that Mehmed 'Ali had complained to Commod. Elliott over the presence of an American consul in Syria who was not under the control and direction of the U.S. consul in Egypt. At the Viceroy's request Elliott reported this matter directly to the President of the U.S. and added his own recommendation that an American consul-general be appointed at Alexandria with power to appoint consular agents in Syria where necessary. Elliott also submitted a report to the Sec. of the Navy. See *Letter Book of the U.S.S. Constitution, Cruising in the Mediterranean, Commodore I. D. Elliott, U.S.N.*, unnum. ltr. to Maj. Gen. Andrew Jackson, Pres. of the U.S.A., at Sea, Oct. 10, 1836; *ibid.*, ltr. no. 54 to Hon. M. Dickerson, Sec. of Navy, Alexandria, Oct. 5, 1836.

United States had a Mediterranean naval squadron that regularly visited the important ports of the Turkish Empire, including Alexandria. This procedure, known as "showing the flag," was designed, among other things, to instill in the minds of Ottoman officials a wholesome respect for American power. But on the whole the United States used her Navy as an instrument of national policy quite sparingly compared with such foreign Powers as Britain and France. This may be explained at least in part by the fact that the United States had comparatively fewer interests at stake in the area. A few examples suffice to show the scope of United States practice. In the "Jaffa outrages" of 1858, Consul-General De Leon used the threat of naval reprisal in his effort to secure satisfactory reparation for the assaults on American citizens. It is instructive, however, to contrast this with the "Bird incident" of 1834, in which Rev. Isaac Bird, an American missionary at Damascus, was beaten and threatened by some of Ibrahim Pasha's soldiers. When a request for assistance was made to Commodore D. F. Patterson, commanding the United States Mediterranean Squadron, he replied rather testily that he could not be expected to answer the application of every consular agent to put pressure on the Egyptian Government.[25] A final illustration is the recommendation of Agent and Consul-General Richard Beardsley at Cairo that at least one American warship be kept in Egyptian waters during the winter months. It would have, he pointed out, a "beneficial effect upon American interests."[26]

A third cause of friction between the United States and Egypt was the matter of protection of Turkish subjects. It was admitted on all sides that the capitulations entitled the Western Powers to extend their protection to all Ottoman citizens legitimately employed as dragomans, consular agents, clerks, guards and the like. The privileges conferred on these individuals were so considerable that other Turkish subjects also sought and

[25] D. D., Turk., 3, desp. no. 137 from D. Porter, Constantinople, Sept. 9, 1883; ibid., desp. no. 174, Jan. 18. 1834.

[26] C. D., Eg., 7, desp. no. 56 from R. Beardsley, Cairo, Jan. 7, 1873.

secured the benefits of foreign protection. This latter group were referred to collectively as protégés. This situation inevitably led to abuses in the sale of protection. Nasim Sousa described what happened:

> . . . Then followed the sale of patents of protection to wealthy Ottoman subjects who found in the capitulatory privileges security and economic advantages. In virtue of the patent the foreign protection was not confined to the purchaser only, but it was extended to all the family. It was hereditary and could be transferred for a consideration. These patents of protection were rather limited, at the beginning, to those who could afford to buy them; but the situation took a different aspect when the limitation was removed and the patents were issued on a large scale for political purposes. . . .[27]

Sousa also declared that "a French ambassador was reported to have received a sum exceeding 400,000 francs from this source [sale of protection] and a British ambassador 2,000 to 3,000 pounds from the same source."[28]

Small wonder, therefore, that the Turkish Government strongly opposed this much-abused protégé system and strived to curtail it. As early as 1842 the Sultan requested the Western Powers not to extend their protection to Turkish subjects not legitimately employed by them. Also, in 1852 the Porte began issuing a series of regulations, some limiting and others prohibiting altogether the grant of protection to Ottoman citizens. But neither pleas nor prohibitions met with much success. The Western Powers, relying on their capitulatory rights and realizing the weakness of the Ottoman Empire, gave way only grudgingly on this point down to World War I.[29]

The United States appears to have been relatively guiltless on this score. Hodgson, in his 1834 report, noted that John Gliddon, while American consular agent at Alexandria, had

---

[27] Sousa, *op. cit.*, pp. 100-101.

[28] *Ibid.*, p. 98.

[29] *D. D., Turk.*, 9, desp. no. 124 from Porter, U.S. Min. Resident, Constantinople, July 2, 1842; Sousa, *op. cit.*, pp. 101-12.

been offered a thousand dollars by an Egyptian for a grant of protection but had quite properly refused. Only 50 non-American citizens were under United States protection in Egypt in 1852. This figure had reached 197 by 1867, but of these 149 were Greeks to whom De Leon had given protection in 1854.[30]

In 1850 the Department of State issued a basic statement of policy, the first of a long series of instructions to American consuls in Egypt regarding protection of non-American citizens:

> I was well aware of the custom of the representatives of Christian powers in the Barbary States to extend the protection of their flags over many individuals who are not citizens of their respective countries, and who can not be properly considered as officials, such as brokers, interpreters, etc., etc. But whilst I deem it the duty of our consuls to protect American citizens, and necessary and useful official persons connected with their consulates, they ought scrupulously and carefully to abstain from all interference in behalf of individuals who are neither citizens nor have any rightful claim to our protection; and, the more especially, when such protection is likely to bring the American consul into any kind of conflict with the rights and prerogatives of the representatives of friendly powers. . . .[31]

The Department qualified its attitude slightly in 1853. It admitted then to De Leon that it would be unjust to withdraw protection suddenly from persons who had previously enjoyed it, albeit without authorization, but reiterated that no new protégés were to be added without the consent of the Secretary of State. Consul-General De Leon, while admitting that his predecessors may have been guilty of some excesses, offered the humanitarian response of the man in the field to the Department's cold, logical position. "Justice," he wrote, "compels me

[30] *D. D., Turk.*, 6, unnum. desp. from Hodgson, Mar. 2, 1835; *C. D., Eg.*, 1, unnum. desp. from R. B. Jones, U.S.C.G., Alexandria, May 12, 1853; *ibid.*, 4, desp. no. 81 from C. Hale, U.S.A.C.G., Alexandria, Apr. 15, 1867.

[31] *C. I., B. P.*, 14, inst. no. 7 to D. S. Macauley, Alexandria, Jan. 14, 1850.

[32] *C. D., Eg.*, 2, desp. no. 8 from De Leon, Mar. 2, 1854; see also *C. I., B. P.*, 14, inst. no 3 to De Leon, Dec. 23, 1853.

to add that humanity may plead their apology while the conduct of the Egyptian Government in the same matters has been little short of infamous and neither respectful nor just towards our own Government. At a distance these matters seem trivial, but I assure you, Sir, that they are of consequence in fixing the American status in Egypt, now and hereafter."[32]

De Leon was very soon presented with an opportunity for putting his sentiments into practice. Shortly after the outbreak of the Crimean War in 1854, the Greeks, taking advantage of the Sultan's involvement, invaded Thessaly and Epirus. In retaliation the Porte ordered the Egyptian Pasha to expel the entire Greek colony except those enrolled as *re'aya* (non-Muslim subjects). 'Abbas Pasha complied, ordering the thousands of Greek residents in Egypt to leave the country within fifteen days. On his own initiative De Leon gave protection to large numbers of these unfortunates. Approval of the United States Government was asked after the fact.[33] The Department of State, however, failed to comment on De Leon's handling of this incident, though it did show initial interest, not acted upon, in his report of a suggestion from the grateful Greek Government that Greece might favorably consider a United States request for a naval base on the Greek island of Amargos.[34]

In 1864, Francis Dainese, acting United States consul-general at Alexandria, became involved in a serious dispute with the Egyptian Government over his efforts to extend protection to two non-American citizens. Dainese finally struck the American flag, severing relations without authorization from the Department of State. Upon the arrival in Egypt of the new agent and consul-general, Charles Hale, relations were restored and the

---

[33] *C. D., Eg.,* 2, desp. nos. 10 and 11 from De Leon, May 4 and June 4, 1854; compare De Leon, *Khedive's Egypt,* pp. 83-84, for some variation in the figures.

[34] *C. D., Eg.,* 2, desps. no. 12 and 19 from De Leon, July 6, 1854, and Feb. 6, 1855, resp.; *C. I., B. P.,* 14, inst. no. 9 to De Leon, Sep. 19, 1854. The Greek Govt. also expressed its appreciation for De Leon's services through the U.S. Min. to France. See *D. D., Fr.,* 36, desp. no 25, from John Mason, U.S. Min., Paris, June 24, 1854.

controversy was amicably settled.[35] The Department seized this occasion to reaffirm most emphatically its stand on protection: "Hence forward you will grant no protection to any person whomsoever not actually a citizen of the United States by birth, or complete naturalization, or to any other person not actually employed in the consulate."[36] In 1866, Consul-General Hale reported that he was following the instruction of 1864 regarding protection but that he believed exceptions should be made in instances where hardship might follow its strict application. The Department replied that the rule was categorical, and added that Hale's attitude showed "a want of appreciation of those views and instructions of the Department in relation to the matter, which have been signally disregarded by some of your predecessors."[37]

It is apparent from the above discussion that the United States never seriously abused the protégé system and that, beginning in 1850, the Department of State made serious efforts to restrict American protection to legitimately employed Turkish subjects, though receiving only reluctant cooperation from the early American consuls-general in Egypt.

One final word should be added regarding protection. United States–Egyptian relations were more or less untroubled by a related problem that was the source of much bad feeling in other parts of the Turkish Empire: the dispute over whether Ottoman subjects could emigrate to America, become naturalized citizens, and then return to Turkey secured by United States protection. The Porte, insisting that such persons never lost their Turkish

[35] *C. D., Eg.,* 3, desps. nos. 54, 55 and 56 from F. Dainese, Acting U.S.C.G., Alexandria, July 21, Aug. 4 and 12, 1864; *ibid.,* desp. no 2 from Hale, U.S.A.C.G., Alexandria, Aug. 27, 1864; for Dainese's version of this affair and his subsequent lawsuit, see F. Dainese, *The History of Mr. Seward's Pet in Egypt: A Memorial to Congress in Regard to Charles Hale, Consul to Egypt, December 26, 1866* (Washington, 1867 [?]); Dainese v. Hale, 8 D.C. 86, 1 MacArthur 86 (1873); Dainese v. Hale, 91 U.S. 13 (1875).

[36] *C.I., B.P.,* 14, inst. no. 4 to Hale, Oct. 3, 1864.

[37] *C. D., Eg.,* 4, desp. no. 64 from Hale, Nov. 12, 1866; *C. I., B. P.,* 14, inst. no. 26 to Hale, Dec. 11, 1866.

citizenship without special permission, treated them as such upon their return to the Empire. The United States Government protested vigorously, but there was little it could do. Armenians, and later Lebanese, chiefly were involved in this controversy. The issue did not arise in Egypt because practically no Egyptians emigrated to the United States—or anywhere, for that matter.[38]

A special facet of protection of Turkish subjects created a fourth problem—the use of such persons as consular agents. Ottoman citizens thus employed enjoyed, of course, the privileges of the capitulations. Indeed, this was their only practical incentive, for they received no salary and in the case of Egypt, almost nothing in fees. The general United States practice was to permit American representatives in Egypt to select their own consular agents, subject to approval by the Department of State. United States consular agents in Egypt were almost exclusively foreigners—in the port cities, Europeans; in the interior, Egyptians.[39]

Soon, however, both the United States Government and the Sultan adopted policies aimed at discouraging the employment of Turkish subjects as consular agents. On the part of the United States, this position probably sprang from the feeling that only American citizens were able adequately to represent the national interest and defend the country's honor. Correspondingly, the Sublime Porte also must have been concerned over the loss of control and revenues. Whatever the motivation, in 1853 the Department of State issued a circular forbidding the employment of foreigners as consular agents. This prohibition was then incorporated into the Consular Regulations. But there was an important exception to this rule, "in cases of absolute necessity."[40] Undoubtedly the policy of the United States Government was influenced in part by the even stronger feelings of the Porte on this subject. The Sultan's attitude was finally crystalized in

[38] Gordon, *op. cit.*, pp. 326-40; Issawi, *op. cit.*, p. 47.

[39] *C. I., B. P.*, 14, inst. no. 11 to Macauley, Feb. 8, 1851; *C. D., Eg.*, 1, desp. no. 18 from Macauley, June 20, 1850.

[40] *D. D., Turk.*, 7, desp. no. 355 from Porter, Oct. 17, 1835; *ibid.*, 12, desp. no. 53 from G. P. Marsh, U.S. Min., Constantinople, Sept. 5, 1853; *U.S. Cong. Regs.* (1868), p. 159.

Article 6 of the Ottoman Regulations of 1863 regarding foreign consulates. In substance it is the same prohibition as that expressed by the United States. An exception "for urgent cases" was included, but with a proviso that such appointments would be provisional only and, further, that Turkish citizens would lose the right to foreign protection when they ceased to be employed as consular agents.[41] The Porte was able to control the situation by an additional requirement that consular agents must secure an exequatur from the Imperial Divan (Council) before being permitted to exercise their functions.[42]

The United States was faced with a practical difficulty in this matter; if Turkish subjects could not be employed as consular agents, Americans would remain without representation in much of Egypt and other parts of the Ottoman Empire as well. Not only did few American citizens permanently reside in Egypt (some forty-odd in 1873), but most of those in Upper Egypt were disqualified from serving because they were missionaries. Faced with this impasse, the United States could legitimately invoke the exception of "absolute necessity" mentioned above. Egyptians were in fact utilized as consular agents until World War I, but this representation was not achieved without some struggle. Periodically the Porte raised objections that were answered with increasing difficulty.[43]

A survey by Agent and Consul-General E. E. Farman in 1877 disclosed that in addition to Alexandria, Suez and Port Sa'id, there were United States consular agencies at Mansurah, Asyut, Luxor, Kena, Tanta, Bani Suwayf, Girga (Jirja) and Khartum. This number was gradually reduced in Upper Egypt, however, so that by 1904 all except the agency at Asyut were closed. The retention of the consular agencies in Upper Egypt for so long did not reflect any important American commercial interests

---

[41] Feller and Hudson, *op. cit.,* pp. 480-81.

[42] *Ibid.*

[43] *D. D., Turk.,* 12, desp. no. 53 from G. P. Marsh, U.S. Min., Constantinople, Sept. 5, 1853; *C. D., Eg.,* 32, desp. 317 from J. G. Long, U.S.A.C.G., Cairo, Jan. 10, 1903; De Leon, *Khedive's Egypt,* pp. 426-27; *D. D., Turk.,* 7, desp. no. 355 from Porter, Constantinople, Jan. 27, 1835.

in that area. Indeed, as Agent and Consul-General Richard Beardsley observed in 1875, if trade were the only consideration, all the consular agencies in Egypt except the one at Alexandria could have been abolished. But these consular agents were of distinct service to American tourists.[44] The agents were even more important to the American missionaries in Egypt. The work of the American Mission, in which these consular agents played a significant and often stormy role, will be treated in a later chapter.[45]

----

[44] It was reported in 1903 that approximately 4,000 of them annually visited the Upper Nile.

[45] *C. D., Eg.*, 10, desp. no. 307 from R. Beardsley, U.S.A.C.G., Cairo, May 4, 1875; *ibid.*, 13, desp. no. 117 from E. E. Farman, Apr. 6, 1877; *ibid.*, 32, desp. no. 405 from F. G. Morgan, V.C.G., Cairo, Oct. 28, 1903; *ibid.*, 33, desp. no. 32 from J. W. Riddle, U.S.A.C.G., Cairo, June 20, 1904; *ibid.*, 33, desp. no. 46 from Morgan, Aug. 18, 1904; *D. I., Turk.*, 8, inst. no. 325 to J. G. A. Leishman, U.S. Min., Constantinople, Mar. 19, 1903.

CHAPTER IV

Egypt and the American Civil War

The outbreak of civil war in America in April, 1861, had a constrictive effect on United States relations with Egypt. Trade between the two countries virtually disappeared. While normal diplomatic and consular intercourse continued, the only political issues that aroused much attention in Washington were those that might affect the outcome of the war. Even these were largely peripheral. Egyptian and Turkish neutrality presented no real problem. But United States involvement in the Civil War made possible the interesting and little-known, though relatively minor, incident of the despatch of Sudanese troops for service with the French in Mexico. Moreover, the Civil War crucially provided Egypt with a golden opportunity to expand and develop the production of its excellent long-staple cotton.

EGYPTIAN AND TURKISH NEUTRALITY

One early question to which the United States desired an immediate and favorable response was Turkish and Egyptian neutrality. What Washington feared was not, of course, direct aid to the Confederates in the form of armed intervention, but rather, covert assistance to Rebel privateers. In approaching this problem the Sultan was forced to move with a certain caution. For although the Unionist Government represented legitimacy and although the Sublime Porte—with its memories of Mehmed 'Ali and the Greeks—had no desire to encourage rebellion of any sort, British and French circles at Constantinople were sympathetic to the Confederate cause. Nevertheless, by a series of decrees of growing severity, issued in 1861–1862, the Ottoman Government finally arrived at a position with which even the President of the United States expressed himself as being wholly satisfied. All of these Turkish rulings dealt with the significant subject of privateering. As a first step, in June, 1861, Ottoman subjects and foreigners in the Empire alike were forbidden to fit out vessels designed for depredations against United States commerce. Then, in March, 1862, privateers were forbidden entrance into Turkish ports, either alone or with prizes, except in the case of marine damage, when a reasonable layover for repairs was permitted. Finally, in May of the same year this prohibition was made absolute.[1]

The Egyptian Viceroy, Muhammad Sa'id Pasha, made his own contributions to this "benevolent neutrality." In November, 1861, he issued a decree aimed directly at the Southern insurgents, excluding from Egyptian ports any vessel bearing an unrecognized flag. As further evidence of his good will he offered to sell a quantity of rifles to the United States Government—a tender, however, declined with thanks.[2] There was a report in September, 1863, that Sa'id was acting as a dummy in the purchase of two British ironclads ultimately destined for use by the South. But investigations by United States representatives in London, Paris and Alexandria proved it to be unsubstantiate.[3]

Despite success in securing Turkish and Egyptian neutrality, the United States Government remained worried over the pos-

---

[1] *D. D., Turk.,* 17, desp. no. 3 from J. P. Brown, Chargé, Constantinople, June 11, 1861; *ibid.,* desps. nos. 14 and 19, Mar. 26 and May 6, 1862; *D. I., Turk.,* 2, insts. nos. 23 and 26 to E. J. Morris, U.S. Min., Constantinople, May 5 and June 4, 1862.

[2] *C. D., Eg.,* 3, desps. nos. 10 and 11 from W. S. Thayer, U.S.C.G., Alexandria, Nov. 13 and 19, 1861; *C. I., B. P.,* 14, inst. no. 10 to Thayer, Mar. 17, 1862.

[3] *D. D., G. B.,* 83, desps. nos. 486 and 492 from C. F. Adams, U.S. Min., London, Sept. 3 and 8, 1863; *ibid.,* pvt. ltr. from C. Wilson, Chargé, London, Sept. 16, 1863.

sibility of Confederate privateers operating in the Mediterranean. To meet the anticipated threat the Department of State instructed Consul-General William Thayer at Alexandria to employ a secret agent who could visit the ports of the Ottoman Empire to secure information that might be useful in preventing attacks on American commerce. Thayer was further directed to seize the papers of any vessel wholly or partly owned by Confederates if he had reason to suspect its employment as hostile to the United States. Such precautions, however, proved needless; at no time during the Civil War did Rebel raiders operate in the Mediterranean. The report of the presence of the *Sumter* at Cadiz in January of 1862 did, it is true, cause considerable alarm in Egyptian maritime circles, and for a while shippers at Alexandria would not charter American vessels. Thayer even requested naval assistance. But the arrival of Union warships off Gibraltar relieved the tension.[4]

SUDANESE TROOPS IN MEXICO

The normally good relations existing between the United States and Egypt were marred during the Civil War by a minor, if unusual, incident in which Sudanese troops were sent to serve with the French forces in Mexico. In 1861, taking advantage of United States involvement in the Civil War, France, Spain and England had occupied Vera Cruz, ostensibly for the purpose of protecting their financial investments. In April, 1862, England and Spain withdrew, leaving Napoleon III in sole occupation. By 1863, French troops had taken Mexico City and in April, 1864, Archduke Maximilian of Austria was made Emperor of Mexico. The United States, although outraged by the flouting

---

[4] *C. I., B. P.,* 14, unnum. confid. inst. to Thayer, Alexandria, Nov. 7, 1861; *ibid.,* insts. nos. 8 and 14, Mar. 1 and June 21, 1862; *C. D., Eg.,* 3, unnum. confid. desp. from Thayer, Jan. 15, 1862; *ibid.,* desps. nos. 14, 16 and 17, Jan. 24, Feb. 17 and Mar. 13, 1862; Serpell, *op. cit.,* pp. 348-49.

of the Monroe Doctrine, at the time was powerless to do more than protest.[5]

On January 7, 1863, it was disclosed in Alexandria that some five hundred Sudanese had been secretly placed on a French transport for service with Napoleon III's forces in Mexico. The nature of the *quid pro quo*, if any, for the Egyptian Viceroy is not mentioned in Department of State correspondence. Information from Paris indicated that these troops were destined for garrison duty at Vera Cruz and had been selected "because the black race is not subject to yellow fever. . . ."[6]

The Turkish, British and American governments had received no advance notice of this action. The United States obviously opposed such a move, but made no official protest at this time. The Ottoman and British governments were stirred because the incident seemed to indicate that an agreement had been reached between Napoleon III and Viceroy Sa'id, amounting to virtual recognition of Egypt's independence. However, the affair appeared amicably settled when the Egyptian Pasha apologized to all concerned and promised not to repeat it in the future.[7]

Despite the promises and assurances cited above, some nine hundred more Sudanese were ready for embarkation to Mexico

---

[5] T. A. Bailey, *A Diplomatic History of the American People* (New York, 1946), pp. 378-91; H. I. Priestley, *The Mexican Nation: A History* (New York, 1935), chap. xxi; J. F. Rippy, *The United States and Mexico* (New York, 1926), chaps. xiii-xv.

[6] *D. D., Fr.*, 52, desp. no. 258 from Wm. L. Dayton, U.S. Min., Paris, Jan. 23, 1863; New York *Times*, Feb. 17, 1863; *C. D., Eg.*, 3, desp. no. 26 from Thayer, Alexandria, Jan. 9, 1863.

[7] *Ibid.*, desp. no. 27 from Thayer, Alexandria, Jan. 18, 1863; *D. D., Turk.*, 17, desp. no. 46 from E. J. Morris, U.S. Min., Constantinople, Jan. 15, 1863. On Jan. 27, 1863, Thayer wrote to John Bigelow, U.S. chargé in Paris, that "the Minister of Foreign Affairs and the French Consul General assured me it was a small affair of 500 negroes or so. I told his Excellency the story of the maid who excused her frailty by saying her baby was a little one. This converted him. . . ." J. Bigelow, *Retrospections of an Active Life* (New York, 1909), I, 598.

in August of 1865. This time no secrecy was attempted; the American agent and consul-general at Alexandria was informed in advance. The Egyptian Government's position was that these troops were merely replacements and therefore were part of the original agreement with the French. The Porte had also been consulted and had consented to the arrangement. On this occasion the United States Government protested strongly to both.[8]

The most vigorous American representations, however, were made in Paris. The successful termination of the Civil War now permitted the United States Government to turn full attention to the Mexican question. The use of the Sudanese in Mexico was, of course, only one aspect of the larger problem of achieving the evacuation of all foreign troops, chiefly French, from that country. The burden of the United States complaint was that the Sudanese troops had reportedly been seized en masse in the same manner as slaves and sold into the service of a state they never knew existed. Quite naturally the American Government objected to slavery, whatever its guise, in a neighboring country. The French Foreign Minister was at first inclined to stand on his country's right to obtain troops from any ally and to refuse to question the manner of their recruitment. Under continued American pressure, however, the French Government agreed to inquire into the facts, promising not to use the Sudanese if coercion actually had been employed. In the end no Sudanese replacements were sent from Egypt.[9]

Strong French influence in Egypt was reflected also in Constantinople, where Emperor Maximilian's envoy to the Porte was

[8] *C. D., Eg.,* 4, desps. nos. 41, 44, 45, 46 and 52 from C. Hale, U.S.A.C.G., Alexandria, Aug. 26, Oct. 27, Nov. 13, Nov. 18, 1865, and Jan. 18, 1866; *D. D., Turk.,* 19, desp. no. 130 from E. J. Morris, Constantinople, Oct. 29, 1865; *D. I., Turk.,* 2, inst. no. 93 to Morris, Sept. 21, 1865; *C. I., B. P.,* 14, inst. no. 13 to Hale, Sept. 21, 1865.

[9] *D. I., Fr.,* 17, insts. nos. 264 and 302 to J. Bigelow, U.S. Min., Paris, Sept. 20 and Nov. 6, 1865; *ibid.,* inst. no. 278, Jan. 29, 1866; *D. D., Fr.,* 58, desp. no. 177 from Bigelow, Paris, Sept. 22, 1865; *ibid.,* 59, desps. nos. 184 and 186, Oct. 13 and 18, 1865; *ibid.,* desp. no. 235, Jan. 5, 1866; *C. I., B. P.,* 14, inst. no. 16 to Hale, Alexandria, Nov. 27, 1865; *ibid.,* unnum. inst., Dec. 14, 1865; Bigelow, *op. cit.,* III, 189 ff.

warmly received and a preliminary agreement reached to exchange consulates. French forces were withdrawn from Mexico in 1867. And with the return of the Sudanese troops to Egypt in May of that year, the incident ended amicably without seriously straining United States–Egyptian relations.[10]

COTTON DIPLOMACY

The great expansion of Egyptian cotton production was without doubt the most significant development in Egypt during the American Civil War. Its repercussions were as important politically as economically. "One can not study the history of Egypt during the last half of the nineteenth century," observed Edward M. Earle, "without being profoundly impressed by the importance of the American Civil War in the making of modern Egypt; without realizing that the production of Egyptian cotton, stimulated by the blockade of Southern ports, contributed materially to the development of important British interests in Egypt; without feeling that the resulting increase in cotton exports from the Nile Valley to Lancashire was a factor in the eventual British occupation of Egypt. . . ."[11] It should be added that there was a definite connection between the sudden Egyptian cotton prosperity and the building of the Suez Canal; this will be discussed in a later chapter.

The diplomatic strategy of the Confederate States was built around cotton. The commanding position acquired by the South as primary supplier of this staple to the British textile industry is reflected in Great Britain's import figures. In 1860, for example, of a total of 1,390,938,752 pounds of cotton imported, 1,115,890,-608, or about 80 per cent, derived from the United States; of the

---

[10] D. D., *Turk.*, 19, desp. no. 133 from E. J. Morris, Constantinople, Nov. 22, 1865; C. D., *Eg.*, 4, desp. no. 88 from Hale, Alexandria, June 8, 1867.

[11] E. M. Earle, "Egyptian Cotton and the American Civil War," *Political Science Quarterly*, XLI (Dec., 1926), 520. Earle's article on this subject is excellent, although he did not make full use of the U.S. National Archives material.

remainder, 14 per cent came from India, 3 per cent from Egypt, and smaller amounts from the British West Indies, Brazil and other countries. Southern leaders were convinced that if the North effectively shut off England's major source of raw cotton the effects on the Lancashire textile industry and indeed on the entire British economy would be so disastrous as to force the United Kingdom to intervene actively on the Confederate side.[12]

As anticipated, the outbreak of the Civil War in 1861 and the imposition of a northern blockade on the southern ports brought a sharp drop in the amount of American cotton imported into Great Britain. In 1862 it had fallen to 13 million pounds, and by 1863 had reached a low of 6 million pounds. A small number of mill owners were driven to bankruptcy and a great many workers to unemployment by the resulting curtailment of British textile output. The distress of the operatives was keenest during 1862, before industry adjustments had taken place and before other sources of cotton production could be expanded. Poor Law Board figures in England showed 508,293 on public charity in December, 1862, the peak of unemployment. It is estimated that the Lancashire cotton famine rendered destitute approximately two million people. Such conditions created an explosive situation that, coupled with continuing propaganda and agitation carried on by Confederate agents and pro-Southern groups in England, greatly alarmed Secretary Seward and Minister to Great Britain Charles F. Adams. The question of intervention in the American Civil War by Britain and France, both individually and jointly, was hotly debated in the press and in Parliament. For a variety of reasons, however, not just the alleged anti-slavery sentiments of

[12] C. F. Adams, "The Confederate Cotton Campaign: Lancashire, 1861-1862," *Trans-Atlantic Historical Solidarity*, (Oxford, 1913), pp. 57-84; F. L. Owsley, *King Cotton Diplomacy: Foreign Relations of the Confederate States of America* (2nd ed. rev., Chicago, 1959), chaps. i, ii, iv, v and *passim*. For figures on British cotton imports, 1852-1882, see *G.B., A.P.*, Statistical Abstract for the United Kingdom, cmd. 3878, LXXI (1867), 50-51; *ibid.*, cmd. 2599, LXXVI (1880), 60-61; *ibid.*, cmd. 3663, LXXVI (1883), 64-65; cf. L. B. Schmidt, "The Influence of Wheat and Cotton on Anglo-American Relations during the Civil War," *Iowa Journal of History and Politics*, XVI (1918), 400-439.

the British and French textile workers, neither country intervened.[13]

One of the factors that successfully deterred England and France from entering the war on the side of the South was the increased production in India, Egypt and elsewhere; the British hoped to find a permanent replacement of the United States as their chief source of raw cotton. As early as 1857, English merchants had formed the Cotton Supply Association. The purpose of this organization, with headquarters at Manchester, was to develop non-American sources of cotton. India, as a British possession, was given earliest and closest attention, but Egypt, Brazil and other countries were also encouraged. With the advent of the Civil War, such efforts were intensified. France made similar, if less intense, endeavors. As a result of considerable financial assistance and high prices, cotton imports from India into England increased from roughly 200 million pounds in 1860 to a peak of just over 600 million pounds in 1866. At the end of the American Civil War, India was supplying 85 per cent of England's cotton needs. However, this Indian, or "Surat," cotton, was unpopular with the British textile trade, being described by one observer as "short, harsh, brittle and dirty."[14]

The failure of Indian cotton to meet the qualitative tests opened the door for Egypt's permanent expansion into this field. Cotton of an inferior quality was indigenous to Egypt, and its use goes back to Pharaonic times. But cotton became truly significant only after the discovery in 1820 of a new type known as Jumel or Mako. The ambitious Mehmed 'Ali pushed cultiva-

-----

[13] *C. D., Manchester, Eng.,* I, desp. no. 4 from H. W. Lord, U.S. Con., Manchester, May 1, 1862; *ibid.,* unnum. desp. July 3, 1862; see generally Dept. of State correspondence with C. F. Adams, U. S. Min., London, 1861-1865; Owsley, *op. cit.,* chap. iv; C. F. Adams, *op. cit.,* pp. 70-84; S. Bernstein, "The Opposition of French Labor to American Slavery," *Science and Society,* 17 (1953), No. 2, 136-54.

[14] J. A. B. Scherer, *Cotton as a World Power* (New York, 1916), p. 268; Owsley, *op. cit.;* Earle, *op. cit.,* pp. 524-27; F. A. Logan, "India: Britain's Substitute for American Cotton, 1861-1865," *Journal of Southern History,* 24: 472-86 (Nov., 1958). For statistics on Indian cotton imports into England, see *G.B., A.P.* (1867, 1880 and 1883).

tion of this high-grade, long-staple cotton, with the result that exports multiplied from approximately 20,000 pounds in 1821 to 18.6 million pounds in 1831. By 1860 the export figure had reached 43 million pounds. The Pasha's plans to make Egypt a cotton manufacturing center, however, were not pursued by his successors.[15]

During the Civil War the British strove to increase Egyptian cotton output also. In July, 1861, representatives of the Manchester Cotton Association went to Egypt to encourage the expansion of cotton acreage in that country. Instructions and superior seed were furnished by the Association. And at the Viceroy's suggestion, British merchants began making advances to the *fallahin* on their future crop. The Sublime Porte, desirous of reaping the benefit of rising cotton prices, instructed all provincial governors in the Turkish Empire to promote the cultivation of cotton as energetically as possible. In 1862, Sa'id Pasha, after a trip to England, reported that he had "advised" the *fallahin* to plant one-fourth of their land in cotton. He also established fifty steam cotton-cleaning companies.[16]

In March of 1862, Consul-General William Thayer advised the Department of State that the Viceroy of Egypt was going to England to attend an exhibition of agricultural and manufactured products in London. Thayer suggested it would be a good idea if he went along to counteract "the insidious effect of the clique of Southern Commissioners, one of whom was my predecessor [De Leon]."[17] Secretary of State Seward replied confidentially that Thayer should by all means go to England with the Pasha,

---

[15] F. Charles-Roux, *Le Coton en Egypte* (Paris, 1908), chap. i; G. R. Gliddon, *A Memoir on the Cotton of Egypt* (London, 1841); John Bowring, "Report on Egypt and Candia," *G.B.*, *A.P.*, cmd. 277, XXI (1840), 19-21, 29-32; De Leon, *Khedive's Egypt*, pp. 206-10. For Egyptian cotton exports, 1821-1860, see *C. D.*, *Eg.*, 3, desp. no. 31 from W. S. Thayer, U.S.C.G., Alexandria, Mar. 5, 1863, and *Comm. Rels.* (1863), pp. 528-35.

[16] *C. D.*, *Eg.*, 3, desps. nos. 6 and 10 from Thayer, Aug. 28 and Nov. 13, 1861; *ibid.*, desp. no. 23, Nov. 5, 1862; *D. D.*, *Turk.*, 17, desp. no. 3 from E. J. Morris, U.S. Min., Constantinople, Oct. 8, 1861; Earle, *op. cit.*, 531-33.

[17] *C. D.*, *Eg.*, 3, pvt. ltr. from Thayer, Mar. 13, 1862.

especially since "the cotton manufacturers of England are just now studying how to increase the cotton cultivation in Egypt, as well as in India." Secretary Seward went on to define United States policy on the cotton question:

It would be a pleasing duty, under proper circumstances to study how to promote, through the agencies of our foreign intercourse, the growth and cultivation of cotton in our own country, and to extend the market for its consumption. But at the present conjuncture, the great mass of cultivators of cotton in the Southern states attempt to cast off their allegiance, and have submitted themselves to the guidance of a treasonable faction, who, with their consent, and using all the forces derived from that important element of our national strength, to overthrow the Republic. They are desperately attempting to impoverish the country at home, and involve it in foreign wars by destroying the cotton already gathered, and preventing the further cultivation of that staple.

Under these circumstances it has seemed to the Government an obvious duty to cast about and examine the capacities of other countries for cotton culture and stimulate it as must as possible, and thus to counteract the destructive designs of the factious monopolists at home.[18]

In a somewhat similar vein Seward wrote to Minister E. J. Morris at Constantinople:

The decline of the cotton culture in the United States is an unavoidable result of the war. But is there not some very valuable instruction in the fact that the cotton culture is reviving so rapidly in Turkey. I wish that our insurgent citizens could allow themselves time to think that the way of wisdom, at least in the present age, is the path of peace.[19]

If the above-quoted statements were intended in fact to enunciate an active policy of the United States Government to stimulate cotton production outside the United States, there is

[18] *C. I., B. P.,* 14, confid. inst. no. 12 to Thayer, Apr. 8, 1862; see also *ibid.,* insts. nos. 17 and 17½, Dec. 2 and 15, 1862.

[19] *D. I., Turk.,* 2, inst. no. 43 to Morris, Dec. 13, 1862.

no record in the Department of State correspondence to show that any concrete assistance was offered in Egypt or Turkey. It is possible, however, that advice and encouragement were given informally by the United States representatives in those countries.

The net result of the various types of assistance, expanded cotton acreage and the stimulus of high prices was an amazing increase in Egyptian cotton production. Total Egyptian cotton exports jumped from 60 million pounds in 1861 to approximately 274 million pounds in 1865—a gain of some 350 per cent. Most, but not all, of this cotton went to England. In 1861, for example, out of the total of 60 million pounds exported, some 40 million pounds was sent to Great Britain, about 15 million to France and the remainder to Austria and other countries. Between 1861 and 1865, Egypt furnished about 12 per cent of the cotton imported by the United Kingdom and the Continent.[20]

Meanwhile the value of Egyptian cotton spiraled upward from about $7 million in 1861 to a peak of $77 million in 1865. The sudden burst of prosperity brought with it, however, considerable inflation. Although tremendous profits were made, the price of cotton fluctuated with the tide of battle in America. When the news of the end of the Civil War reached Egypt, the bottom fell out of the cotton market, causing a financial crisis. Many speculators were ruined, and great hardship overcame the *fellahin,* who had difficulty repaying the advances made them by the European capitalists. The situation was somewhat alleviated by a relief program instituted by the Viceroy.[21]

The immediate effects of the termination of the Civil War were certainly painful in Egypt, but the permanent results of that war on Egyptian cotton were more crucial. Although cotton

---

[20] Earle, *op. cit.,* pp. 534-35; *C.D., Eg.,* 3, desp. no. 15 from Thayer, Alexandria, Jan. 27, 1862. For Egyptian cotton exports for 1861-1866, see *ibid.,* desp. no. 18 from C. Hale, Alexandria, Feb. 24, 1865, and *ibid.,* 4, desp. no. 93, June 17, 1867; cf. Earle. *op. cit.,* p. 535, for slightly different figures. For 1867-1884 Egyptian cotton exports, see A. E. Crouchley, *The Economic Development of Modern Egypt* (London, 1938), pp. 134-35.

[21] *C.D., Eg.,* 3, desps. nos. 18 and 32 from C. Hale, Alexandria, Feb. 24 and June 14, 1865; *ibid.,* 4, desp. no. 93 from Hale, June 17, 1867; *Comm. Rels.* (1864), pp. 483-84.

exports fell in 1866 to some 178 million pounds and reached a low of 125 million pounds in 1868, the figure had climbed again to 243 million pounds by 1877.[22] Fortunately for Egypt, manufacturers discovered that Egyptian long-staple cotton was particularly adaptable for the spinning of fine yarns. After the Civil War, Egyptian cotton was even absorbed in increasing quantities by the growing American textile industry. But cotton was not an unmixed blessing for Egypt. To the dangers of a one-crop economy were added problems of soil depletion and irrigation. Perhaps an even greater peril to Egypt was the dependence of her economy on the British textile industry. This meant in turn that the United States and other nations were to encounter persistent obstacles in their commercial relations with Egypt. Of greater moment, as Earle has pointed out, English manufacturers acquired such strong ties to Egyptian cotton production that pressure to protect their interest was a prominent factor, at least in the background, of the British occupation of Egypt.[23]

---

[22] *C.D., Eg.*, 4, desp. no. 93 from C. Hale, Alexandria, June 17, 1867; Crouchley, *op. cit.* For the comparative decline of Indian exports to England in the post–Civil War period, see *G.B., A. P.* (1867, 1880 and 1883).

[23] T. Ellison, *The Cotton Trade of Great Britain* (London, 1886), p. 143; Issawi, *op. cit.*, p. 67; Earle, *op. cit.*, p. 545.

CHAPTER V

Americans in the Egyptian Military Service

EMPLOYMENT OF THE AMERICANS

Isma'il Pasha, who became Viceroy of Egypt in 1863, inherited his grandfather's ambitions. Supplementing a normally large income with profits from "Civil War cotton prosperity" and with enormous and injudicious foreign loans, he was able to indulge a passion for public works in a manner and with consequences that will be discussed in a later chapter. The Viceroy also determined to free himself from the restraints of the 1841 Egyptian settlement. In return for increased tribute, he had obtained from the Sublime Porte in 1867 a *firman* conferring upon him the title of Khedive (a Persian word signifying Prince or Viceroy) and the right to make certain non-political treaties, such as those regarding customs duties.[1] So strong was the impression abroad that the Sultan was losing control over his richest province that the Turkish Minister to Washington felt compelled to send a note to the Department of State asserting that there had been no change in Egypt's basic relationship with the Ottoman Porte.[2]

These new political gains seemed only to whet Isma'il's appetite. In 1869 he embarked on a course of building Egypt's armed strength. He realized, however, that this could be done

---

[1] Text in Hurewitz, *op. cit.*, pp. 100-101. In 1873 these rights and privileges were widened yet further and consolidated in a new *firman*. See *For. Rels.* (1874), pp. 1179-81.

[2] *Notes from Turk. Leg.*, 1, note no. 53 from Blacque Bey, Turk. Min., Washington, Jan. 18, 1868.

only with the assistance of foreign military advisers. And although French Army influence had been paramount in Egypt since the days of Mehmed 'Ali, the new Khedive chose to call in American officers. There were several reasons for this. The rising young giant of the West had impressed the world with the bravery, skill and strategy shown on both sides during the Civil War. Emperor Napoleon III's rather hasty evacuation of Mexico in 1867 had shown already the new respect for American power. Undoubtedly, availability also played a part in Isma'il's decision; a large number of military personnel, available and eager for adventure, remain as a by-product of every large war. The United States formed a pool from which were drawn the American officers who entered the military service of the Egyptian Government. Finally, the Khedive was predisposed toward Americans because of the demonstrated absence of any United States territorial design on Egypt.

In a welcoming speech made to a group of the first American officers arriving in Egypt, Isma'il reiterated the reasons for their employment, and spoke in guarded terms of his long-range ambition for independence:

> I welcome you, gentlemen, to my country. I desire to express to you my appreciation of your prompt response to my invitation. I may say to you, in absolute confidence that you are expected to see active service very soon. Your experience in the late war with the States in America, and the lack of selfish interest in Egypt on the part of your country, are the motives which suggested Americans for the proposed service. . . . I count upon your discretion, devotion and zeal to aid me in the establishment of the independence of Egypt. . . .[3]

Colonel Charles Chaillé-Long, one of the American officers, furnished further testimony regarding Isma'il's plans for independence. Before taking an oath to support the Khedive, he asserted, he was confidentially informed that "aside from the reorganization of the Egyptian Army, the real and immediate object of our employment was nothing less than to strike a blow

---

[3] C. Chaillé-Long, *My Life in Four Continents* (London, 1912), I, 32.

for the independence of Egypt and to sever that country from the tyranny of the Turkish yoke."[4]

The first of the American contingent, General Thaddeus P. Mott, "U.S. citizen," formerly of the United States Army, arrived in Egypt in January, 1870. He and his brother, Henry A. Mott, a lawyer in New York City, were assigned the original task of selecting American officers for military service with the Khedive. They were assisted by General William T. Sherman, who (together with General Charles P. Stone) assumed responsibility for the "recruitment," after Mott had left the Egyptian service following a quarrel with Stone. Over the period 1869–1883 some fifty-five Americans were employed in Egypt. This group included both former Confederate and former Union officers. Not all of the officers served simultaneously, however. Owing to resignation, discharge, death or disability, there were never over thirty in the country at one time.[5]

---

[4] *Ibid.*, pp. 16-17.

[5] Chief sources for this American "venture" are: *U.S. Consular Despatches*, Egypt, 1869-1883 (marred at times by the intemperance of the U.S. agents and consuls-general); *General William T. Sherman Papers* (Manuscript Division, Lib. of Congress, Washington), Vols. 32-60 (1872-1883), *passim* (there are many letters from Gen. Chas. P. Stone to Sherman here); P. Crabites, *Americans in the Egyptian Army* (London, 1938), *passim* (Crabites had access to the Dept. of State Post Records in Cairo and to much unpublished material in the Egyptian archives, but his treatment of the subject is sketchy and sometimes inaccurate in detail); W. B. Hesseltine and H. B. Wolf, *The Blue and the Grey on the Nile* (Chicago, 1961), *passim* (the authors have uncovered many new manuscripts and letters in the U.S.; however, their work is rather popular and anecdotal); Frederick J. Cox, who reportedly is writing a book on this subject, has written several scholarly articles (to be referred to below) on specific aspects of the problem (Cox utilizes Egyptian sources extensively); finally, many of the participating officers wrote autobiographical accounts of their activities, e.g., Chaillé-Long, *op. cit.*, and E. Warren, *A Doctor's Experiences in Three Continents* (Baltimore, 1885). (These books provide interesting color but should be used with discretion.)

There is a difference of opinion regarding the total number of American officers who went to Egypt. Crabites, *op. cit.*, chap. ii, says it was 50; Hesseltine and Wolf, *op. cit.*, Appendix, pp. 253-60, list 44. Each of these authors has some obvious omissions.

REACTION OF THE POWERS

The United States Government made it very clear that the American officers in khedivial employ did not constitute an official American military mission. Washington did not wish either to arouse the suspicions of Britain or France or to offend the sensibilities of the Turkish Sultan, who would certainly have regarded an official mission as provocative. The hands-off attitude of the United States Government was clearly expressed in an instruction, dated November 29, 1875, to the American consul-general in Cairo:

> In this connection I have to call your attention to that portion of your despatch in which you refer to the "American Officers" now in Egypt. No American officers are now in service in Egypt. It is presumed that you intend to refer to certain natives of the United States who have accepted service as officers of the Egyptian Army, but these gentlemen can not be considered as American officers and should not be so designated in official communications.[6]

Such diplomatic propriety, however, did not worry the Khedive, who at an official reception asked the United States consul-general to thank the President "for permitting so many distinguished officers to leave their country for the service of Egypt."[7]

Notwithstanding official pronouncements on the subject, the United States Government actually did provide considerable assistance to American citizens in the military employ of the Khedive. Several times it aided individual officers in collecting back pay and other compensation from the Egyptian Govern-

---

For excerpts from a standard contract used in hiring the American officers, see Crabites, *op. cit.*, pp. 8-11; for a complete copy, see *C.D., Eg.*, 7, desp. no. 112 from H. A. Babbitt, U.S.V.C.G., Alexandria, July 10, 1873.

[6] *C.I., Eg.*, 16, inst. no. 237 to R. Beardsley, U.S.A.C.G., Cairo, Nov. 29, 1875.

[7] *C.D., Eg.*, 6, desp. no. 1 from G. H. Butler, U.S.A.C.G., Alexandria, May 28, 1870.

ment. The Khedive, on the whole, dealt most generously with the American military advisers, although after the creation of the Egyptian Public Debt Commission in 1876, the Americans, together with all other army officers, failed to receive their wages in full. Almost all Americans were dismissed, many without payment of their arrears in salary. At this point the United States Government, acting through its agent and consul-general in Cairo, applied diplomatic pressure to secure favorable settlements in a number of cases. The action was taken, curiously enough, even though the Americans in their contracts of service had expressly waived all rights to United States protection and though the Department of State had stated in 1871 that it would, therefore, not even employ the customary good offices.[8]

The War Department also cooperated by permitting officers on active duty in the United States Army to secure leaves of absence, thus enabling them to serve in Egypt. The arrangement was not made public until 1876, when the House of Representatives passed a resolution requesting information on all regular United States Army officers who "are now or have been since the year 1870, in the military service or pay of foreign governments. . . ."[9] Secretary of War William W. Belknap furnished the names of four regular United States Army officers on leave and in the employ of the Egyptian Army. According to Colonel Chaillé-Long, writing in 1912, the total of such officers was nine. Belknap carefully noted that leave was not granted to any for the express purpose of enabling them to enter foreign service. Indeed, it was stated that one officer's application for leave to join the Egyptian Army had been refused, but that ordinary

---

[8] *C.I., B.P.,* 15, inst. no. 51 to Butler, Alexandria, Oct. 5, 1871; cf. *C.D., Eg.,* 15, desp. no. 254 from E. E. Farman, Cairo, July 15, 1878, where, for example, medical indemnity was secured for Cols. W. E. Dye and R. E. Colston; Crabites, *op. cit.,* pp. 255-56; New York *Times,* Aug. 11, 1878. There is no discussion in the U.S. correspondence of the interesting points of international law raised by these cases.

[9] *Cong. Rec.,* U.S. 44th Cong., 1st Sess., Vol. 4, Pt. 1, pp. 293-94, Jan. 6, 1876.

leave had been granted. Thus were the forms preserved.[10] The files of the War Department also disclose evidence tending to establish a direct causal relationship between applications for leave and military service in Egypt, notably two letters from General Charles P. Stone, Chief of Staff of the Egyptian Army, addressed to the War Department. One requested that leave be granted a United States Army officer to authorize him for service as inspector of arms being manufactured for the Egyptian Government at the Remington Arms plant at Ilion, New York; the second asked that another regular Army officer's leave of absence be extended to allow him to remain in the Khedive's service for another year.[11]

From the beginning, France and Great Britain had objected to the presence of the American military advisers in Egypt. The French smarted over the loss of their previous influence in this field; the British were nervous about a potential threat to the integrity of the Turkish Empire; and both feared Egyptian ambitions in Africa and were apprehensive for the security of their large investments in Egypt. But in the face of the officially correct position of the United States Government, neither made any diplomatic protest to Washington. The same was true of the Ottoman Porte, which had even greater cause for alarm.

British and French efforts to get rid of the "American Military Mission" in Egypt were directed instead toward Khedive Isma'il

---

[10] "Army Officers who have Signified their Intention of Entering Foreign Military Service," ltr. from W. W. Belknap, Sec. of War, Jan. 15, 1876, in compliance with Resol. of House of Reps., U.S. 44th Cong., 1st Sess., H. Ex. Docs., Vol. 10, No. 78. Cf. Chaillé-Long, *op. cit.*, I, 38-39.

[11] *Dept. of the Army, Register of Ltrs. Received*, Vol. 185, War Office, No. 8175 précis of ltr. from Chief of Ordnance, Oct. 14, 1875, referring to request of Chas. P. Stone; *ibid.*, Vol. 182, No. 8854, précis of ltr. from Gen. Chas. P. Stone, Cairo, Oct. 3, 1874. For efforts that were made to implement Gen. Stone's request, see *Gen. Wm. T. Sherman Papers*, Vol. 41 (Sept. 24-Dec. 3, 1875), ltr. from Gen. O. M. Poe, ADC, to Sherman, Washington, D.C., Sept. 24, 1875.

and the Turkish Sultan. Unofficial protests, for instance, were made to the Egyptian Pasha in 1870. Similarly, it was reported from Constantinople that the British Ambassador was organizing a movement among the European Powers, together with the Porte, to force the Khedive to discharge the Americans. Warnings were also given to Nubar Pasha, the Egyptian Foreign Minister then in Europe, of the fatal consequence if his master persisted in such belligerent conduct, calculated "to excite the suspicions of the Porte and raise the apprehensions of the Powers."[12]

None of the warnings and protests had any immediate effect on Isma'il. In the end, however, the British and French triumphed, albeit circuitously. The ambitious Khedive was spending beyond his means. He finally became "bankrupt" in 1876, and an Anglo-French control over Egyptian finances was established. The end was now in sight for the American military advisers, as indeed it was for Isma'il himself. By June of 1878 all the American officers except General Stone and Colonel A. M. Mason had been discharged. The reason given in the dismissal order was "the necessity for reducing the expenses of the government."[13]

THE "AMERICAN MILITARY MISSION" IN ACTION

Before attempting to assess the achievements of the Americans employed in the Khedive's military service, it is necessary to discuss certain disruptive factors affecting the group as a whole, since these colored its outlook and conditioned its effective operation. For one thing, Isma'il himself had warned his new advisers that they might encounter much jealousy in the Egyptian Army officers. The warning proved all too accurate. As one

---

[12] Crabites, *op. cit.*, pp. 43-45; *C.D., Eg.*, 6, desps. nos. 7 and 32 from G. H. Butler, Alexandria, July 7 and Dec. 30, 1870; *D.D., Turk.*, 21, desp. no. 367 from E. J. Morris, U.S. Min., Constantinople, July 1, 1870.

[13] *C.D., Eg.*, 15, desp. no. 245 from E. E. Farman, U.S.A.C.G., Cairo, July 3, 1878.

result of the hostility, the Americans found themselves confined largely to staff and technical work.[14]

The presence under a single command of former Confederate and Union officers, recently such bitter enemies, inevitably resulted in friction. It was reported, for instance, that the Southerners so intrigued against General Mott, a Northerner who was senior of the Americans, that the Khedive was forced to relieve him of his field command and make him a personal aide-de-camp. Mott soon resigned from the Egyptian service. The fact that four former Confederate officers who had been employed as generals were reduced to the rank of colonel upon their arrival in Egypt produced further dissension. The British and French tried in various ways to exploit such rivalry among the Americans.[15]

A final source of trouble stemmed from the antagonism that developed between George H. Butler, the American agent and consul-general, and certain of the American officers. Butler came into conflict first with General Stone, Chief of Staff of the Egyptian Army, who accused the consul-general, in the spring of 1872, of interfering with the promotion and decoration of Colonel Vanderbilt Allen. The Khedive himself, while visiting Constantinople later that year, added his own complaint in an interview with the American Minister to Turkey. Although Butler strenuously denied the allegations, he received a reprimand from the Department of State. Even more serious and certainly more spectacular was the bitter feud between the consul-general and several of the former Confederates on Stone's staff. The hostility was climaxed by a sensational brawl in a public restaurant of Alexandria on June 12, 1872. There were conflicting versions of the incident, both as to details and as to responsibility. The

---

[14] *Ibid.*, 6, desp. no. 19 from G. H. Butler, Alexandria, Oct. 20, 1870; Crabites, *op. cit.*, pp. 43-49.

[15] *C.D., Eg.*, 6, desp. no. 7 from Butler, July 7, 1870. Crabites, *op. cit.*, p. 11. Cf. Hesseltine and Wolf, *op. cit.*, pp. 63-64, who assert that there was no friction between wearers of the Blue and the Gray.

affair ended when Butler boarded a ship for Europe on emergency leave granted by the Department of State.[16]

Despite countless difficulties besetting the Americans, they contributed considerably to the military life of Egypt. Charles Pomeroy Stone, West Point graduate and former Union officer, was appointed Chief of Staff of the Egyptian Army, with the rank of brigadier general. For one week in October, 1870, General Stone was actually Commander in Chief of the Egyptian Army. He was then decorated and directed to turn over command to an Egyptian officer, Ratib Pasha. For a few weeks during "the Suez Canal Incident of 1874" Stone was in command of the Egyptian troops deployed in the Canal area. This, however, was an exceptional circumstance. The Americans were not given command of Egyptian troops but rather were used for staff work, training and inspection, survey and mapping, and the like.[17]

One of the principal tasks of General Stone and his fellow Americans was the reorganization of the Egyptian Army. On Stone's recommendation a modern staff was created for the first time. The action itself required the institution of several basic

[16] *C.I., B.P.,* 15, insts. nos. 63 and 109 to Butler, Alexandria, May 14 and July 22, 1872; *C.D., Eg.,* 6, desp. no. 109 from Butler, June, 1872. For Butler's version of the brawl, see *ibid.,* desp. no. 114, July 14, 1872. For criticism by the Egyptian Govt., see *D.D., Turk.,* 24, unnum. confid. desp. from G. H. Boker, U.S. Min., Constantinople, July 11, 1872; *ibid.,* desps. nos. 34 and 36, July 18 and 25, 1872.

[17] *C.D., Eg.,* 6, desp. no. 19 from Butler, Alexandria, Oct. 20, 1870; F. J. Cox, "The Suez Canal Incident of 1874," *Cahiers d'Historie Egyptienne,* IV (Oct., 1952), 194-204; De Leon, *Khedive's Egypt,* pp. 247-50; Hesseltine and Wolf, *op. cit.,* chap. iv.

Gen. Stone had been a controversial figure during the Civil War, being imprisoned for a time without charges following the disastrous defeat of troops under his command at the battle of Ball's Bluff on Oct. 21, 1861. For biographical data on Stone, see G. W. Cullum, *Biographical Register of Officers and Graduates of the United States Military Academy at West Point* (Boston, 1891), II, 214-19; D. Malone (ed.), *Dictionary of American Biography* (New York, 1936), XVIII, 72; *The National Cyclopedia of American Biography* (New York, 1901), XI, 215-16; Hesseltine and Wolf, *op. cit.,* pp. 4-9.

reforms, such as the establishment of a staff college, a competent map division and a small-arms munitions factory. In addition, a complete military code was prepared, following American and British lines. Essential to the success of the entire program was the emphasis placed upon the eradication of illiteracy in the Egyptian Army. A khedivial decree required that candidates for military promotion be able to read and write. By 1873 the literacy rate in the Army had risen to 75 per cent. Pushing the program a step further, a system of schools for soldiers' children was inaugurated.[18]

The Americans also reinforced Egypt's defense. The coast was heavily fortified with torpedoes, guns and other equipment. In addition, great quantities of ammunition were purchased in the United States, partly from the Rodman Gun Company but more especially from the Remington Arms Company, where over a million dollars' worth was ordered. These bellicose preparations naturally aroused the suspicions of the Porte. In May, 1871, therefore, the Sultan ordered the Khedive to discontinue such fortifications and to ship all coastal guns to Constantinople. Isma'il complied reluctantly, and one report held that only the older guns were sent. Indeed, there were rumors of impending conflict between Turkey and Egypt as late as 1874. But Isma'il was not a Mehmed 'Ali. Besides, the British and French were more strongly entrenched and more alert to protect their growing interests in Egypt. The Khedive was therefore forced to expend his military energies in the Sudan and Central Africa.[19]

General Stone and his fellow Americans were full participants in the important and often spectacular scientific exploration and military reconnaissance in the Sudan and East Central Africa.

---

[18] C. P. Stone, "Military Affairs in Egypt," *Journal of the Military Service Institution of the United States,* V, No. 18 (June, 1884), 154-83; Crabites, *op. cit.,* pp. 47-52.

[19] *C.D., Eg.,* 6, desps. nos. 47, 55 and 56 from Butler, Alexandria, Mar. 30, April 29, and May 17, 1871; *ibid.,* desp. no. 60, May 27, 1871; *ibid.,* 9, desp. no. 220 from R. Beardsley, Cairo, Aug. 15, 1874; *C.I., Eg.,* 16, inst. no. 96 to E. E. Farman, Cairo, Mar. 28, 1878; F. J. Cox, "The American Naval Mission in Egypt," *Journal of Modern History,* 26 (1954), 173-78.

Prominent among the expeditions undertaken for the Khedive were those to the Sudanese provinces of Darfur and Kordofan (1873–1874), to the sources of the Nile (1874) and to Abyssinia (1875). Suspicion spread among many Europeans that these so-called scientific expeditions were part of a studied Egyptian plan for territorial aggrandizement. Two full-scale military campaigns in fact were undertaken in Abyssinia, but both resulted in disastrous defeat for the Egyptian forces. An attempt was made to fasten blame for these failures on the American staff officers, although they were not in command and their advice was not followed.[20]

Criticism might be leveled against the effectiveness of American training in view of the poor showing made by the Egyptians during the 'Arabi revolt, especially at the battle of Tel-el-Kabir in 1882. It should be noted, however, that according to some observers, bribery and treachery played an important part in the British victory. General Stone offered two explanations for the Egyptian debacle. He alleged that the British made free and timely use of the Khedive's treasure; he argued also that the trained and capable officers remained faithful to the Khedive, with the result that "the British had to fight only the body of the Egyptian Army without its brains."[21]

A particularly interesting contemporary criticism of the "American Military Mission" to Egypt appeared in the *Nation* in connection with a review of Colonel William M. Dye's book on the subject:

[20] For a copy of Gen. Stone's report summarizing the results of Egyptian exploration during 1874–1876, see De Leon, *Khedive's Egypt*, Appendix F; see also Crabites, *op. cit.*, pp. 53 ff.; Stone, *op. cit.*, Hesseltine and Wolf, *op cit.*, chaps. vii–xi; *C.D., Eg.*, 7, desp. no. 47 from Beardsley, Alexandria, Dec. 15, 1872; W. W. Loring, *A Confederate Soldier in Egypt* (New York, 1884), Pt. II, *passim;* also memoirs of other Americans who served in Egypt cited in Bibliography.

[21] Stone, "Military Affairs," p. 181. See also "Stone Pasha and the Secret Despatch" (ltr. from C. P. Stone, Oct. 8, 1886), *Journal of the Military Service Institution of the United States*, VIII (Mar., 1887), 94–95, for an interesting account of how valuable information regarding 'Arabia's forces and intensions was smuggled out of Cairo in 1882 and delivered to Gen. Stone, who in turn made it available to the British.

"This Egyptian incident" is the first instance in which Americans, in any numbers, have entered a foreign service for the purpose of "lifting it from the ruts" or "rejuvenating" it, and the experience should be carefully considered by any officers who may be tempted in the future with offers of colonelcies and generalcies in any state which has relapsed into semi-barbarism. After nearly five years of it Colonel Dye records his opinion as follows: "If in these remarks enough has not been said to indicate that no intelligent foreigner should ever serve under an Egyptian, I wish to state definitely to those having an interest in the progress of the country, that an intelligent foreigner can accomplish little in Egypt unless he has unlimited power entrusted to him." And we may add that, in Egypt or in any other state incapable of correcting its own vices, the chances of unlimited power being entrusted to any foreigner are very small.[22]

It is true also that when Khedive Isma'il became enmeshed in the British and French financial web, Americans were for the most part dismissed, and their influence collapsed almost entirely. In the long view the American "military mission" was only a short interregnum in the continuing Anglo-French struggle for control over Egypt.

Nevertheless, much can be adduced regarding positive contributions of Americans in the Egyptian military service. Not only was a competent staff organization introduced into the Army for the first time, but the Sudan was won back for Egypt, and at one time Egyptian influence reached as far south as the equator. The Americans served the Khedive bravely and loyally, and in turn were honored and trusted by him. At least five American officers were killed or died while on active duty and many others were injured or disabled. It can be said with some justification, therefore, that the period of the American military advisers represented a sort of peak of United States influence in Egypt prior to World War I. And yet it was a characteristic of American policy as well as one of the secrets of sustained American popularity in Egypt and the rest of the Near East that the United States Government never attempted to make political capital out of good will flowing from such undertakings.

---

[22] "American Influence in Egypt," *Nation*, XXXII (Feb. 3, 1881), 77.

CHAPTER VI

Canals, Courts and Creditors

THE SUEZ CANAL

The United States took little part in controversies surrounding the early development of the Suez Canal. Active participants were the English and the French. Nevertheless, crucial American diplomatic decisions of a later day regarding this vital waterway cannot be properly understood without an appreciation of the basic background. This will be presented in the light of United States reactions to events and issues as they occurred.

Since ancient times, various plans for connecting the Red and Mediterranean seas by a canal through Egypt had been considered. The modern history of the Suez Canal began with Napoleon's expedition to Egypt in 1789; another Frenchman, Ferdinand De Lesseps, finally was responsible for the successful construction of the present canal across the Isthmus of Suez.[1]

De Lesseps was able to realize his great ambition largely because his old friend, Sa'id Pasha, made Viceroy of Egypt in 1854, responded to the Frenchman's enthusiasm and gave the necessary permission. The first Suez Canal concession granted to De Lesseps, dated November 30, 1854, stipulated in part that the concession would run for 99 years from the date of the opening of the canal; that the tolls would be the same for all nations; that 15 per cent of the net profits would go to the Egyptian Government, 10 per cent to the "Founders," and 75 per cent to the canal company; and that the company statutes

---

[1] Hoskins, *op. cit.*, chaps. ii-xii; C. W. Hallberg, *The Suez Canal* (New York, 1931), pp. 23-114. Hallberg's book is one of the best single volumes in the extensive literature on this subject.

were to be subject to the approval of the Egyptian Government. A special "footnote" specified that work on the canal was not to commence until after authorization from the Porte had been obtained.[2]

After a competent engineering commission had reported that a maritime canal across the Isthmus of Suez—in its opinion the only feasible route—could be easily constructed for an amount not exceeding 200 million francs, De Lesseps obtained from Sa'id a second act of concession, on January 5, 1856. The new *firman* elaborated upon the earlier one of 1854, and annexed to it were the approval Statutes of the Universal Company of the Suez Maritime Canal (Compagnie Universelle du Canal Maritime de Suez). The Statutes specified, among other things, that the Company would be capitalized at 200 million francs, represented by 400,000 shares of 500 francs each (Art. 6); that the Company would be managed by a Council of 32 members representing the principal nations interested in the Canal (Art. 24); that resolutions of the general meeting would be taken by a majority vote (Art. 50), each owner of 25 shares being entitled to one vote up to an absolute maximum of ten votes (Art. 51); and that the Company would be an Egyptian Company with its corporate seat at Alexandria, but with its domicile for legal and jurisdictional purposes at Paris (Art. 73).[3]

To a certain extent De Lesseps' success in securing the original concessions for the canal sprang from luck and good timing, but there can be no denying his skill, tact and pertinacity in overcoming British opposition and in securing the Sultan's permission, since England's influence at Constantinople in the person of its Ambassador, Lord Stratford de Redcliffe, was extremely great. Lord Stratford at the Porte and Lord Palmerston in London were bitter foes of the canal plan because of its French

[2] For an English translation, see P. Fitzgerald, *The Great Canal at Suez* (London, 1876), I, 293-96; for a French version see A. T. Wilson, *The Suez Canal* (London, 1939), pp. 173-75; see generally F. de Lesseps, *Recollections of Forty Years* (London, 1887), Vol. I, *passim*.

[3] For an English abstract see Fitzgerald, *op. cit.*, I, 310-23; for a French text in full see Wilson, *op. cit.*, pp. 179-91.

origin and its potential threat to British imperial communications wth India. The undisguised hostility of the British Government was mitigated somewhat because the energetic De Lesseps managed to rally warm support in the House of Commons and among British merchants.[4]

Leaving no stone unturned in his search for assistance, De Lesseps issued a circular, dated October 21, 1857, to the Ministers of Foreign Affairs of all the important Powers asking aid for his canal project. One of the addresees of this circular was "James Buchanan, Minister of Foreign Affairs of the U.S. [*sic*]." On the same date, De Lesseps wrote a private letter to President Buchanan:

Sir: The Honorable Representative of the United States at Alexandria has shown the most favorable disposition, in his own name and that of his Government, towards the enterprise of cutting the Isthmus of Suez.

This consideration and my friendly relations with the United States, where many of my relatives have become citizens, justify me in commending to you specially the official letter which I have the honor to address to you on the present situation of the Suez canal, which will shorten by more than 2,000 leagues the maritime distance from Bombay to New Orleans, Boston, and New York.

The liberal and generous policy of the American Union has always defended the freedom of the seas, and if any one other selfish and exclusive policy should show itself to obstruct the free communication between the Mediterranean and the Indian Sea, the principle of the freedom of the sea would receive serious injury. In that case the intervention of the Agent of the United States at Constantinople would be perfectly justifiable, aside from motives of national interest concerning the commerce and navigation of the Union. Besides this, the execution of the canal of the two seas, which one day will be the most useful auxiliary of the American canal of the two oceans, will give at a future day to the United States the occasion and the right of intervention in the councils of European diplomacy to effect, with the concurrence of France, this inevitable solution.

---

[4] Hallberg, *op. cit.*, pp. 119-59; Wilson, *op. cit.*, pp. 15-22.

The respect of private property on the seas and the abolition of the blockade of commercial ports, extending over commerce from the enemy the legislation which already governs the commerce of neutrals [sic].[5]

Apparently the United States answered neither of these communications. In like manner the Department of State ignored a request from Chargé d'Affaires J. P. Brown at Constantinople in February, 1858, for instructions on the United States position regarding De Lesseps' plea to the Porte for permission to begin work on the canal. Brown's personal disposition toward the canal project was disclosed in a letter that De Lesseps had written to the French Ambassador at the Porte in the previous month.[6]

With a great show of bravado De Lesseps sought to force the issue in November, 1858, by offering shares of the Suez Canal Company for sale. Some 200,000 of the total of 400,000 shares were bought in France, and the Egyptian Viceroy bought 64,000. In an effort to secure international participation, shares were sold in Belgium, Italy, Spain and other countries. An allocation of 85,506 was made to England, Austria, Russia and the United States, but neither individuals nor the governments of these countries participated at this time.[7]

Having successfully launched his company and having acquired some working capital, De Lesseps took another bold step by commencing with Egyptian laborers preliminary operations on the canal in April, 1859, without first securing the required authorization from the Porte. But British pressure brought a work-stoppage order from the Sultan on June 1, 1859. "The combination," Consul-General De Leon wrote,

---

[5] De Lesseps' italics; English translation in J. E. Nourse, "The Maritime Canal of Suez," U.S. 48th Cong., 1st Sess., S. Ex. Docs., Vol. 7, No. 198, p. 41; original French text in F. de Lesseps, *Lettres, Journal et Documents pour Servir à l'Histoire du Canal de Suez* (Paris, 1875-1885), II, 134-35.

[6] D.D., Turk., 15, desp. no. 11 from J. P. Brown, Chargé, Constantinople, Feb. 28, 1858; Nourse, *op. cit.*, p. 40.

[7] Hallberg, *op. cit.*, pp. 158-59; Wilson, *op. cit.*, p. 22. Cf. P. Crabites, *The Spoliation of Suez* (London, 1940), chap. vii, for a criticism of De Lesseps' handling of the stock subscriptions.

was too strong and the pressure too heavy for Said, bold as he was, to disobey. He summoned to his councils the consuls general of the other powers and demanded of them if they would sustain him in resisting this order. None would promise him anything more than moral support, and turning to the American he impatiently asked:

"Your Government is not afraid of the English! Would they support me with ships in case I should resist?" "Certainly not, your Highness!" was the prompt reply; "Suez and India are very far from America, and her interests there are very small indeed!"

"Well then," responded the Viceroy, "poor Lesseps must go to the wall; but it is a great shame. *Mais que voulez-vous?* Egypt is a little place, and I am a little monarch!"[8]

Nevertheless, construction was resumed, chiefly by Europeans. This resulted in a second, sterner injuction from the Porte on September 19. In response, the consular corps at Alexandria (including the French consul-general) agreed unanimously to recall their nationals from the job. No Americans appear to have been involved.

In reporting these events, De Leon advised the Department that some American capital (amount unspecified) had already been invested in the Suez Canal Company, with a prospect of more in the future. He also stated that since De Lesseps was contemplating a lawsuit on this issue in which American interests would be involved, he had reserved the United States position in the matter.[9]

Napoleon III's intervention saved the day for De Lesseps, however. The United States Minister in Paris reported early in November, 1859, that "M. Ferdinand de Lesseps, the President of the Canal Company called in person to say that it would be extremely agreeable to his Majesty the Emperor if the Government of the United States would lend its countenance to this scheme intended to benefit the world."[10] There is no record of

---

[8] Nourse, *op. cit.*, p. 61.

[9] C.D., Eg., 2, desp. no. 51 from De Leon, Alexandria, June 18, 1859.

[10] D.D., Fr., 46, desp. no. 6 from R. Calhoun, Paris, Nov. 8, 1859.

any affirmative United States action as a consequence of this plea, but similar French pressure on Austria and Russia produced sentiments favorable to the canal; as a result the Viceroy permitted work to be resumed. Faced with a *fait accompli* in the form of an already partly completed canal, the British in 1863 made a final and unsuccessful effort to frustrate the project by attacking the Egyptian *corvée*, or system of forced labor, which was the Company's chief source of workers. With this failure, England's diplomatic defeat was complete. On March 19, 1866, the Turkish Sultan issued a definitive *firman* authorizing completion of the canal.[11]

After some anxious moments the inauguration of the opening of the Suez Canal was celebrated on November 17, 1869, with great pomp and circumstance, as promised by De Lesseps. European royalty, the Khedive of Egypt and many other dignitaries were present as sixty-seven vessels proceeded through the canal in triumphant procession. Cairo was also the scene of many festivities, including the performance of a new opera, *Aïda*, that Verdi composed especially for the occasion.[12]

The United States was the only Western nation of any size and importance not officially represented at the opening of the Canal. Sir Arnold Wilson suggested as a reason for such a conspicuous absence that "in 1869 the Alabama question was very actively at issue."[13] It is difficult to see, however, how the "Alabama question" was involved in this matter, which was more than anything a moment of personal triumph for De Lesseps. A more likely explanation is that the United States Government was piqued at the manner in which it had been invited to attend the celebration. On July 21, 1869, the American Legation in Paris received a letter from Khedive Isma'il

---

[11] Hallberg, *op. cit.*, pp. 160-215; Wilson, *op. cit.*, pp. 23-27; Fitzgerald, *op. cit.*, I, 333-34.

[12] *C.D., Eg.*, 5, desp. no. 184 from C. Hale, Alexandria, Nov. 24, 1869; Wilson, *op. cit.*, pp. 27-40; Nourse, *op. cit.*, pp. 72-74. For a contemporary account see New York *Times*, Nov. 18 and 19, Dec. 2, 13 and 20, 1869.

[13] Wilson, *op. cit.*, p. 39, n. 2.

addressed to the President of the United States, inviting him or a representative to be present at the opening of the Canal.[14] Chargé d'Affaires Hoffman at Paris informed the Department on August 12 that the Porte and Isma'il were at odds over Isma'il's right "to invite sovereigns to be present at any public celebration in Egypt."[15] Upon receipt of this information the Department of State replied that in view of the complications between the Sultan and the Khedive, the President had decided not to send a representative to the Canal inauguration.[16] About this time the Secretary of State presumably had an off-the-record conversation with the Turkish Minister to Washington about the matter, because on September 2 the Department sent the Turkish Legation the following unofficial note:

> Upon further examination of the letter of the Viceroy of Egypt to the President, and in consideration of the irregular way in which it was received, my impression is that it would be a breach of confidence and a discourtesy towards that functionary to furnish you with a copy of it, even unofficially.
>
> The invitation which it gives for the President to attend the opening of the Suez Canal will not of course be accepted and the letter itself seems to take this for granted.[17]

The attitude of the United States Government cannot be attributed wholly to Turkish pressure, which certainly did not make itself felt effectively in other capitals. The New York *Times* special correspondent in Cairo explained the improper delivery to the United States of an invitation to the Canal opening through the American Legation in Paris merely as a manifestation of the general confusion surrounding the whole affair. He accounted for official Washington's reaction as a case of "indifference at home to the desirability of a prominent repre-

---

[14] For a copy of this letter see *D.D., Fr.,* 65, desp. no. 33 from W. Hoffman, Chargé, Paris, Aug. 4, 1869.

[15] *Ibid.* desp. no. 37, Aug. 12, 1869.

[16] *D.I., Fr.,* 18, inst. no. 13 to Hoffman, Aug. 24, 1869.

[17] *Notes to Turk. and Greek Legs.,* 1, unofficial note to Blacque Bey, Turk. Min. to Washington, Sept. 2, 1869. There is no record of any Turkish note to the Dept. on this subject.

sentation."[18] This analysis appears quite sound and is in line
with the general lack of official American interest in the Suez
Canal in this early period.

Of the total cost of construction of the Suez Canal—over 400
million francs, or more than double the original 1855 estimate—
Egypt, by the most conservative estimate, paid more than one-
half of the full amount, or over 200 million francs. This consisted
primarily of payment for shares in the Canal Company, indemnity to the Company for the loss of the *corvée,* or forced
labor, cost of cutting the Sweet Water canal, and recompense
for surrender of certain rights by De Lesseps. Naturally the
Egyptian Government could raise such an amount only with the
assistance of foreign loans, but in a real sense it can be said
that the Suez Canal was partly built by the extraordinary Egyptian cotton profits made possible by the American Civil War.
Egyptian cotton exports, for example, rose 500 per cent between
1860 and 1865, and the value of the cotton crop increased over
400 per cent in the same period—from approximately $12 to
$64 million.[19]

The new Suez Canal was not originally a financial success.
In its search for increased revenues the Company adopted a
new system of measuring the tonnage of ships entering the
Canal. As a result Canal tolls were raised by some 30 per cent.
This led first to an indecisive lawsuit, then to diplomatic pro-
tests, and finally to the proposal for an international conference
to establish a system for measuring ship tonnage on a universally
agreed basis. In January, 1873, following notification by the
British Ambassador at Washington of the intention of the
Turkish Sultan to hold such a conference, the Department of

---

[18] New York *Times,* Dec. 2, 1869.

[19] Figures cited above are in round numbers, as there is considerable
variation among the authorities. See Farman, *op. cit.,* pp. 210-11; De
Leon, *Khedive's Egypt,* p. 417; Hallberg, *op. cit.,* p. 217; Lord Cromer,
Modern Egypt (New York, 1908), I, 11; Earle, *op. cit.,* pp. 534-35;
Crouchley, *Economic Development of Modern Egypt,* pp. 133-34; Wilson,
op. cit., p. 26, n. 1, and pp. 41-44.

State authorized its Minister at Constantinople to attend, provided that the United States was not bound by the conference conclusions. From then on until October, 1873, when the Powers finally met, there was a remarkable interchange of correspondence between Washington and Constantinople in which the Department tried in various ways to justify its non-participation. For some time it was stoutly maintained that the United States Government had never been formally invited. The real reason for the absence of an American delegate at the conference probably lies in this instruction from the Department, dated November 3, 1873:

> . . . it is obvious that we have little direct interest in the matter, as the flag of the United States is seldom seen in that canal, and it is not likely to be seen there often in comparison with those nations whose tonnage employed in foreign commerce may comparatively be much less than ours.[20]

Omitting technical details, the Constantinople conference adopted the British, or "Moorson," system of measuring tonnage instead of the French system. De Lesseps at first refused to accept this decision, and he agreed, in April, 1874, only after the Khedive, acting on orders from the Sublime Porte, had despatched an armed force under the command of General Charles P. Stone and two Egyptian warships to the Suez Canal. In 1874 the United States accepted the conclusions of the conference, and in 1877 concurred in the 1876 modifications.[21]

One final development with regard to the Suez Canal requires brief discussion. In November, 1875, Disraeli startled the

---

[20] *D.I., Turk.,* 3, inst. no. 147 to G. H. Boker, U.S. Min., Constantinople, Nov. 3, 1873; cf. *ibid.,* 2, inst. nos. 69, 126 and 139 to Boker, Jan. 14, Aug. 28 and Oct. 8, 1873.

[21] *C.D., Eg.,* 8, desp. no. 193 from R. Beardsley, Alexandria, Apr. 29, 1874; *Notes to Turk. and Greek Legs.,* I, Notes to Aristarchi Bey, Turkish Min., Washington, Dec. 30, 1874, and Mar. 23, 1877; Cox, "Suez Canal Incident of 1874"; cf. Hallberg, *op. cit.,* p. 227, who incorrectly states that the Egyptian troops used to put pressure on De Lesseps were commanded by an Englishman.

diplomatic world with his precipitate purchase of Khedive Isma'il's 176,602 Canal Company shares. Over the years this investment has proved a notable financial success. But if this move was designed to effect increased British control over the Suez Canal Company, it can only be regarded as a failure, since by Company statutes (Art. 51) no one shareholder was entitled to more than ten votes irrespective of the number of shares owned or controlled. It is true that in 1876 the British Government secured the right to appoint three members on the Board of Directors and that in 1884 seven more directors (out of a total of thirty-two) were to be chosen by private English interests; yet at best this could mean only minority participation in the direction of a company that remained until 1956 under French administrative control.[22]

Following the outbreak of the 'Arabi revolt of 1882, the strategic and commercial significance of the Suez Canal proved most decisive in compelling Great Britain to initiate the forceful action that led eventually to her occupation of Egypt. And as long as Britain retained physical control of the Suez Canal area, it mattered little in whose hands the administration of the Company rested.

Despite the general lack of United States concern over Suez Canal affairs, when the Company was first formed in 1858, an American, Paul Forbes, was one of the three vice presidents. Forbes acted in this capacity, however, only from December 20, 1858, until November 13, 1860, when he resigned. After him, no American served in the Company's administration until the appointment of S. Pinkney Tuck to the Board of Directors on June 8, 1948.[23] The explanation for Forbes' appointment prob-

---

[22] Hallberg, *op. cit.*, pp. 229-77. Cf. Cox, "Suez Canal Incident of 1874," pp. 203-4, who insists on the crucial importance of the Khedive's sale of his share to Great Britain both in the history of the Canal and in the history of modern Egypt.

[23] Forbes was a member of the banking house of R. B. Forbes, Boston. See personal letter from the Asst. Director General, Suez Canal Co., Paris, July 30, 1952; *D.D., Fr.*, 14, desp. no. 6 from W. R. Calhoun, U.S. Min., Paris, Nov. 8, 1859; J. Charles-Roux, *L'Isthme et le Canal de Suez* (Paris, 1901), I, 291-92.

ably is to be found in De Lesseps' original concept of universality as a basis for the Suez Canal Company's ownership and direction. The subsequent omission of Americans in the administration of the Company resulted from United States failure on almost every level, especially commercial, to participate in Suez Canal activities. The virtual absence of American shipping through the Canal is best shown by a sampling of traffic statistics (Table 1).

TABLE 1

SUEZ CANAL TRAFFIC, 1870–82
(In Thousand Tons)

Year	United States	Great Britain	Total
1870	0	289	436
1871	4	546	761
1872	1	1,060	1,439
1875	5	2,181	2,941
1880	1	3,461	4,376
1882	0	4,126	5,076

Source: A. T. Wilson, *The Suez Canal,* pp. 135-36.

THE MIXED COURTS OF EGYPT

In contrast to its generally disinterested attitude toward Suez Canal problems, the United States was actively involved in the origin and development of the Mixed Courts of Egypt. The reason lies in the capitulations enjoyed by the United States and other Western Powers in Egypt and in the rest of the Ottoman Empire. The extent and abuses of these rights and privileges not unnaturally resulted in Egyptian and Turkish efforts to seek alleviating reforms.

It was apparent from an early date that none of the foreign Powers benefiting from the capitulatory regime would voluntarily abandon the system as a whole and that all could be counted on to oppose most modifications of detail. The United States, no exception, in the long run proved more reluctant to give up privileges than any of the others. The Sultan and the Viceroy, therefore, could hope only for piecemeal relief. The Mixed Courts represented the most substantial reforms achieved in Egypt.

The earliest experiment in any form of mixed tribunal took place in Turkey in 1820, when France, Great Britain, Austria and Russia agreed orally to set up mixed commissions on an *ad hoc* basis in cases involving nationals of different states. These courts operated successfully until 1864, when the French court at Aix-en-Provence declared them to be of no binding legal authority. In Egypt, Mehmed 'Ali failed in his ambition to abolish the consular courts and subject all Franks to Egyptian law, to be based on the Code Napoléon. He was no more successful with a primitive sort of voluntary mixed court, composed of Franks, Muslims and Re'aya (Christian subjects of the Sultan). Subsequent efforts in Turkey, however, were more fruitful. In 1849, Sultan Abdul Mejid established a special tribunal for commercial cases involving Turkish subjects and foreigners where the value exceeded 1,000 piastres. There were two judges of the foreigner's nationality and three Turkish judges, one of whom presided. Special codes were drafted for the use of these tribunals.

The Porte made ineffectual efforts to introduce similar courts into Egypt in 1856 and again in 1860. In the first instance the plan failed because of the solid opposition of the foreign consuls and the indifference of Sa'id. The second attempt, in 1860, though actively supported by the Viceroy and approved by the five major European Powers, was abandoned because of opposition from the smaller Powers led by the American consul-general at Alexandria. The fiery De Leon addressed some caustic comments to the Egyptian Foreign Minister on this point:

Whatever may be the real or supposed obligations conferred on the Egyptian Government by any of the Powers in 1841, or at any other period, at this date every representative of a foreign government here, great and small, enjoys the right of exclusive protection of his own subjects or citizens, under treaty stipulations, in which the rights and privileges conceded "to the most favored nations" place all foreign agents on the same footing. Under such circumstances, as the representative of my Government here, I will never surrender those rights, nor resign into irresponsible hands, my high prerogative of demanding and enforcing justice for my people, from prince or peasant, in Egypt and its dependencies.[24]

Despite De Leon's efforts, the old system of mixed tribunals was reorganized in Alexandria and Cairo in 1861; but again it proved unsatisfactory and unworkable. There matters rested until Nubar Pasha, the able and energetic Egyptian Prime Minister, began his campaign in 1867 for completely new mixed courts in Egypt.

In 1867, Nubar Pasha addressed his famous note to Khedive Isma'il, strongly indicting the whole system of justice developed in Egypt, "contrary alike to the spirit and letter of the capitulations," and urging that a complete reform be instituted. In essence his plan provided for the creation of an independent Egyptian judiciary composed of seven judges—the president and three others to be Egyptian, the vice president and two others to be foreigners. Subsidiary commercial and civil courts were to be established to try all cases between Westerners and Egyptians. Crimes committed by foreign citizens were to be tried by European judges and juries. The plan was communicated to the United States and to the European Powers. An instruction to Agent and Consul-General Charles Hale at Alexandria, dated January 13, 1868, expressed the United States Government's initial disinterested good will:

---

[24] De Leon, *Khedive's Egypt*, pp. 301-2; see also *C.D., Eg.,* 2, unnum. desp. from De Leon, Alexandria, May 1, 1856; *ibid.,* desp. no. 56, Aug. 24, 1860; Hinckley, *op. cit.,* pp. 151-55; Scott, *op. cit.;* J. Y. Brinton, *The Mixed Courts of Egypt* (New Haven, 1930), pp. 9-13. Brinton was an American who served as a judge on the Mixed Courts of Egypt, and his book is the best in English on this subject.

The United States, owing to their remoteness from Egypt, have less direct interest in the question than the European Christian powers. They have also, perhaps, more confidence in the safety and success of Government reforms, even in those countries which have not been completely administered within the range of international law as established by Christian nations. . . .[25]

The Department of State meanwhile sought the attitude of the British Government regarding Nubar's proposal. The American Minister to London reported in May, 1868, that the British were lukewarm to the project. However, by June of that year, under prodding from the Egyptian Government, they had changed their minds and agreed to participate in a discussion of the suggested changes.[26]

In 1869 a conference of the capitulatory Powers, including the United States, was held in Alexandria for the purpose of studying the proposed judicial reform. From its inception Nubar Pasha's plan had been under attack, especially from the French, and he was forced to make a number of important concessions —notably, to allow a majority of European judges in courts of all levels and to permit reconsideration of the whole system at the end of five years.[27]

On March 16, 1870, the Department of State issued a strongly worded instruction to Consul-General Hale at Alexandria endorsing in principle the object and plan of the proposed courts, but making reservation regarding the necessity for congressional approval of any alterations in the United States–Turkish Treaty of 1830. For some unknown reason this instruction was withdrawn; we have no further indication of the Department's at-

---

[25] *C.I.*, *B.P.*, 14, inst. no. 49 to C. Hale, U.S.A.C.G., Alexandria, Jan. 13, 1868.

[26] *D.I.*, *G.B.*, 21, inst. no. 2156 to C. F. Adams, U. S. Min., London, Apr. 13, 1868; *D.D.*, *G.B.*, 83, desp. no. 1583 from Adams, London, May 2, 1868; *ibid.*, desp. no. 57 from B. Moran, U.S. Min., London, June 20, 1868.

[27] *C.D.*, *Eg.*, 5, desp. no. 192 from Hale, Alexandria, Jan. 25, 1870.

titude until 1873, when Minister George Boker at Constantinople was informed that the decision of the United States Government would be decisively influenced by that of the great European Powers whose immediate stakes in Egypt were larger.[28]

Nubar Pasha worked busily and effectively in the capitals of Europe and at the Porte. A second conference on judicial reform in Egypt was held at Constantinople in 1873. To meet new French objections, more concessions were made, principally in the exclusion of criminal jurisdiction except for a few cases such as offenses against judges and officials of the courts. By late 1873, England, Austria, Russia, Germany and the Turkish Sultan had agreed to the new court proposals. In order to force the hands of the French, the Egyptian Government was extremely eager to secure the consent of the United States. Khedivial disappointment at Washington's delay in responding was reflected by despatches to the Department from American representatives at Alexandria and Constantinople.[29]

On December 1, 1873, the President of the United States formally asked Congress for its assent to modify the legislation providing for consular jurisdiction in the Ottoman Empire, as affecting the new Mixed Courts of Egypt. At long last Congress granted the necessary authorization on March 23, 1874; and on March 27, President Grant issued a proclamation suspending in part the operation of the Act of 1860 so as to accept the jurisdiction of the new Egyptian tribunals.[30]

The new Mixed Courts of Egypt were inaugurated by the Khedive on June 28, 1875, with great ceremony, "in the absence, and in anticipation, of French approval." The stratagem worked, and the French soon fell into line. Fourteen capitulatory Powers

---

[28] *C.I., B.P.,* 15, inst. no. 83 to Hale, Mar. 16, 1870; *ibid.,* tel. to Hale, Apr. 11, 1870; *D.I., Turk.,* 2, inst. no. 88 to Boker, Constantinople, Apr. 14, 1873.

[29] *C.D., Eg.,* 8, desp. no. 125 from R. Beardsley, U.S.A.C.G., Alexandria, Sept. 10, 1873; *D.D., Turk.,* 24, desp. no. 113 from Boker, Constantinople, May 29, 1873; Brinton, *op. cit.,* pp. 32-36.

[30] *U.S. Stats. at Large,* Vol. 18(3), pp. 23-24; J. D. Richardson (comp.) *A Compilation of Messages and Papers of the Presidents, 1789-1908* (New York, 1909), VII, 235, 238, 390-91.

agreed to the new regime in Egypt. These were Austria, Belgium, Denmark, France, Germany, Great Britain, Greece, Holland, Italy, Norway, Portugal, Russia, Spain and the United States of America.[31]

The Mixed Courts of Egypt were officially installed on January 1, 1876, and began to hear cases on February 24, 1876. By the terms of its charter there were three Courts of First Instance at Alexandria, Cairo and Zaqazig (later at Mansurah), each of which had seven judges: four foreigners and three Egyptians. At Alexandria there was also a Court of Appeals composed of eleven judges: seven foreigners and four Egyptians. Article 9 of the charter provided that "these Courts shall have exclusive jurisdiction over all litigation in civil and commercial matters between natives and foreigners or between foreigners of the same nationality or of different nationalities, outside of the law of personal status." The courts also had jurisdiction over real-estate actions between Egyptians and foreigners of the same or different nationalities. It is important to remember, however, that the whole area of criminal law and bankruptcy as it affected foreigners lay outside the jurisdiction of the new courts; this remained, as before, within the competence of the consular courts. Article 40 of the charter stipulated that the system of the Mixed Courts was to be tried in Egypt for a five-year period. The Western Powers were then to have the option of renewing the arrangement with the Egyptian Government or of returning to their earlier practice.[32]

The United States Government did not, in general, manifest much interest in the day-to-day operations of the Mixed Courts of Egypt. This attitude prompted the following comment from the American consul-general at Cairo, in justification for his independent action on an Egyptian proposal to abolish the Court of First Instance at Mansurah:

---

[31] Brinton, *op. cit.*, pp. 38-40.

[32] For an English translation of the charter of the Mixed Courts, as amended to 1930, see Brinton, *op. cit.*, Appendix E, pp. 370-82.

> According to the instructions I have heretofore received, the Government of the United States does not wish to enter into the details of the organization and workings of the International Courts of Egypt, and prefers not to examine the various questions that are constantly arising in this connection.[33]

For this reason the many interesting legal and technical aspects of the conduct of the Mixed Courts will not be presented.[34] Instead, discussion will be confined to two issues of a more political nature with which the United States Government did concern itself: the appointment of judges and the competence of the Mixed Courts to pass on the validity of khedivial decrees.

Considerable diplomatic negotiation preceded the final agreement that the six Great Powers (France, England, Russia, Italy, Austria and Germany) and the United States, who had participated in the second conference on judicial reform in Egypt, should have one judge each on the Court of Appeals and a minimum of one judge each on the Courts of First Instance. A few changes, of course, were made in this arrangement later on. In 1889, for instance, the right to representation in the Mixed Courts was extended to Greece.[35]

On the selection of foreign judges Article 5 of the charter of the Mixed Courts provided:

> The nomination and choice of Judges shall belong to the Egyptian Government; but in order that it may be assured as to the guarantees presented by the persons whom it may select, it shall address itself unofficially to the Ministers of Justice abroad, and authorization of their own Government.[36]

This article, so obviously the result of compromise, very shortly was tested. In April, 1874, the Department of State asked the Egyptian Government whether Victor E. Barringer, formerly

---

[33] *C.D., Eg.,* 17, desp. no. 488 from E. E. Farman, U.S.A.C.G., Cario, May 10, 1881.

[34] For a good analysis of these problems see Brinton, *op. cit.,* pp. 40 ff.

[35] *C.D., Eg.,* 9, desp. no. 284 from R. Beardsley, Cairo, Mar. 5, 1875; Brinton, *op. cit.,* pp. 71-72.

[36] Brinton, *op. cit.,* p. 371.

Attorney General of North Carolina, would be acceptable as the American judge on the Court of Appeals. The Khedive replied that he had no objection to Barringer, but since the right of appointing judges belonged to Egypt, he feared that United States recommendations in this instance might be misconstrued by the other Powers. The Khedive finally accepted Barringer, though insisting that the manner of selection not be taken as a precedent. The fears of the Egyptian ruler were quickly realized as all the Powers soon began to appoint their quotas of judges. The United States designated George L. Batcheller of New York and Philip H. Morgan of Louisiana as judges on the Courts of First Instance in 1875 and 1877, respectively.[37] The conflict on this point remained quiescent until shortly after the British occupation of 1882, when the Egyptian Government, backed by the English, tried to reassert its right to appoint all foreign judges on the Mixed Courts. This led to a serious dispute with the United States.

Of graver international consequence was Khedive Isma'il's denial of the competence of the Mixed Courts to pass on the validity of his decrees. The question arose in the following manner: Bills of exchange were drawn by the director of the Daira (the Khedive's private estates) on the Egyptian Minister of Finance. Some of these bills came into the hands of one Caesar Capri, a French subject, who brought suit in the Mixed Courts to recover payment. The Daira, which had refused to honor the bills, set up as a defense khedivial decrees postponing payment on said instruments. The court of Appeals at Alexandria ruled against the Daira. Isma'il then issued a circular to the Powers stating that he was not bound by the decisions of the Mixed Courts.[38] The British Government replied by requesting the

---

[37] *C.I., B.P.,* 15, inst. no. 118 to Beardsley, Cairo, Apr. 10, 1874; *C.D., Eg.,* 8, desp. no. 199 from Beardsley, May 27, 1874; see Brinton, *op. cit.,* pp. 393-94, for a list of American judges serving on the Mixed Courts of Egypt from their inception to 1930.

[38] *C.D., Eg.,* 12, desp. no. 7 from E. E. Farman, U.S.A. C.G., Cairo, May 26, 1876; *ibid.,* desp. no. 64, Oct. 17, 1876; the judgment of the court in the Capri case is given in Van Dyck, *op. cit.,* Pt. II, pp. 29-36.

United States and other Powers involved to participate in a joint protest to the Khedive. The United States agreed, instructing its agent at Cairo to join with his colleagues in denouncing Isma'il's action. The Secretary of State even hinted at a withdrawal of United States assent to the whole system of the Mixed Courts in Egypt. "The question presented," he explained, "is perhaps of less interest to the United States than to most of the European powers, by reason of our comparatively small political and our unfortunately small commercial relations with Egypt. But we are not without interest and have participated in the organization of the new tribunals in Egypt."[39]

This attempt to present a united front against the Khedive failed because the French refused to participate. The stalemate that ensued was only one of many financial grievances held against Isma'il by the British and French, and led ultimately to his deposition as Khedive.

THE FINANCIAL PRELUDE TO THE BRITISH OCCUPATION

The position of the United States during the Egyptian financial crisis was of considerable interest. In the early stages, for the most part, America remained aloof while the chief protagonists, Great Britain and France, engaged in intricate financial maneuvers designed to impose their joint will on Khedive Isma'il. This response, or rather lack of response, probably stemmed from the traditional American principle of non-intervention in the affairs of Europe, extended to cover Egypt, although the Department of State never clearly articulated the view. By the mid-1870's, European rivalries and intrigues in Egypt had reached such intensity that the country was in imminent danger of being occupied by one or more of the contestants. Indeed, the fate of the Nile Valley and the Suez Canal was being decided in

[39] *C.I., Eg.,* 16, inst. no. 27 to Farman, Cairo, Nov. 25, 1876; see also *Notes from Br. Leg.,* 101, note from Sir E. Thornton, Br. Min., Washington, D.C., Sept. 15, 1876; *Notes to Br. Leg.,* 17, note to Thornton, Nov. 28, 1876.

London and Paris, rather than in Cairo and Constantinople. It is all the more amazing, therefore, to find evidence in 1879 and 1880 suggesting that the Department of State was considering more active intervention in Egyptian political affairs. This new policy, however, if it can be so styled, did not take hold and the United States soon reverted to her more modest role.

The root of Egypt's economic troubles lay in Khedive Isma'il's orgy of borrowing and spending. Mention has been made of Isma'il's military ambitions, which constituted a considerable drain on the country's economy, but it was only a fractional part of the vast amounts disbursed for various public works. Orthodox British opinion, for which Lord Cromer was the spokesman, maintained that Isma'il Pasha was a wastrel and that all the borrowed money, except for the amount contributed to the Suez Canal constructions, was squandered. In contrast, a number of early American observers, including De Leon and E. E. Farman, have emphasized such beneficial and constructive accomplishments of the Khedive's regime as railway and harbor construction and increase in tillable land. This view was resurrected in the interwar years by Pierre Crabites, among them. Recent writers, notably Charles Issawi, have tried to present a more balanced picture.[40]

It was soon evident that Egypt's finances were in a precarious condition. In 1871 the American consul-general at Cairo had reported confidentially to the Department of State that the local discount rate on Egyptian Treasury bonds was 25 per cent and rising and that if rumors were correct, a loan might be sought in New York, since the Khedive's credit was so poor with European bankers. No American loans were sought, but by 1875 the situation had so deteriorated that at the request of the Khedive, Hon. Stephen Cave, H.M. Paymaster-General, made a special on-the-spot survey of Egyptian finances. His report revealed that Egypt's debt, acquired at exorbitant interest rates ranging from 12 to 27

---

[40] Cromer, *op. cit.*, I, 11; cf. De Leon, *Khedive's Egypt*, pp. 168-75; Farman, *op. cit.*, chap. 23; P. Crabites, *Ismail: Maligned Khedive* (London, 1933); Issawi, *op. cit.*, pp. 23-24.

per cent, surpassed £60 million. The Cave report painted a black picture of corruption, waste, extravagance and unproductive spending, but concluded that the situation could be salvaged.[41]

The Egyptian financial crash came on April 18, 1876, when the Khedive deferred payment on the Treasury bills for three months. Two days earlier he had suspended payment on bonds issued by the Director of the Daira (Khedive's private states) and had become involved in a court action and then a diplomatic dispute with the Western Powers. Following this admission of "bankruptcy," Isma'il issued a decree dated May 2, 1876, establishing a "Caisse" (Commission) for the service of the public debt of Egypt which was consolidated at £91 million. The direction of the Caisse was placed in the hands of European commissioners.[42]

The British Government, reluctant at this point to intervene in the internal affairs of Egypt, did, however, give unofficial support to the Goschen-Joubert mission, representing British and French bondholders. The mission succeeded, among other things, in securing the appointment of two controllers general: one English, to supervise tax collection, and one French, to supervise spending. The British Government refused at this time to appoint its controller general, but did name Captain Evelyn Baring (later Lord Cromer) as a member of the Debt Commission in March, 1877.[43]

The years 1877 and 1878 were black ones for Egypt. A low Nile, and the drain on the Egyptian Treasury in furnishing assistance to the Sultan in the Russo-Turkish War, aggravated existing financial difficulties. Many government workers and a large part of the Egyptian Army, including almost all of the Americans employed as staff officers, were discharged. There was

---

[41] *C.D., Eg.*, 6, desp. no. 49 from Butler, Cairo, Apr. 5, 1871; *ibid.*, pvt. ltr. from Butler, Apr. 6, 1871; *G.B., A.P.*, Egypt no. 4 (1876), Correspondence regarding Mr. Cave's Special Mission to Egypt, cmd. 1396, LXXXIII (1876), 87 ff.

[42] *Ibid.*, Egypt no. 8 (1876), cmd. 1484.

[43] *Ibid.*, Egypt no. 2, cmd. 2233, LXXVIII (1879), 239-79; *C.D., Eg.*, 13, desp. no 79 from E. E. Farman, Cairo, Dec. 8, 1876.

every indication that the interest on the unified debt could not be met. French bondholders refused to agree to a moratorium, and the British Government reluctantly joined in the pressure for payment, which was made by ruinous sacrifices on the part of the *fallahin*.[44]

Commenting on the seriousness of the situation in Egypt, Consul-General E. E. Farman suggested that the only remedy was to lower the high interest rates on the bonded debt. He then recommended that the United States intervene actively to help secure this reduction.[45] Refusing to concur, the Secretary of State replied, in part:

> . . . You intimate that the rate of interest is exorbitant and might be reduced by negotiations on the part of other powers with the British and French Governments. In this opinion I can not at once concur. Certainly it would scarcely be advisable for this Government at least alone to enter into such a negotiation. It would not comport with our practice to undertake it jointly with other powers, especially if it is not known that any citizen of the United States is a judgment creditor against the Egyptian Government. It is understood that the habits of that government have been prodigal and the embarrassments of which you speak are their natural and inevitable result from which governments can not expect to be exempt any more than individuals.[46]

Farman, evidently undeterred by this rebuff, became in his despatches even more critical of British and French financial policy in Egypt. Furthermore, the Secretary's statement that he would keep the matter under advisement left the door open for possible future United States intervention.

The year from June, 1878, to June, 1879, was one in which Great Britain and France coordinated their policies closely to force more reforms on Isma'il. After some dispute the Khedive had agreed to a full-fledged investigation into Egyptian finances by an international commission of inquiry. The commission's pre-

---

[44] *Ibid.*, 15, desp. no. 249 from Farman, Cairo, June 9, 1878; *G.B.*, A.P., Egypt no. 2, pp. 301-5; Cromer, *op. cit.*, I, 34-35.

[45] *C.D., Eg.*, 14, desp. no. 210 from Farman, Feb. 18, 1878.

[46] *C.I., Eg.*, 16, inst. no. 94 to Farman, Mar. 20, 1878.

liminary report of August, 1878, sharply criticized Egyptian financial methods. Its recommendations included the establishment of a system of ministerial responsibility and the transfer of the Khedive's estates to secure an additional loan. Isma'il grudgingly consented to these changes. Nubar Pasha was named President of the Council of Ministers; Rivers Wilson, an Englishman, and M. de Blignières, a Frenchman, were appointed Ministers of Finance and Public Works, respectively.[47]

The Egyptian Government, already harassed by a rapidly deteriorating economy, soon faced an explosive situation. Large numbers of Egyptian Army officers who had been either discharged or retired on half pay without being compensated for arrears due them were inadvisably permitted to concentrate in Cairo. On February 18, 1879, occurred what Cromer called the "first mutiny." The army malcontents seized Nubar Pasha and Rivers Wilson and held them captive in the Finance Ministry. They were finally released uninjured, but only after the personal intercession of the Khedive, who promised to arrange for back pay. This incident contained the germ of the 'Arabi revolt. The alarmed European consuls requested that warships be sent to Alexandria. The American consul, on the other hand, reported that there was no immediate danger, but was pleased when the U.S. corvette *Wyoming* arrived in Egyptian waters. It would, he wrote, give the impression that the United States intended to maintain her rights if attacked.[48]

Events moved swiftly thereafter. Isma'il forced the resignation of Nubar Pasha and reorganized the government, dismissing Wilson and his French colleague. More authority was assumed by the Khedive, including the power to restrict and abolish the rights of creditors by placing certain revenues outside the jurisdiction of the Mixed Courts. The action drew an immediate protest from the Western Powers. Finally, on June 18, 1879, Sir

---

[47] *G.B., A.P.*, Egypt no. 2, pp. 342-517; Cromer, *op. cit.*, I, chaps. iii, iv.

[48] *C.D., Eg.*, 15, desps. nos. 281 and 286 from Farman, Cairo, Feb. 22 and Mar. 24, 1879; *G.B., A.P.*, Egypt no. 5 (1879), cmd. 2397, LXXVIII (1879), pp. 48-49.

F. Lacalles, the acting British agent, was instructed to join with the French agent in advising Isma'il to abdicate. The Khedive hesitated and referred the matter to his suzerain, the Turkish Sultan. The end came on June 26, when Isma'il received the now famous telegram addressed to "The ex-Khedive Isma'il Pasha," informing him that he was deposed in favor of his son, Tawfiq. The new Khedive was duly installed on August 14 and invested soon after with a new *firman* substantially like the one of 1873, except for a restriction on the size of the peacetime army and the elimination of the right to borrow unrestrictedly.[49]

Farman, the American consul-general, viewed this whole proceeding with a somewhat jaundiced eye. In a rather caustic despatch, dated March 21, 1879, he observed:

> It is impossible to account for the course pursued by England and France towards Egypt on any purely financial grounds. The group of stock speculators at Paris and London . . . are of course only interested in questions of finance . . . but their governments, and especially the English, must have had some other object in view. It would almost seem to a disinterested observer that the object was to provoke a revolt if possible to have an excuse to take possession of the country.[50]

Whatever their ultimate objective, the British and French had achieved the limited success of replacing the independent-minded Isma'il with the more pliable Tawfiq. But Egypt was still in desperate financial straits. In late August, 1879, the new Khedive proposed to create an impartial commission of liquidation as one means of assisting in the solution of the Egyptian debt question.

At this juncture the United States Government, which hitherto had abstained from entering the international financial negotiations in Egypt, despite the urgings of its consul-general, suddenly cabled Vice Consul-General N. D. Comanos on August

---

[49] *Ibid.*, pp. 87-163; *ibid.*, Egypt no. 3, cmd. 2352, pp. 5-14; *C.D., Eg.,* 15, desps. nos. 303, 307 and 314 from Farman, Cairo, June 20, June 27 and July 16, 1879.

[50] *C.D., Eg.,* 15, unnum. desp. from Farman, Mar. 21, 1879.

27, 1879, "to ask that this Government be represented in the proposed Liquidation Commission."[51] The unexpected action is difficult to explain. It may possibly be accounted for by the cumulative effect on Secretary of State William M. Evarts of Consul-General Farman's vigorous reporting and his presence in the United States at the time on leave. Be this as it may, there was no doubt about the Khedive's pleasure at receiving such an application. However, Tawfiq was unable to give an immediate reply, as he had yet had no response from the leading European governments concerning his proposal. The Khedive then made a general appeal for greater American intervention in Egyptian affairs. "He desired me to do what I can," Comanos replied,

> to encourage the United States to take part in the solution of the difficulties which surround the Egyptian Government with reference to the claim of the creditors and the action of the Governments of Europe, for he considers that the influence of the Government of the United States, it being free from motives of self interest and unbiased by prejudice, cannot but result in advantage and gain to Egypt.[52]

Suspicion that the cable of August 27 requesting American representation on the Liquidation Commission did not reflect a permanent change in the standard United States policy of non-intervention is increased by press coverage of the incident in the United States. Following up a report from London that such a request had been made, New York *Times* reporters interviewed President Hayes, who expressed surprise, stating that there had been no Cabinet discussion of the matter. Secretary of State Evarts was away from Washington at the time, but Second Assistant Secretary of State William Hunter, just back from his vacation, advised that he could not imagine the Secretary's taking such action without consulting the President. "Why, what folly it would be," Hunter continued, "for our Government to meddle with the Egyptian Debt. There is not a man in America who is interested in that debt to the extent of $100. No Sir, you

---

[51] *C.I., Eg.,* 16, unnum. tel. to N. D. Comanos, Cairo, Aug. 27, 1879.
[52] *C.D., Eg.,* 16, desp. no. 332 from Comanos, Cairo, Sept. 1, 1879.

may be assured that the Consul never was authorized to act in the matter, and further, that he never did act as reported. Our policy is to let the political affairs of the old world alone."[53]

The contradiction between Hunter's statement of United States policy and the telegraphic instruction of August 27 was never reconciled. Admittedly, both Hunter and the President may have been speaking in ignorance of the real facts, but a statement that one might have have expected from the Secretary of State clarifying the situation never was made in the press or in any instruction to Cairo. The reason may be that not long after, the British and French managed to sabotage the Khedive's proposed impartial Commission of Liquidation and to substitute their own plan—a plan in which the United States was not invited to participate.

The first step in this Anglo-French campaign forced upon the new Khedive a reinstatement of the system of controllers general. This was done by decree, dated September 4, 1879. Comanos reported from Cairo that the Egyptian Government remained silent regarding its proposed Commission of Liquidation.[54] In due course the British and French, this time in Paris, drafted their own proposal for an Egyptian debt-liquidation commission, to be composed of British, French, German, Austrian, Italian and Egyptian representatives, but excluding the United States, Russia and the smaller European Powers.

Agent and Consul-General Farman reacted violently against the new proposal. He contended that the "honor and dignity of our Government" would be seriously compromised by seeking representation on such a commission. "The situation," he argued, "has now wholly changed. Egypt is virtually in the hands of irresponsible quasi-representatives of France and England, and the negotiations in relation to the commission have been carried on in Europe instead of Egypt."[55] Farman also recommended not giving formal consent or sanction of any act

---

[53] New York *Times*, Sept. 3, 1879.

[54] *C.D., Eg.*, 16. desp. no 335 from Comanos, Sept. 6, 1879, enclosing copy of the decree.

[55] *Ibid.*, desp. no. 372 from Farman, Cairo, Mar. 8, 1880.

of the new commission. Individual American creditors, he asserted, would thus retain freedom of action. He estimated that
Egyptian bonds and claims against the Egyptian Government
belonging to United States citizens and those under its protection, as of December 31, 1879, amounted to not less than $1
million out of a total of nearly $500 million. Farman admitted
this was a small amount compared to the European claims, but
he objected on principle, regardless of the amount involved, to
the fact that "any number of European Governments could be
permitted to arbitrarily determine how much of this should be
paid and the manner and time of payment."[56]

A Commission for the Liquidation of Egyptian debts was
established by khedivial decree of March 31, 1880. It was empowered to determine the revenues to be placed at the disposal
of the creditors. On April 5, 1880, another decree nominated
members of this commission as follows: two British, one of whom
was Rivers Wilson, as president; two French, and one each for
Germany, Austria, Italy, and Egypt. As previously indicated,
the United States was omitted.[57]

The United States Government now was requested to adhere
to the debt-liquidation program. A note to this effect of June
12, 1880, from the British Minister in Washington enclosed a
copy of the decree of March 31 and also a prior declaration of
London by which the five European Powers agreed not only
to be bound in advance by the decisions of the Commission but
also to approach non-signatories for their adhesion. The aim was
to secure the assent of all Powers subscribing to the system of
Egyptian Mixed Courts in order that all creditors might thereby
be bound.[58]

On June 28 the Department of State instructed Farman in

[56] *Ibid.* For Farman's estimate of Egypt's total debt, see *ibid.,* desp. no.
370, Feb. 14, 1880.

[57] *Ibid.,* 17, desps. nos. 381 and 388 from Farman, Apr. 5 and 8, 1880;
B.F.S.P., LXXI (1879-1880), 548-51, contains copies of these decrees in
English.

[58] *Notes from Br. Leg.,* 105, note from Sir E. Thornton, Br. Min.,
Washington, June 12, 1880.

Cairo to advise the Egyptian Government that although it was
not considered necessary to participate in the Debt Liquidation
Commission, "the United States reserve their relations to the
Egyptian Government in case they should have any interests
to protect calling for diplomatic representation."[59] A qualification
was added, however, to the effect that if the Egyptian Government could show that it was embarrassed by this action, the
American Government would reconsider its position.

The Law for the Liquidation of the Egyptian Debt was
proclaimed on July 17. But the British Government was upset
by the United States' reserved adherence. In a confidential note
of July 28, H. M. Minister Victor Drummond in Washington
complained to the Department that its position virtually destroyed the value of its acceptance. Additional pressure was
applied by the Austrian, French, German and Italian governments and by the Khedive. Finally the United States Government instructed its agent at Cairo on September 6, 1880, to
"recall your qualified adhesion, the adhesion itself being in
accordance with your instructions and admitting no reserve."[60]

Thus, by midsummer of 1880 the British and French apparently had the Egyptian situation firmly in hand. The Anglo-
French working agreement still operated harmoniously. Khedive
Tawfiq had succumbed to pressure; and the United States had
retreated from her stubborn opposition. However, Egypt was
still in bad financial shape, and the surface calm was soon to be
broken by the violent eruption of Egyptian nationalism and
the 'Arabi revolt, bringing with it the eventual British occupation of Egypt in 1882.

---

[59] *C.I., Eg.*, 16, inst. no. 170 to Farman, June 28, 1880.
[60] *Ibid.*, inst. no. 183 to Farman, Sept. 14, 1880; *Notes from the Br.
Leg.*, 105, confidential note from V. Drummund, Br. Min., Washington,
July 28, 1880. For a copy of the Law of Liquidation see *B.F.S.P.*, op. cit.,
pp. 557-76. As a *quid pro quo* for United States assent, the wily Farman
forced a favorable settlement of the long-pending claims of the Remington
Arms Co., and of Judge P. H. Morgan, former Judge of the Mixed Courts,
for disputed salary, *C.D., Eg.*, 17, personal and confidential letter from
Farman, Cairo, June 22, 1880.

CHAPTER VII

The British Occupation of 1882

No sooner had the British and French completed the re-organization of Egyptian finances than they faced the 'Arabi revolt, which gradually assumed a violently nationalistic, anti-foreign character. As the situation deteriorated in the winter of 1881–1882 and following months, attempts to solve the problem were made by England and France, by the European Powers in conference in Constantinople and by the Turkish Sultan. These rather involved negotiations are discussed in some detail, since they provide a necessary background for properly appreciating the important but little-konwn United States endeavor to help the Sublime Porte and the British Government reach a settlement in Egypt. The American attempt aborted, and the British fleet bombarded Alexandria on July 11, 1882. American sailors and marines assisted in the exciting and dangerous task of restoring order to the chaotic city, but they did not participate in the subsequent occupation of Egypt by the English.

THE 'ARABI REVOLT

The original disaffection of the Egyptian Army officers was caused by discontent over their financial treatment. Only later did the army clique led by Colonel Ahmad 'Arabi merge with and dominate the rising tide of Egyptian nationalism. The first of these so-called mutinies had forced the retirement of Nubar Pasha, viewed as a tool of the Western Powers. The second, in January–February, 1881, sprang from dissastisfaction over promotions. Again the rebels were successful, this time forcing the dismissal of the Minister of War. Emboldened by their victories, the Egyptian Army officers staged a third, more serious revolt. The occasion for the outbreak was the ordering of the third Egyptian infantry regiment from Cairo to Alexandria. 'Arabi and his fellow officers surrounded the Khedive's palace with 2,500 men and artillery. Three demands were presented to Tawfiq: dismissal of the Ministry, creation of a representation chamber and enlargement of the Army to 18,000. The intimidated Khedive gave way, and asked Sharif Pasha to form a new cabinet. The mutineers then dispersed to barracks on the promise that the other two demands were being referred to the Sultan. Following the last outbreak, the American consul telegraphed the Department of State urging the despatch of United States warships to Alexandria and Port Sa'id to protect American citizens.[1]

The Sharif Ministry was soon formed, but the intrigues and double dealings that were to characterize this whole period began almost immediately. The Khedive and 'Arabi separately telegraphed the Sultan for troops; the first hoped that Sharif Pasha would resign, and the second that Tawfiq would abdicate. Turkish intervention was stoutly resisted by the British and French. When the Sultan sent not troops but commissioners headed by Fuad Bey, they instructed their respective agents at Cairo on October 5, 1881, to advise "the Government of His Highness to receive the expected Turkish envoys with all the honors due their rank, but to firmly oppose any interference on their part in the internal affairs of Egypt."[2]

This suggestion was followed by the despatch of Anglo-French warships to Alexandria, for the announced purpose of lessening panic among the foreign population and serving as a refuge in case of disturbances. By mid-October, 1881, however,

---

[1] *C.D.*, *Eg.*, 18, unnum. tel. from S. Wolf, U.S.A.C.G., Cairo, Sept. 11, 1881; *G.B.*, *A.P.*, Egypt no. 3, cmd. 3161, LXXXII (1882), 1-3; Cromer, *op. cit.*, I, 176-81. For a careful survey of available sources concerning the 'Arabi revolt see R. L. Tignor, "Some Materials for a History of the Arabi Revolt," *Middle East Journal*, 16 (Spring, 1962), 239-48.

[2] *G.B.*, *A.P.*, Egypt no. 3, *op. cit.*, pp. 35-36.

an agreement had been reached whereby the naval vessels were ordered home; in return the Turkish commissioners were recalled to Constantinople. In December the U.S.S. *Nipsic* appeared on the scene, but as the situation was then quiet, her captain was advised she was not needed.[3]

Simon Wolf, the United States consul-general in Egypt, close friend of 'Arabi in this period, reported to the Department in November, 1881, that the Colonel was violently nationalistic and had advocated using force, if necessary, to protect Egypt from foreigners. Wolf also claimed credit for persuading 'Arabi to defer armed revolt at this time. "There would have been," he asserted, "another uprising had I not been on such intimate relations with 'Arabi. I pointed out to him the insufficiency of their preparations, that England was too great a power to trifle with, and that the best thing to do was to educate his people to a high plane of citizenship, and the time might come, but not then, to throw off what he called 'the yoke.' I succeeded in my efforts and received great credit not only from the Khedive but from my colleagues."[4] Following a later interview, Wolf wrote that Colonel 'Arabi, then Minister of War, had modified his bellicose stand; while still desirous that Egypt manage her own internal affairs, he would not avoid international obligations.[5]

Léon Gambetta, an eager imperialist, became Foreign Minister of France in November, 1881. He was the author of the controversial joint Anglo-French note presented to the Khedive on January 8, 1882. The note, which sought to bolster Tawfiq's position, had precisely the reverse effect, arousing widespread anxiety. The other great European Powers—Germany, Austria,

---

[3] *Ibid.*, pp. 51-70; *C.D., Eg.*, 18, desp. no. 45 from N. D. Comanos, V.C.G., Cairo, Dec. 24, 1881.

[4] S. Wolf, *Some Reminiscences at Home and Abroad* (Washington, 1914), p. 13.

[5] *C.D., Eg.*, 18, desps. nos. 32 and 58 from S. Wolf, Cairo, Nov. 10, 1881 and Feb. 27, 1882. Wolf resigned his commission on June 1, 1882, and as result the U.S. was represented in Egypt in these very critical days, until Oct., 1882, by N. D. Comanos, a Greek merchant, who acted as vice consul-general. See *ibid.*, 19, unnum. desp. from Wolf, Washington, June 1, 1882.

Russia and Italy—hastened to get on record as opposing any change in the Egyptian status quo without agreement by the Concert of Europe. The Turkish Sultan immediately protested that such direct dealings with the Khedive amounted to a denial of his sovereignty. In Egypt the nationalists and military groups, now drawn closer together, were able to oust Sharif Pasha. On February 5, Mahmud Pasha Sami became President of the Council of Ministers, and the increasingly popular 'Arabi was named Minister of War.[6]

Despite Gambetta's resignation on January 31, 1882, and his replacement by the non-interventionist government of Charles de Freycinet, the British and French governments continued their close cooperation in Egyptian affairs. On May 6, 1882, Lord Granville instructed Sir E. Malet, the English agent and consul-general at Cairo, to use care in seeing that any advice he gave the Khedive would be identical with that offered by the French agent.[7]

An alleged plot by the Circassian officers in the Egyptian Army against 'Arabi Pasha and the Egyptian Ministry's unauthorized convocation of the Chamber of Notables convinced London and Paris both of the desirability of sending warships again to Alexandria to uphold the Khedive's authority and of preventing any intervention by the Porte. In a revealing despatch of May 14, Malet confined to Lord Granville that he and the French agent were agreed that the political advantage of warships at Alexandria outweighed any danger to Europeans in Cairo.[8] On May 15, Sir Beauchamps Seymour, the British Admiral in command in Egyptian waters, was directed to support the Khedive and protect British and Europeans, "landing forces, if required, for the latter object, such forces not to leave the protection of the Ships' guns without instruction from home."[9]

[6] G.B., A.P., Egypt no. 2 (1882), cmd. 3106, LXXXII (1882), 2-3; *ibid.*, Egypt no. 5, cmd. 3230, pp. 36-84; G. Young, *Egypt* (London, 1927), pp. 114-16; Cromer, *op. cit.*, I, 227-35.

[7] G.B., A.P., Egypt no. 7, cmd. 3249, p. 106.

[8] *Ibid.*, p. 132.

[9] *Ibid.*, p. 138.

The instruction, never revoked, became crucially important in later efforts to assess blame for the burning and pillage of Alexandria.

As tension and anti-foreignism mounted, other nations, among them the United States, augmented the assemblage of naval vessels. The Khedive was advised to take advantage of the presence of the Anglo-French fleet to dismiss the cabinet and form a new one under Sharif Pasha. But 'Arabi Pasha refused to resign and continued military preparations despite contrary orders from Tawfiq. The Egyptian Ministry finally did resign on May 27, labeling the Khedive a mere puppet. Nevertheless, 'Arabi was restored to office after an ultimatum from the Egyptian Army. Confronted with this state of affairs, the British Government suggested to the French Government that Turkish troops be sent to Egypt, but the French objected. The two Powers finally agreed to propose to the other European states that a conference on the Egyptian question be called at Constantinople.[10]

'Abdul Hamid II, the Turkish Sultan, would have no part of any conference on the Egyptian question or of any collective action. For the Sultan, as Young has suggested, "could not act as policeman against what had become a Pan-Islamic movement."[11] Besides, he apparently felt capable of salvaging the situation by sending a new mission to Egypt headed by Dervish Pasha and Sheikh Admed Es'ad. With characteristic duplicity secret instructions were issued to Dervish to support the Khedive and oppose 'Arabi, while at the same time Es'ad was directed to work closely with the rebellious Egyptian Army group.[12]

On June 11, 1882, Alexandria was the scene of a bloody riot in which Europeans were attacked by Egyptian mobs. Some two hundred persons were killed, about one-fourth of them Westerners, and many more wounded, including the British, Italian and Greek consuls. There were no American casualties. The affray, believed to have started in the early morning with

---

10 *Ibid.*, Egypt no. 8, cmd. 3251, pp. 7-60.

11 Young, *op. cit.*, p. 118.

12 *Ibid.*, p. 119; Cromer, *op. cit.*, I, 284-86.

a street brawl between an Egyptian donkey boy and a Maltese British subject, did not end until late afternoon, and then only after Egyptian military intervention, the local police remaining conspicuously aloof. Authorities are still not of one mind on the complicity of the Khedive or of 'Arabi in the affair.[13]

The U.S.S. *Galena,* Commander O. A. Batcheller, U.S.N., commanding, had reached Alexandria on June 10 in time to provide protection to American families and many others as well. An Italian sailing ship was hired to take care of the overflow that could not be accommodated on board the warship. The acting American consul-general immediately requested the Secretary of State to ask that two more naval vessels be sent to Egypt.[14]

Strenuous efforts were now made to launch the Constantinople conference. On June 13, Britain and France had proposed to the European Powers that the Sultan be invited to send troops to Egypt to restore order, subject to the condition that no change be introduced in the status quo as based on the existing *firmans.* When no action was taken on this suggestion, Lord Granville instructed Lord Dufferin, British Ambassador to Turkey, to urge an immediate convocation of the conference with or without the Porte. The first meeting of the Six-Power conference on Egypt, however, was not held until June 23. The United States was not represented. Meanwhile the Sultan played a dangerous game. He not only declined an invitation to attend the conference but further exacerbated the situation by giving 'Arabi Pasha a high Ottoman decoration. On June 26 the European Powers at Constantinople signed a self-denying protocol in which they pledged not to take any territorial or other advantage in consequence of concerted action. It is worth noting that the eventual

---

[13] Cromer says there is no convincing evidence against either. See *ibid.,* I, 286-88. Cf. Young, *op. cit.,* pp. 120-21, and W. S. Blunt, *Secret History of the English Occupation of Egypt* (London, 1907), pp. 497-534, who believed the Khedive implicated. See also *C.D., Eg.,* 19, desp. no. 83, bis from Comanos, Cairo, June 12, 1882.

[14] *Ibid.,* desps. nos. 83 and 87 from Comanos, June 10 and 19, 1882; *ibid.,* unnum. and undated tel., marked "received June 13, 1882."

English occupation of Egypt was technically not covered by the above agreement, since it was made independent of any decision of the conference.[15]

In Egypt many foreigners were overcome with panic, some fleeing the country. The British Government, alarmed by continuing Egyptian military preparations, issued a basic instruction to Admiral Seymour, dated July 3, 1882:

> Prevent any attempt to bar channel into port. If work is resumed on earthworks or fresh guns mounted, inform Military Commander that you have orders to prevent it, and, if not immediately discontinued, destroy earthworks and silence batteries if they open fire, having given sufficient notice to population, shipping, and foreign men-of-war.[16]

The same day a supplementary instruction was sent to the English Admiral: "Before taking any hostile action, invite cooperation of French Admiral; but you are not to postpone acting on your instructions because French decline to join."[17] A despatch from Lord Lyons, British Ambassador at Paris, showed the need for such an amendment; it reported the French Council of Ministers' refusal to order the use of force for halting the fortification of Alexandria, because such a step would constitute an act of war that the French legislature must first sanction. In reply Lord Granville wrote on July 6: "What we were doing seemed to me to be an act of legitimate, and indeed, necessary self defense."[18]

Several days of fruitless negotiation ensued; and on July 9, Admiral Seymour telegraphed the fateful message to the British Admiralty:

> Guns are now being mounted in Fort Silsili. Shall give foreign Consuls notice at daylight tomorrow morning, and com-

---

[15] *G.B., A.P.*, Egypt no. 11, cmd. 3295, LXXXII (1882), 44-81; *ibid.*, Egypt no. 17, cmd. 3391, LXXXIII (1882), 30-33.

[16] *Ibid.*, p. 69.

[17] *Ibid.*, p. 74.

[18] *Ibid.*, p. 90.

mence action twenty-four hours after unless forts on isthmus and those commanding entrance to harbour are surrendered.[19]

The Admiralty concurred, but ordered the substitution of "temporarily surrendered for the purpose of disarmament" for "surrendered." The foreign Powers were advised of this intention, and the ultimatum as amended was sent to the Egyptian military governor of Alexandria on July 10. Raghib Pasha, President of the Council and Foreign Minister, replied on the same day that the proposal was unacceptable, stating:

> . . . it [the Egyptian Government] cannot perceive that it has taken any measures which can be regarded as a menace to the English fleet by works, by the mounting of new guns, or by other military preparations.
>
> Nevertheless, as a proof of our spirit of conciliation and of our desire to a certain extent to accede to your demand, we are disposed to dismount three guns in the batteries you have mentioned, either separately or together.
>
> If in spite of this offer you persist in opening fire, the Government reserves its freedom of action and leaves with you the responsibility of this act of aggression.[20]

The correspondence ended sometime in the early morning of July 11 with a terse message from Admiral Seymour to Raghib Pasha: "I have the honor to acknowledge the receipt of your communication of yesterday's date, and regret that I am unable to accept the proposal contained therein."[21]

AN AMERICAN EFFORT AT GOOD OFFICES

The issue was now drawn at Alexandria; both participants and onlookers anxiously awaited the promised sunrise bombardment of the Egyptian fortifications by the British fleet on July

---

[19] *Ibid.*, p. 105.

[20] C. F. Goodrich, *Report on the British Naval and Military Operations in Egypt, 1882* (Washington, 1883), p. 11.

[21] *Ibid.*

11. Before discussing this dramatic event, it is necessary to examine the diplomatic developments in Turkey in the six preceding feverish days. The Great Power representatives at the Constantinople conference had proved incapable of devising any solution of their own, thus giving the British relatively free rein. The Turkish Sultan, who had been acting independently through his commissioners in Egypt, now frantically sought the good offices of the United States to effect an arrangement with Great Britain. The attempt, though abortive, is of considerable interest because of the new light it throws on British intentions regarding Egypt.

On July 5, 1882, United States Minister Lewis Wallace at Constantinople cabled the Sultan's request to the Department of State:

> Sent for by the Sultan today. He would be greatly pleased if United States would offer its good offices to bring about amicable settlement of Egyptian affairs between his Government and England. I telegraph at his request. If particulars needed, inform me. Hostilities imminent.[22]

In a later despatch Wallace quoted the Sultan's explanation for choosing the United States. "Your country is," the Sultan stated, "the only one I can rely upon for friendly services. It is the only one not asking my money; it is not waiting for a partition of my territory."[23]

Secretary of State Frederick T. Frelinghuysen replied the next day:

> Your cipher telegram was informally communicated to Granville through British Minister here. Granville suggests that before you can be usefully employed you should be made acquainted with all that has passed regarding Egypt between the British Government and the Porte and between the Sultan and Lord Dufferin. After so acquainting yourself you can advise the

---

[22] *D.D., Turk.*, 39, unnum. cipher tel. from Lewis Wallace, U.S. Min., Constantinople, July 5, 1882.

[23] *Ibid.*, confid. desp. no. 110, July 20, 1882..

Department of your conclusions with any information you may deem important. We await your answer.[24]

The American Minister's next communication to the Department on July 9 was full of hope. He had sounded out both the Sultan and Lord Dufferin to get their sides of the story. "Comparing the statement of the two point by point," he wrote, "I am very confident that the intermediation will be agreeable to both parties and reach an amicable result. The trial should be made."[25] The next day, however, Wallace felt the situation was hopeless. He telegraphed Washington: "British Admiral notifies he will open fire on forts in Alexandria Tuesday morning at four. Granville permits this. Good offices useless."[26]

Upon receiving word of the impending British bombardment of Alexandria, the Sultan appealed for a postponement to Lord Dufferin, who sent a telegram to Lord Granville on July 10.[27]

The Sultan has replied that he would send a categorical answer to my communication by 5 o'clock tomorrow; at the same time, that he requested that the bombardment of Alexandria might be delayed. I informed His Majesty, in reply, that I would transmit his message to your Lordship, but that I could hold out no hope, if the conditions required by Admiral Seymour (which I had communicated this morning to the Secretary of State by your Lordship's direction) were refused, that the line of action determined would be modified.[28]

The British Ambassador also telegraphed Admiral Seymour at 3:30 A.M. on July 11 (hour of receipt not shown):

I do not know what are your exact instructions and whether

[24] *D.I., Turk.*, 3 unnum. cipher tel. to Wallace, July 6, 1882; see also *Notes from Br. Leg.*, 108, pvt. ltr. from L. S. Sackville-West, Br. Min., Washington, July 6, 1882.

[25] *D.D., Turk.*, 39, unnum. cipher tel. from Wallace, Constantinople, July 9, 1882.

[26] *Ibid.*, unnum. cipher tel., July 10, 1882.

[27] Exact time sent not given; notation of receipt shown as July 11, but hour not specified.

[28] *G.B., A.P.*, Egypt no. 17, cmd. 3391, LXXXIII (1882), 121.

you have any discretion left to you in the matter. If you have, as the Turkish note can not reach Lord Granville in time for him to communicate with you before the hour you have named for opening fire, it might be well to delay action for three or four hours, in order that Lord Granville may judge whether the Turkish communication is of a nature to modify his present decision.[29]

Lord Dufferin's efforts were useless, for the bombardment of Alexandria took place as scheduled at 7:00 A.M. on July 11. Sa'id Pasha, the Turkish Foreign Minister, immediately protested, claiming he had been given to understand that Dufferin had agreed to telegraph to London and to Admiral Seymour in order to delay the bombardment in anticipation of an early Turkish decision. The British Ambassador replied the same day, pointing out that Sa'id had not made the request until 2:00 A.M. on the eleventh, and in view of the delay in encoding and the difference in time the British could not be blamed "if events have outstripped diplomatic action."[30]

Lord Dufferin appears to have done what he could to secure postponement of the bombardment. His telegram to Lord Granville apparently did not arrive until late in the morning on July 11, and we are informed by Minister Wallace that "it is said (I do not know with what truth) that Seymour got the message not to fire 20 minutes too late."[31] Wallace raised one query about Dufferin, however. On July 10, after notice of Seymour's ultimatum had been received in Constantinople, the Sultan asked Wallace to request the British Ambassador to postpone firing until 5:30 P.M. on the eleventh. Wallace conveyed this message, but Dufferin declared he could not consider it as official. The American Minister commented that this was peculiar, since he had just borne a note from Dufferin to the Sultan. The hour of this incident is not known, but it possibly delayed the official

---

29 *Ibid.*, p. 122.

30 *Ibid.*, pp. 122-24, 163.

31 D.D., *Turk.*, 39, confid. desp. no. 110 from Wallace, Constantinople, July 20, 1882.

Turkish request made by Sa'id at 2:00 A.M. on the eleventh.[32]

Minister Wallace assigned to Lord Granville and the British Government primary blame for the failure of the United States' attempted good offices. He made this point in a forthright despatch to the Department of State:

> . . . presuming Lord Dufferin had transmitted to his chief the important fact that the Sultan was seeking the intermediation of a Power which might fairly be supposed as friendly to England as it was to Turkey—a circumstance in itself declarative of an intent both pacific and yielding—it looked very much as if the British Premier had purposely answered the overture of His Majesty with an order to load the guns and fire . . . —as if England had objects of her own in view, and made up her mind not to be satisfied with anything Turkey might do or conclude . . . —in short, as if, with or without consent, peaceably, if she could, forcibly, if she must, she had started in to possess herself of the Suez Canal and Egypt, the latter as an appurtenance. If so it was useless to offer intermediation. I confess the reflection intensified an interest in the business. The pending dispute relative to the Panama Canal and the Clayton-Bulwer Treaty came to mind. Precedents are never so useful as in the practice of International Law.[33]

Wallace expressed this same idea even more forcefully later in the same despatch. "In short," he continued, "I became perfectly satisfied that it was not in the Sultan's power, by promises or concessions, to avert the bombardment—*unless he made the English Government a quit claim deed for the Canal and Egypt.*"[34]

---

[32] *Ibid.*

[33] *Ibid.*

[34] *Ibid.,* Wallace's italics. Wallace's own autobiography is silent on this incident; see *Lew Wallace: An Autobiography* (New York, 1906), Vol. I, chap. xiii. McKee's book on Wallace has a short statement on this subject, but no new material is added; see I. McKee, *"Ben Hur" Wallace* (Los Angeles, 1947), pp. 203-4. The contemporary American press was aware that something was going on, but reported only that Wallace was shuttling back and forth between the Porte and the British Embassy. See New York *Times* and New York *Herald,* July 7-11, 1882.

The Secretary of State answered Wallace's lengthy report by summarizing the measures taken in Washington. After stating that the United States would have been glad to offer good offices but could not without being assured that Great Britain as well as the Sultan would agree, he concluded: "As Lord Granville did not communicate in any form an assurance, it was not considered advisable to take any definite steps to that end and the bombardment began without receipt of any information as to his view."[35]

The American Minister, in a note to the Turkish Foreign Minister, asserted that the United States Government was able to do no more in the absence of British consent "and the failure was with the English authorities exclusively."[36] The incident was closed with an exchange of notes between Wallace and Dufferin in which Dufferin attempted to justify his actions. The British Ambassador denied that he had promised to communicate with Admiral Seymour, or that he had recommended United States good offices.[37]

Dufferin's correspondence with the British Foreign Office, as contained in *Great Britain, Accounts and Papers for 1882*, fails to mention Minister Wallace's efforts. And without examining the complete British files on the subject, it is difficult to judge definitively. The evidence at hand is not conclusive either way. Playing a far from praiseworthy part in this affair, the Sultan by his refusal to cooperate in any proposals submitted by the European Powers must have been very exasperating. The London *Times* reported "that the British Government were unable to give effect to Said Pasha's request because the Turkish Prime Minister could not offer any guarantee that Arabi Pasha would acquiesce in the demands of Lord Seymour."[38] Nevertheless, the British Government presumably was under moral obligation to exhaust all peaceful remedies before seeking a solution through

---

[35] *D.I., Turk.*, 3, confid. inst. no. 73 to L. Wallace, Constantinople, July 21, 1882.

[36] *D.D., Turk.*, 39, desp. no. 111 from Wallace, Aug. 8, 1882.

[37] *Ibid.*, desp. no. 115, Aug. 15, 1882.

[38] July 13, 1882.

such violent means as bombardment. The knowledge that Lord Granville had been informed of the American offer of good offices as early as July 6 without making a real effort to encourage or utilize it lends credence to Wallace's accusation that the British had made up their minds to take Egypt and were not interested in trying to reconcile their differences with the Sultan.

THE BOMBARDMENT OF ALEXANDRIA AND ITS AFTERMATH

Since the facts of the British bombardment of Alexandria and the events flowing therefrom are well known, only the barest outline will be presented, based, wherever possible, on American eyewitness accounts. Emphasis will be given to the courageous and useful service performed by United States sailors and marines in assisting in the restoration of law and order in Alexandria following its destruction by fire and pillage.[39]

On June 18, 1882, Rear Admiral J. W. A. Nicholson, U.S.N., and his entire European squadron were ordered to Alexandria. Meanwhile the U.S.S. *Galena*, which had arrived on June 10, was actively engaged in offering protection to refugees. These included not only some 50 Americans (chiefly missionaries and their families) but also about 250 Europeans. In view of overcrowding on the *Galena*, her captain, Commander Batcheller, assumed responsibility for chartering a small Italian steamer in

---

[39] The most important American sources are: *Navy Department, European Squadron, Ltrs. from Rear Adm. J. W. A. Nicholson;* Goodrich, *op. cit.;* Consular Despatches, Egypt, 1881-1883; Farman, *op cit.;* C. Chaillé-Long, *Three Prophets: Chinese Gordon, Mohammed Ahmed (the Maahdi), Arabi Pasha—Events before and after the Bombardment of Alexandria* (New York, 1884); Chaillé-Long, "The Burning of Alexandria: American Marines at the Historical Egyptian Massacre," *Evening Star* (Washington), June 2, 1907; F. J. Cox, "Arabi and Stone: Egypt's First Military Rebellion, 1882," *Cahiers d'Histoire Egyptienne,* VIII (Apr. 1956), 155-75; Cox, "American Naval Mission in Egypt"; *Gen. Wm. T. Sherman Papers,* Vol. 59, Ltr. from Gen. Chas. P. Stone, Cairo, Oct. 30, 1882, to Sherman; New York *Herald,* reports of its special correspondent, C. T. Barnard, for July, 1882.

which he housed the refugees. He was assisted in this work by Baron J. de Menasces, United States consular agent at Alexandria, who personally guaranteed the full amount of the charter. Menasces then obtained a leave of absence and was replaced by Colonel Charles Chaillé-Long. This American, who had served in the Egyptian Army, won high praise for his work both before and after the bombardment.[40]

Despite the absence of open violence since the June 11th riots, panic and wild rumors circulated among foreigners, both in Alexandria and in Cairo, during the last days of June and the first week in July, 1882. In the midst of all this, N. D. Comanos, acting United States consul-general, made the startling request of Commander Batcheller that United States naval officers and men—in disguise, but armed—be sent to Cairo to defend the American consulate. Batcheller refused, pointing out that his men might be seized and shot as spies if caught, and further, that Cairo had had no government since the Khedive had fled to Alexandria.[41]

By June 27, Admiral Nicholson had arrived at Alexandria to take command of the American naval forces, which consisted now of the U.S.S. *Lancaster*—Nicholson's flagship—the U.S.S. *Quinnebaug*, the U.S.S. *Nipsic* and the U.S.S. *Galena* (the *Galena* was ordered away to Tripoli on the morning of the bombardment). An additional 130 persons of various nationalities were given protection on the American ships. Colonel Chaillé-Long and N. D. Comanos, the last two Americans on shore except General C. P. Stone and his family, were ordered on board the United States warships upon receipt of the news on July 10 that Admiral Seymour would begin bombarding the Egyptian forts in the morning. General Stone, at this time still Chief of Staff of the Egyptian Army, was with the Khedive at

---

[40] *Navy Dept., Ltrs. to Flag Officers Commanding Stations*, Vol. 8, p. 318, cable to Adm. Nicholson, June 13, 1882; *Ltrs. from Adm. Nicholson*, pp. 51 ff., Ltrs. nos. 46, 48 and 55, June 27 and 30 and July 15, 1882, U.S.S. *Lancaster*, Alexandria.

[41] *Ibid.*, no. 48, June 30, 1848.

Ramleh, just outside Alexandria; at his insistence his wife and daughters remained in Cairo.[42]

On the evening of July 10 foreign warships crowded Alexandria harbor. The thirteen ships of the British Navy held the center of the stage. But United States, Greek, Austrian, German, Italian, Russian, Egyptian and Turkish vessels were present, as observers. The French fleet had withdrawn to Port Sa'id. By nightfall all neutral ships had anchored behind that part of the English fleet stationed outside the bar of the harbor.[43]

Admiral Seymour officially reported the commencement of hostilities as follows:

At 7 A.M. on the 11th I signaled from the *Invincible* to the *Alexandra* to fire a shell into the recently armored earthworks termed the Hospital battery and followed this by a general signal to the fleet, "attack the enemy's batteries," . . . . The action terminated successfully at 5:30 P.M. when the ships anchored for the night.[44]

On the morning of the twelfth the British ships resumed firing. During the day the Egyptians asked for two flags of truce, and by nightfall 'Arabi's forces had evacuated the forts and the city. The British losses were small—six killed and twenty-seven wounded. According to General Stone, Egyptian losses amounted to about 115 killed and about 350 to 400 wounded. 'Arabi's men fought stubbornly and several of Seymour's ships were hit; no guns were disabled, however, and their fighting qualities remained unimpaired.[45]

---

[42] *Ibid.*, p. 61, no. 54, July 14, 1882, Alexandria, U.S. flagship *Lancaster*; *C.D., Eg.*, 19, desps. nos. 90 and 91 from N. D. Comanos, Acting Con.-Gen., Alexandria, June 18 and 23, 1882; Farman, *op. cit.*, pp. 314-17; Chaillé-Long, *Three Prophets*, pp. 134-51; New York *Herald*, July 8, 1882. For Stone's detailed and very interesting account of these events, see Cox, "Arabi and Stone."

[43] Goodrich, *op. cit.*, p. 12; Ltrs. from Adm. Nicholson; Farman, *op. cit.*

[44] Quoted in Goodrich, *op. cit.*, pp. 33-34.

[45] *Ibid.*, pp. 36-45; Ltrs. from Adm. Nicholson; Chaillé-Long, *Three Prophets*, pp. 152-60; New York *Herald*, July 12, 1882; *Army and Navy Journal*, XIX (July 15, 1882), 1168-69; Cox, "Arabi and Stone."

On the evening of July 12 parts of the city of Alexandria were observed to be in flames. It is still a matter of debate whether this was expressly instigated by 'Arabi Pasha. In any event the city was given over to destruction by fire and looting for several days. Not until the evening of July 13 did the British land a small force of sailors and marines to occupy the inner harbor and wharves; they did not, however, penetrate the interior of the city until July 15. As a result the British have been widely criticized for their failure immediately after the bombardment to land a force to preserve law and order. The delay, according to Cromer, was apparently ordered by the British Cabinet to show the world that Great Britain was not contemplating an occupation. The matter came up for sharp debate in the House of Commons. Prime Minister Gladstone admitted that under the terms of Admiral Seymour's instructions of May 15, which had not been superseded, he had discretionary power to land troops at any time for preserving order. But Gladstone specifically upheld Seymour's conduct and his exercise of judgment. When pressed by the opposition for an explanation why no specific command had been given to make a landing, the Prime Minister insisted that the evacuation of Alexandria and its subsequent burning and pillage were contingencies that the Government could not possibly have anticipated.[46]

No such diplomatic niceties restrained the Americans. Colonel Chaillé-Long made three reconnaissances into the city in the morning and afternoon of July 13 in advance of any military forces. At his request Admiral Nicholson—urged by the British and with the approval of the Khedive—landed about 150 United States sailors and marines on the morning of July 14. The American forces proceeded to the center of Alexandria; after reopen-

---

[46] *Hansard's Parliamentary Debates*, Vol. 272 (July 11-27, 1882), 3rd series, pp. 286, 718, 901-4 and *passim;* the New York *Herald*, July 15, 1882, commented editorially that the events following the British bombardment were anticipated "everywhere else but in Her Majesty's cabinet councils"; Goodrich, *op. cit.*, p. 75; Chaillé-Long, *Three Prophets*, pp. 160-68; *Army and Navy Journal*, XIX (July 15, 1882), 1164; Cromer, *op. cit.*, I, 297-98.

ing the United States consular agency, it did yeoman work there in fire fighting and preventing looting, saving several public buildings, including the Palace of Justice. Marines from Germany and other nations soon followed, but not until July 15 did British marines take over the main responsibility for security. The bulk of the American force was then withdrawn, leaving only about thirty-five Marines on shore; on the eighteenth the detachment was reduced to seven, employed until the twenty-fourth on guard duty for the consular agency in Alexandria. Admiral Nicholson received commendations from the British, Dutch, Norwegian and Swedish governments for his services to nationals of those countries before, during and after the bombardment.[47]

Americans, both military and civilian, came through those terrible days unscathed. General Stone's wife and three daughters, who had remained in Cairo, had some uneasy moments, but on August 8 were escorted safely to Port Sa'id. The archives of the United States agency and consulate-general, which had been lost in the course of Vice Consul-General Comanos' headlong flight to Alexandria, were found intact in the railway station at Cairo.[48]

While American participation in the stirring events at Alex-

---

[47] R. S. Collum, *History of the United States Marine Corps* (Philadelphia, 1890), pp. 218-19; H. A. Ellsworth, *One Hundred Eighty Landings of the United States Marines*, Pt. I (no place given, 1934), p. 75; Chaillé-Long, *Three Prophets;* Chaillé-Long, *Burning of Alexandria;* Goodrich, *op. cit.,* pp. 79-87; *Ltrs. from Admiral Nicholson,* p. 63, no. 56, July 15, 1882; p. 66, no. 59, July 20, 1882; and p. 85, no. 75, Sept. 21, 1882; Farman, *op. cit.,* pp. 318-20; New York *Herald,* July 16-17, 1882. Comanos and Crabites give the time of the American landing incorrectly as the afternoon of July 13. See *C.D., Eg.,* 19, desp. no. 90 from Comanos, July 18, 1882, and Crabites, *op. cit.,* pp. 264-72.

[48] For a lively account of life in Cairo during the 'Arabi revolt, see Fanny Stone, "Diary of an American Girl in Cairo during the War of 1882," *Century,* o.s. XXVIII, n.s. VI (1884), 288-302; cf. *C.D., Eg.,* 19, desp. no. 97 from Comanos, Aug. 3, 1882. Gen. Stone's frantic efforts to insure the safety of his family in Cairo are detailed in *Gen. Wm. T. Sherman Letters,* Vol. 59, Ltr. from Gen. Stone to Sherman, Cairo, Oct. 30, 1882.

andria drew to a happy conclusion, some startling repercussions resounded in the United States, caused primarily by inaccuracies and distortions of newspaper accounts. The American press, using British sources, reported on July 11 that Admiral Nicholson had warned the Egyptians that if they fired upon him, he would reply in kind. Again, on July 14 it was published that after the bombardment the American Admiral and his men had steamed around the British fleet, cheering each British ship in succession. Finally the press wrote that American sailors and marines were landed specifically to assist the British in restoring order.[49]

One effect of the reports was to arouse the ire of the American Anglophobes. On July 17, Rpresentative William E. Robinson (Dem., N.Y.) submitted the following resolution to the House of Representatives:

> Resolved, that the Secretary of the Navy is hereby instructed to communicate to this House any correspondence with or instructions to Commodore Nicholson relative to his extraordinary threat to open fire upon the City of Alexandria upon certain contingencies; and also to inform the House whether he has been informed that American sailors and officers are performing police duty in the City of Alexandria under the British Admiral, and if so, by what authority.[50]

In compliance with the above resolution, the Navy Department advised in substance that Admiral Nicholson was ordered to Alexandria to protect United States interests and was not authorized to become further involved in the war. Correspondence with Nicholson, but only for the period prior to the bombardment, was turned over to the House.[51]

Admiral Nicholson himself finally issued a statement publicly denying the press reports of his alleged involvement in the war

[49] New York *Times*, July 11, 14 and 16, 1882.

[50] *Cong. Rec.*, U.S. 47th Cong., 1st Sess., Vol. 13 (July 17, 1882), Pt. 2, p. 6146.

[51] "Proceedings at Alexandria, Egypt," ltr. from Wm. E. Chandler, Sec. of Navy, July 28, 1882, in response to resolution of the House of Representatives, U.S. 47th Cong., 1st Sess., H. Misc. Docs., Vol. 12, No. 46; New York *Times*, July 22, 25 and 28, 1882.

and pro-British activity. The American force, he said, was put ashore at the Khedive's request and in order to protect American property. Nicholson's conduct, therefore, could presumably be justified, not only on humanitarian grounds but also as being within the scope of his orders, inasmuch as protection was in fact extended to the United States consular agency and to several American business enterprises in Alexandria.[52]

The United States played no further part in the British military occupation of Egypt, nor was she involved in any of the accompanying diplomatic negotiations. Two amusing suggestions of intervention by private American groups, however, are worthy of mention. One was a plan of former Confederate officers in the South for organizing cavalry units to assist the Egyptians, and the other was a scheme by Irish-American groups for sending money and men to aid 'Arabi against the British. Both projects, needless to say, proved abortive.[53]

Although the British occupied Alexandria, 'Arabi Pasha encamped near the city with his Egyptian troops in open defiance of khedivial authority.[54] The British Government sounded out both the French and Italian governments on the proposition of a joint intervention to remove the threat. In spite of continued British pressure a definite French decision not to participate was given on July 29. The Italians also declined to take part in the proposed campaign. The Sultan, on the other hand, finally agreed in principle to send Turkish troops to Egypt. The British Government answered the latest Turkish *démarche* by advising the Porte that Ottoman troops would not be allowed to land in

---

[52] *Ibid.*, July 25, Aug. 18 and 20, 1882.

[53] In the course of an editorial satirizing the Irish proposal, the New York *Times* observed that "it is thought that the money to be given to Arabi by the Philadelphia club will amount to fully $7.50, and it is positively known that the expedition to be sent from this City will consist of three distinct Irishmen." See *ibid.*, Aug. 11, 1882; also Aug. 18 and 20.

[54] On July 13, 'Arabi had become a rebel following his abortive attempt on the person of the Khedive. Gen. Stone felt that owing to the relatively few British and other troops in Alexandria at this time, 'Arabi could easily have retaken the city. See Cox, "Arabi and Stone," pp. 173-75.

Egypt unless the Sultan issued a proclamation denouncing 'Arabi as a rebel, and signed a military convention for cooperation of English and Turkish troops in Egypt. The Turks finally issued an edict condemning 'Arabi and submitted a proposed military agreement. The agreement was found unacceptable by London; hence the days prior to Tel-el-Kabir were filled with fruitless negotiation. It does seem that if there had been a real meeting of the minds on the desirability of Turkish intervention, the terms could have been framed without undue delay. Significantly, not until September 13, the very day of the decisive battle of Tel-el-Kabir, did the British Government decide that all its objections had been met and that the convention could therefore be signed.[55]

All during these negotiations with the Sublime Porte, British military preparation for an assault on 'Arabi's forces were speedily going forward. On August 21, 1882, British troops, under the over-all command of General Sir Garnet Wolseley, moved from Alexandria and landed at Port Sa'id and Isma'liyah. These landings were unopposed because of synchronized action by the British Navy, and because De Lesseps, openly hostile to Great Britain, had convinced 'Arabi Pasha that the British would not dare violate the "neutrality" of the Suez Canal. The British Government denied that the Canal Company concession, which declared the Canal zone to be neutral, had any binding effect; it relied on an authorization from the Khedive of August 9, 1882, "to occupy such points of the Isthmus of Suez as you may deem useful for the free traffic of the canal, the protection of towns . . . and to suppress any force which does not recognize my authority. . . ."[56]

The military campaign in Egypt began in earnest on August 25, with the British occupation of Maharta. The Egyptians fought

---

[55] *G.B., A.P.,* Egypt no. 17, cmd. 3391, LXXXIII (1882), 148-389; *ibid.,* Egypt no. 18, cmd. 3401, pp. 1-60.

[56] *Ibid.,* Egypt no. 17 (1882), p. 311; Goodrich, *op. cit.,* pp. 105-45. Goodrich had been named an official observer with British Army Headquarters. See *D.D., G.B.,* 145, desp.. no. 234 from W. J. Hoppin, U.S. Min., London, Sept. 2, 1882.

well until the crushing British victory of Tel-el-Kabir on September 13. A daylight assault caught the Egyptians almost completely by surprise. A rout ensued. On September 14, Cairo was occupied and 'Arabi seized. With this the rebellion collapsed, and the British were soon masters of Egypt—all in the Khedive's name, of course. The Sultan was informed that the emergency had passed and therefore no Turkish troops were needed. Negotiations regarding the military convention between Turkey and Great Britain were discontinued forthwith.[57]

The British occupation of Egypt in 1882 was one of the most significant events in modern Egyptian history. What started out as a temporary intervention by Great Britain for the purpose of restoring law and order soon ripened into a permanent occupation. To the Egyptians this was a bitter pill, serving as a rallying point for all nationalists. The French reacted with resentment and obstruction in Egypt up to the Entente of 1904. The Sultan, who had played his cards badly, was deprived of the little *de facto* control he still enjoyed in Egypt, though he retained *de jure* sovereignty until 1914. The effect of the British occupation on United States–Egyptian relations will be considered in later chapters.

---

[57] *G.B. A.P.*, Egypt no. 18, cmd. 3401, p. 69; Goodrich, *op. cit.*, pp. 146-61. Col. 'Arabi has been criticized by one of the American officers formerly with the Egyptian Army for not having followed Gen. Stone's earlier advice to the Egyptian Govt.: that Tel-el-Kabir and Zagasig were crucial in the defense of Egypt; that both should be heavily fortified; and that a determined stand should be made there against any invader. S. H. Lockett, "Arabi and his Army," *Nation*, Vol. 35, pp. 257-58, at p. 258; cited in Cox, "Arabi and Stone," p. 159 (Sept. 28, 1882).

CHAPTER VIII

Yankee Traders in Egypt: I

TARIFF PROBLEMS

One motive for concluding the Treaty of 1830 between the United States and Turkey was American desire to share in the lucrative Egyptian trade. This treaty, which gave American merchants the right to trade freely throughout the Ottoman Empire, adopted no specific tariff schedule. Still, Article I provided for most-favored-nation treatment.[1]

Acting on instructions from the Department of State, David Porter, United States chargé d'affairs at Constantinople in December, 1831, negotiated an agreement with the Sultan by which the terms of the French tariff—a 3 per cent ad valorem duty on all articles imported into or exported from Turkey—were made applicable to American traders. Upon expiration of the French agreement in 1832, the Porte tried to force the United States to accept an ad valorem duty of 15 per cent. But by August of that year Porter (at the cost of a substantial bribe) was able to report final success in resisting the proposed increase. The customs duty charged for United States nationals remained, for the time being, at 3 per cent. These and subsequent tariff arrangements with the Porte were naturally expected to apply to Egypt as to other parts of the Ottoman Empire[2]

Shortly after his appointment as United States consular agent at Alexandria in January, 1832, John Gliddon was confronted by Mehmed 'Ali's attempt to raise the Egyptian tariff. To this news Chargé d'Affaires Porter replied that although no present prob-

[1] Malloy, op. cit., II, 1318-20.

[2] D.D., Turk., 2, desp. nos. 29, 37, 69 and 70, from David Porter, U.S. Chargé, Constantinople, Dec. 15, 1831, Jan. 12, Aug. 15 and 18, 1832.

lem existed concerning customs duties in Egypt—since as yet no American vessels visited Alexandria—the future should be safeguarded by strict insistence on the convention agreed to by himself and the Porte. As for any similar, subsequent disputes with the Egyptian Government, Gliddon was instructed first to let France take the lead, then claim like advantages for the United States. The Egyptian Viceroy was not strong enough to defy the Sultan on the issue of regulating his own tariff but did obtain a measure of indirect control over customs through his monopoly ownership of Egyptian agriculture and industry.[3]

On August 16, 1838, England and Turkey entered into a commercial convention by which British subjects were granted the right to buy and sell freely throughout the Ottoman Empire, subject only to 5 per cent duty on imports and 12 per cent on exports. By agreement of November 14, 1839, the arrangement was extended to the United States. If the Anglo-Turkish treaty of 1838 had been applied in Egypt as its terms indicated, Mehmed 'Ali's monopoly system would have been destroyed. The Egyptian Pasha successfully defied the Sultan in this regard until the Egyptian defeat at the hands of the European Powers. The Sultan's *firman* of June 1, 1841, reaffirmed the earlier status by providing expressly that "all treaties concluded or to be concluded between my Sublime Porte and the friendly powers shall be executed in the province of Egypt."[4] By 1842, Mehmed 'Ali's monopolies were destroyed, and once again Egypt was open to free trade.[5]

The next change in United States–Egyptian tariff arrangements was that effected by the United States–Turkish commercial convention of February 25, 1862. This treaty provided in Article I for the customary most-favored-nation treatment in all parts of the Ottoman Empire. Article IV specified an 8 per cent ad valorem duty on exports, the same to be reduced annually until a permanent level of 1 per cent was reached, while Article V

---

[3] *Ibid.*, desp. no. 97 from Porter, Mar. 7, 1833, encl. an inst. from Porter to Gliddon, Mar. 6, 1833; Crouchley, *op. cit.*, pp. 66-89.

[4] *For. Rels.* (1879), p. 1031; Hurewitz, *op. cit.*, pp. 51, 52.

[5] Crouchley, *op. cit.*, pp. 89-90.

called for an 8 per cent ad valorem duty on imports from the United States of America, to be restored if the goods were re-exported within six months. The reduction of the old Turkish land-transfer tax from 3 to 1 per cent was covered by Article VII.[6]

In 1873 the Sultan authorized Khedive Isma'il to make non-political treaties relating to commerce and customs with foreign Powers. Isma'il did not wait long before attempting to exercise his new powers. On April 12, 1874, the American agent and consul-general at Cairo reported that Nubar Pasha, the Egyptian Foreign Minister, had requested the United States to enter into negotiations for a commercial treaty. Inasmuch as the Porte had expressed a desire to review the United States–Turkish convention of 1862, the Department of State preferred to wait before doing anything in Egypt. The American consul was instructed to secure all possible information and to transmit all Egyptian proposals, but in no wise to commit the United States Government. No further developments occurred until 1881, when the Egyptian Government reiterated its desire to revise the United States–Turkish treaty of 1862 as it affected Egypt. But not until 1884 was a commercial convention between the United States and Egypt actually concluded.[7]

COMMERCIAL RELATIONS

In one of his reports to Commodore Porter, dated May 22, 1832, Consular Agent John Gliddon at Alexandria took a dim view of United States–Egyptian trade potentialities. "As to trade," he said, "I see little probability of a regular current of intercourse, since there [are] no articles of bulk which either country wants from the other."[8]

[6] For text in English, see Malloy, *op. cit.*, II, 1321-41.

[7] *C.D., Eg.*, 8, desp. no. 188 from R. Beardsley, U.S.A.C.G., Alexandria, Apr. 12, 1874; *C.I., B.P.*, 15, inst. no. 123 to Beardsley, May 18, 1874; *D.I., Turk.*, 3, inst. no. 39 to G. H. Heap, Chargé, Constantinople, June 16, 1881; *D.D., Turk.*, 37, desp. no. 27 from Heap, July 5, 1881.

[8] *D.D. Turk.*, 2, desp. no. 61 from D. Porter, Constantinople, June 23, 1832, encl. desp. from Gliddon to Porter, May 22, 1832.

Despite such discouraging reports the Department of State, influenced no doubt by Mehmed 'Ali's spectacular successes, sent William Hodgson on a confidential mission to Egypt in 1834 to survey the scene. In addition to reporting on political conditions, Hodgson was instructed to examine the conditions of Egyptian trade and the best means of improving America's commercial position. Egyptian commerce, valued at approximately $17 million in 1832, he reported to be largely in the hands of Turkey, England, Austria-Hungary, Tuscany and France. He pointed out that the absence of existing direct trade between the United States and Egypt was compensated for in part by the fact that considerable American goods were transshipped to Egypt via Europe. Further, he believed that despite the similarity of the chief products of the two countries, such as cotton, rice and grain, many other commodities might profitably be exchanged. The United States could buy, for example, henna, gum arabic and dates, and sell to Egypt timber, coal, cotton goods and other manufactured products. Hodgson also envisaged a flourishing commerce between the United States and Mehmed 'Ali's dominions along the Red Sea and Indian Ocean.[9]

Hodgson's favorable reports apparently played some part in the United States Government's decision in March, 1835, to raise the post at Alexandria from consular agency to consulate, and to permit direct correspondence between the incumbent and the Department of State. Offsetting this affirmative response in an unsigned memorandum in the Consular Bureau of the Department of State, probably written in 1835, after a perusal of Hodgson's reports; it contains some cogent observations on the subject of Egyptian trade:

It does not appear from these considerations that the Pasha wants our commerce or that we could gain anything by an intercourse with him. On the contrary, we should wish that all his plans may fail. If he enters into a treaty with England, it will be most injurious to us. He can supply all the cotton she wants. It will be carried to England in British vessels; in return he will

---

[9] *Ibid.*, 6, unnum. desp. from Hodgson, Washington, Mar. 2, 1835.

take hardware, etc. We could carry him nothing, nor is it probable that our manufacturers will ever let us bring a yard of cloth from him. India productions he can get easily by the Red Sea.[10]

The above memorandum may not have represented the Department of State's considered opinion regarding United States trade with Egypt, but it certainly prophesied the actual trend of commercial relations between the two countries, at least until after the end of the American Civil War.

The paucity of United States–Egyptian trade is highlighted by the fact that between 1832 and 1837 only two American ships stopped at Alexandria. Both arrived from Boston in the summer of 1835 with cargoes of rum, cigars, candles, fish and sugar. Not until 1838 did the first American ship carry Egyptian goods—in this case linseed and two camels—from Alexandria to the United States. War and pirates, however, rendered a brisk trade in Mocha coffee, from Yemen, somewhat irregular and hazardous.[11]

As a part of his grandiose program of industrialization, Mehmed 'Ali purchased from the United States a certain amount of heavy machinery, for example, a rice-hulling mill and a cottonseed mill, employing American mechanics and engineers to put them in operation. George R. Gliddon, for a time United States consul at Cairo, was sent by the Egyptian Government on a mission to the United States to obtain data on other American equipment and to popularize Egypt as a market for American goods. However, such a profitable source of trade for American manufacturers was never fully realized, for after Mehmed 'Ali's death in 1849 his successors allowed his industrial empire to fall into decay.[12]

---

[10] Unsigned memo, entitled "Remarks on the Situation of the Pasha of Egypt," undated except for a pencil notation of "1835," *Report of Bureau Officers (Consular Bureau), Dept. of State,* Vol. 2 (1835-1851).

[11] *C.D., Cyprus, Alexandria, Stancho,* 1, unnum. desp. from J. Gliddon, U.S. Con., Alexandria, Aug. 28, 1835; *ibid.,* desp. no. 9, Jan. 1, 1836; *ibid.,* unnum. desp., July 13, 1838; *ibid.,* unnum. desp. from Geo. R. Gliddon, U.S. Con. at Cairo, New York, Apr. 15, 1837.

[12] *Ibid.,* unnum. desp., Alexandria, May 20, 1840.

Commercial relations between Egypt and the United States were singularly barren in the two decades preceding the American Civil War. Poor consular reporting and the generally inadequate statistics of the era may be partly to blame for America's poor record. But the basic truth is that commercial intercourse of any significance just did not exist between the two countries.[13] An analysis of Egyptian imports and exports for the ten-year period 1853–1862 best illustrates the situation. The United States, ranking tenth out of fourteen countries, is shown to have furnished only a little over $6 million out of a total of Egyptian imports valued at slightly more than $250 million. For Egyptian exports, the United States, buying about $300,000 out of a total of $500 million, ranked eleventh out of thirteen countries.

The content of trade existing between the United States and Egypt prior to 1862 is summarized by Consul-General De Leon in his report of 1859:

> Agricultural products in Egypt and our Southern States must ever prevent any large interchange of commodities, or any brisk trade.
>
> A few vessels per year, ladened with ice, lumber, furniture and provisions, and returning with rags, in pressed bales, gum arabic, in bags, suma, in bales, old iron, natron, and hides constitute the extent of the direct trade between America and Egypt. . . .
>
> Through my recommendation has been the Viceroy been persuaded, during the past two years, to contract for railroad cars, locomotive engines, a large pontoon floating bridge, steam pumping engines and rolling stock for his railroad and various other manufactures.[14]

The American Civil War years and those immediately following represented a low ebb in United States–Egyptian commercial relations. Indeed, for the year 1863 no trade at all was reported. Not until 1873 did commerce between the two countries become stabilized. And from that date on a gradual but steady increase

---

[13] See Appendix B.

[14] *Comm. Rels.* (1859), p. 357.

is apparent. In 1873, for example, Egypt imported goods from the United States valued at $225,406 and exported to America $270,631 worth, while in 1881 the respective figures were: Egyptian imports, $590,058 and Egyptian exports, $423,478—roughly a twofold increase. But in order to put this commercial relationship in proper perspective, the percentages of Egypt's total trade enjoyed by the foreign countries in 1882 should be examined. Great Britain led with 56 per cent; Turkey followed with 11 per cent; France was third with 10 per cent. The United States share, not enough to merit an individual listing, was only approximately 0.2 per cent.[15]

The character of Egyptian exports to the United States in 1873 had not altered appreciably from that of 1859. The bulk of it still consisted of rags, gum arabic, Mocha coffee, old iron and hides. Notable, however, was a radical change in the constitution of Egyptian imports from America—a new emphasis on petroleum. The new orientation is shown by the fact that of the imports from America in 1873 estimated at $368,322, some $367,241 was spent for refined oil. Petroleum, by this time an American monopoly not only in Egypt but in the rest of the Near East as well, showed a steady increase on Egyptian import accounts, from 1,375,687 okes[16] in 1870 to 4,255,568 in 1872. But by 1879 its importation had dropped in quantity to 1,736,420 okes, and in value to $173,240. The eventual loss of American pre-eminence respecting this valuable product will be dealt with in a subsequent chapter.[17]

A brief discussion of American shipping rounds out a survey of United States–Egyptian commercial relations. The port of Alexandria, for centuries one of the best harbors in the Mediterranean, was vastly improved by Isma'il Pasha and grew in importance, becoming the outlet for practically all of Egypt's overseas trade. Merchant ships of all nations came to Alexandria

---

[15] *Comm. Rels.* (1882-1883), II, 76; see also Appendix B.

[16] An oke is two and three-quarters pounds.

[17] *Comm. Rels.* (1872), p. 842; *ibid.* (1873), pp. 1088-89; *ibid.* (1879), I, 281-82.

in increasing numbers, but the American flag was rarely seen there, as Table 2 shows.

TABLE 2

U.S. SHIPPING AT ALEXANDRIA, 1849–79

Year	U.S. Ships	British Ships	Total
1849	2	—	1651
1861	2	214	1844
1876	6	303	2589
1878	10	516	1984
1879	0	1090	3045

Sources: C. D., Eg., 1, desp. no. 10 from D. S. Macauley, U.S.C.G., Alexandria, Jan. 8, 1850; *ibid.*, 3, desp. no. 15 from W. S. Thayer, Alexandria, Jan. 27, 1862; Comm. Rels. (1876, 1878, and 1879), pp. 911, 1124, and 283, resp.

Until 1862, American merchantmen calling at Alexandria in the carrying trade customarily arrived in ballast and left with wheat, other grains and beans for Malta, Marseilles, Smyrna and other Mediterranean ports. After 1864 some Yankee ships began to bring coke and coal from English ports to Egypt; cotton and wheat were the chief outbound cargoes.[18] One of the most serious indictments of Yankee enterprise is to be found in the report that of seventeen steamers loaded with Egyptian goods that left Alexandria in 1880 bound for the United States, fifteen were British and not one was American.[19]

REASONS FOR THE PAUCITY OF UNITED STATES–EGYPTIAN TRADE

The preceding brief account of the arrival in Egypt of Yankee merchants and their activities there up to 1882 shows how completely early hopes for a flourishing United States–Egyptian

---

18 *Ibid.* (1856-1882), *passim.*

19 *C.D., Eg.*, 17, desp. no. 470 from E. E. Farman, U.S.A.C.G., Cairo, Mar. 7, 1881.

commerce had failed to materialize. An important and difficult question follows: Why did the United States not enjoy greater trade with Egypt? The answer is crucial in understanding American relations with Egypt. No solution emerges, however, from evidence so far adduced.

Instructions from the Department of State to United States representatives both in Turkey and in Egypt provide no real clues. Indeed, the matter is largely ignored. In consular reporting from Egypt alone was there any attempt to discuss the problem. The supposed barrier to trade between the two countries is referred to frequently in the early despatches, but this did not long remain true, since especially after the Civil War the United States became a manufacturing country as well. Later American consuls believed that substantial commerce between Egypt and the United States could be developed, and put forward a number of remedial proposals. Consul-General W. S. Thayer, for instance, in 1862 urged a sort of three-cornered trade: American merchandise to be shipped directly to Alexandria; Egyptian cotton and grain to be taken to Marseilles and Liverpool; and finally European goods to be carried to the United States. Another consul, E. E. Farman, pointed out in 1881 that in contrast to the British merchants, Americans neglected to adapt their merchandise to Egyptian needs.[20] Doubtless these and other suggestions, if followed, would have been useful stimulants to trade with Egypt, but none of them reaches the heart of the matter. We shall examine this vital point later. Suffice it to say now that the answer to the question posed above is very complex and includes a consideration of traditional American outlooks on foreign policy and domestic developments within the United States.

---

[20] *C.D., Eg.*, 3, desp. no. 15 from Thayer, Alexandria, Jan. 27, 1862; *ibid.*, 17, desp. no. 470 from Farman, Cairo, Mar. 7, 1881.

CHAPTER IX

The Cultural Impact: I

SPREADING THE GOSPEL, AMERICAN STYLE

American missionaries from their arrival in Egypt in 1854 to 1882 were concerned primarily with establishment and first growth. The American Mission engaged in two main types of activity: evangelism—together with the allied function of the distribution of Bibles and other religious literature—and education.[1] In the beginning these functions were intertwined. The early American missionary in Egypt—and there were few—served in a versatile manner as preacher, teacher and Bible salesman. Even before 1882 two trends were developing: the emphasis on education (and later, on medical work), seen early as a more fruitful approach to the Muslims than the unsuccessful attempts at conversion to Christianity; and a tendency toward separation and institutionalization of its activities, which grew as the Mission expanded.

American missionary work began in Egypt on November 15, 1854, when Rev. and Mrs. Thomas McCague arrived in Cairo; Rev. James Barnett joined them soon after. These missionaries, who had been stationed in Damascus, were sent to Egypt by the Associated Reformed Church, which merged in 1858 with the Associate Church to form the United Presbyterian Church of North America. Americans had been active in mission work in Syria and Anatolia as early as 1821; but in modern Egypt two groups preceded them—the Moravians (1752–1782), about whom little is known, and the Church Missionary Society of Great

---

[1] A permanent medical branch was not established until 1891.

Britain (1815–1848), who attempted unsuccessfully to work through the Coptic Church with the idea of reforming it from within. Greek and Catholic churches also had missions in Egypt, but at least until 1882, the Protestant churches, by common consent, gave the United Presbyterians a free hand in that country.[2]

In 1859 the American Mission won its first converts: two Copts, one Syrian and one Armenian, all members of Eastern Christian churches. And on April 13, 1860, Revs. McCague, Barnett and Gulian Lansing, having been authorized by the General Assembly of the United Presbyterian Church, met and organized a Presbytery of Egypt. The comparative statistical Table 3 shows the subsequent growth of the American Mission in Egypt.

TABLE 3
PROGRESS OF THE AMERICAN MISSION, 1869–79

	1869	1874	1879
American missionaries	19	21	22
Convert workers	27	67	139
Organized churches	2	6	11
Church members	180	596	985
Avg. Sunday attendance	438	986	2,083
Book depots	4	5	5
Books sold	6,446	10,176	20,494

Sources: 11th, 16th and 21st *Ann. Repts.*, U. P. Ch. (1870, 1875 and 1880), pp. 65, 62-63 and 81-82, resp.

---

[2] The work of the American Mission in Egypt is described in its annual reports to the Board of Foreign Missions of the U.P. Ch. of N. Am., in the issues of *Missionary Review of the World* (Princeton and New York, 1878——), in the despatches of the U.S. consuls-general, and in a number of books by the early missionaries themselves, the best of which is A. Watson, *The American Mission in Egypt, 1854-1896* (Pittsburgh, 1904); see also C. R. Watson, *Egypt and the Christian Crusade* (Philadelphia, 1907); C. R. Watson, *In the Valley of the Nile* (New York, 1908); G. Lansing, *Egypt's Princes* (New York, 1865); and R. L. Hogg, *A Master Builder on the Nile: Being a Record of the Life and Aims of John Hogg, D.D.* (New York, 1914). A useful summary is also to be found in W. N. Jamison, *The United Presbyterian Story: A Centennial Study, 1858-1958* (Pittsburgh, 1958).

The progress of the American Mission as shown above is impressive in all categories, especially in church attendance and membership. By 1881 the Mission had one Presbytery, five main stations—Cairo, Alexandria, Asyut, Mansurah, and Al-Madinah in the Fayyum—and in addition, fifty-four outlying stations, mostly in Upper Egypt.[3]

The first reported Bible distribution by the American Mission in Egypt took place in 1856. Book depots for the sale of religious literature opened in Alexandria and Cairo in 1859. In the early days the missionaries themselves went out on long trips preaching and selling Bibles. Rev. Gulian Lansing, describing such a tour of Upper Egypt in a Mission boat (1861–1862), brings alive the ingenuity and flexibility of those pioneer missionaries:

> Stopped today opposite Tanta, going ashore with our box of books we had great trouble to find a beast of burden to carry them. We finally succeeded in impressing a sorry-looking-woe-begone donkey. . . . We too were disposed to be as facetious as our appearance was comical. We met many people coming down to the landing, and they stared at the strange cavalcade. We stopped each man as he came along, and if he wore a light colored turban we asked him, "Do you fast Ramadan or the 'holy forty' (Lent)?" If he said "Ramadan," we said, "Then go in peace, we have only some Christian books to sell." If he said "the 'Holy forty,'" we next interrogated him, "Are you a Copt or 'Tabia' ('adherent')?" There are many Catholics in Tanta, and the Catholics in Egypt are called "adherents" of the Pope. If he said "a Tabia," we said "We have nothing to do with you. We have Bibles to sell, but your priests will not let you read the Bible. But we also bring you word that the Pope is dead; Garibaldi has just killed him." If he said "a Copt," we answered, "You are just the man we want to see. We have some Bibles and other religious books here and sell them very cheap. All we want is the cost of transportation. . . ."[4]

---

[3] *Minutes of 2nd Gen. Assembly of U.P. of N.A.*, Philadelphia, May 23, 1861, pp. 68-69; *23rd Ann. Repts., U.P. Ch.* (1882), p. 6.

[4] Lansing, *op. cit.*, pp. 317-19.

Colporteurs, or selling agents (usually Egyptian converts who received a sales commission), assisted the missionaries in the work of Bible distribution. Later the colporteurs handled this work almost exclusively. The American Bible Society and the British and Foreign Bible Society aided by furnishing books at cost and a few colporteurs. The American Bible Society, with its printing press in Bayrut, translated and printed the Bible in Arabic, Armenian, Turkish and other languages of the area. The American Mission acquired its own press in 1866.[5]

American missionaries arrived in Egypt, as in other countries of the Near East, eager to convert Muslims to Christianity; they met, however, with such fanaticism and opposition that they soon concentrated their attention on the Coptic Christian minority.[6] Most of the new converts thus were Copts. Viewing the Coptic Church, along with the other Eastern Christian churches as "lapsed churches," the American missionaries established their own church, the Protestant or Evangelical Church of Egypt. They criticized the Copts' excessive formalism; their worship of pictures, saints and angels; and their alleged general ignorance and impiety. Hope for converting the Muslims, however, was not permanently abandoned.[7]

Hostility of the Coptic clergy increased almost in direct proportion to the success of the American Mission. An interview which the Coptic Patriarch granted to Consul-General William Thayer and Rev. John Hogg in 1863 furnishes us a rare, direct glimpse of Coptic feeling about American missionaries. Thayer told the Patriarch he should not object to the American Protestants, since they taught only the "Pure Gospel." "Pure Gospel! . . . ," he retorted. "Why have they come to Egypt with

---

[5] A. Watson, op. cit., p. 148; Ann. Repts., Am. Bible Soc. (1857-1882), passim; 7th Ann. Rept., U.P. Ch. (1866), pp. 17-18.

[6] By the 1897 census there were 608,000 Copts in Egypt, out of a total population of some 9.7 million. See Cromer, op. cit., II, 168, 201.

[7] For a brief history of the Coptic Church see C. R. Watson, Valley of the Nile, pp. 44-59; for a bitter attack on Coptic practices, see A. Watson, op. cit., pp. 412-13; D. Finney, Tomorrow's Egypt (Pittsburgh, 1939), pp. 108-9.

their fine talk . . . . We had the Gospel before America was born. We don't need them here to teach us. We know the Gospel better than they do."[8]

Coptic antagonism smoldered but did not develop into an open clash until 1865, when Hogg was sent to establish a permanent station at Asyut, the "capital" of the Upper Nile and the real center of Coptic influence. To meet the threatened "invasion," a Coptic Metropolitan bishop came to Asyut and warned darkly against heretics and their teachings. Nevertheless, Hogg continued his work, organizing schools for boys and girls and starting outstations in the surrounding territory.[9]

When peaceful measures failed, the Coptic hierarchy, allegedly with the tacit consent and encouragement of the Khedive, acted in 1867 to destroy the American Mission once and for all. The Patriarch himself toured the Upper Nile denouncing the Protestants and attempting to discourage attendance at Mission schools and churches. Several prominent Protestant converts and agents of the missionaries were beaten and forced to leave their towns. For the more serious of these attacks the American Mission was able to obtain partial redress through diplomatic channels. The fault, however, did not lie entirely with the Copts. In 1869, for instance, five Protestant converts, all former Copts, literally interpreting the biblical injunction against graven images, destroyed many religious pictures in the Coptic church at Asyut.

In pleasant contrast, the American missionaries enjoyed generally excellent relations with the Egyptian Government. This state of affairs, so different from the situation in Turkey, may be explained in several ways. In the last analysis, Egyptian rulers depended on foreign support for their quasi-independent status vis-à-vis the Turkish Sultan. Consequently any prolonged or violent outbreaks against missionaries would have produced the most serious repercussions. The Western Powers quickly showed a united front in protesting such incidents as did occur. The

---

[8] Hogg, *op. cit.*, p. 108.

[9] 7th *Ann. Rept.*, *U.P. Ch.* (1867), pp. 24-26; A. Watson, *op. cit.*, pp. 177-82; C. R. Watson, *Valley of the Nile*, pp. 146-58.

American Mission won favor also for chiefly confining its evangelical work to the Copts. Yet even proselytizing the Copts would have been dangerous had that minority group entertained separatist ambitions like the Armenians in Turkey, who, when converted, emigrated to the United States to become naturalized citizens and then returned to Anatolia to engage in political intrigues. Official Egyptian recognition of the beneficial results flowing from the Mission's excellent schools further enhanced the Americans' position.[10]

Muslim fanatics engaged in relatively few attacks against the missionaries; the Egyptian Government dealt with them severely when they did occur. The incident involving Faris-el-Hakim, an agent of the American Mission at Asyut, became something of a *cause célèbre*. In 1861, Faris was arrested, charged with enticing a woman to become a Christian. He was beaten by a Muslim crowd, urged on by the Muslim judge. A vigorous protest by the American consul-general brought Faris' release from prison and punishment of those involved. President Lincoln wrote a letter of thanks to the Egyptian Viceroy, Sa'id, for his prompt handling of the incident. "In this case, Honorable Sir and Friend," Sa'id replied, "I have only executed the rule which I have always endeavored to follow in protecting in an equal way and without consideration of creed all those who, either by inclination or for the fulfillment of a duty, sojourn in the country, submitted to my administration."[11] American missionaries regarded the favorable and decisive settlement of the Faris case as an important victory.

10 *C.D. Eg.*, 3, desp. no. 12 from W. S. Thayer, Alexandria, Nov. 26, 1861; see also 19th *Ann. Rept., U.P. Ch.* (1878), pp. 19-20, for a discussion of the difficulties following the public conversion to Christianity of Ahmed Fahmi, a member of a prominent Muslim family.

11 Both letters are quoted in Lansing, *op. cit.*, pp. 342-44; see also M. J. Wright, "Some Bold Diplomacy in the United States in 1861," *American Historical Association Annual Report for 1895* (Washington, 1896), pp. 405-10; A. Watson, *op. cit.*, pp. 127-35; *C.D., Eg.*, 3, desp. no. 5 from Thayer, Alexandria, Aug. 26, 1861.

Sa'id Pasha further favored the American Mission in November, 1861, by a gift of a building in Cairo, valued at $25,000, to be used as a school. Again, in 1862, when the Turkish Sultan visited Egypt, he made donations to benevolent and charitable purposes, including one to "the Protestant Community." The American missionaries eventually received a share of this, amounting to about $600.[12]

When Isma'il became Viceroy in 1863, fanatical Muslims attacked a French citizen, hoping the new ruler would reverse his predecessor's policy of religious toleration. But to the relief of all foreigners, swift punishment followed. Isma'il later received a group of American missionaries and promised them protection and support.[13]

The United States Government's general policy was to afford American missionaries the same protection as it did its other citizens residing in Egypt. In practice, however, the American Mission apparently enjoyed extra diplomatic care and protection —partly because of a recognition of the intrinsic value of its work and partly because of pressure exerted by religious groups and public opinions at home. Even so, consular agents and the scope of protection to be given were points of friction.

The problems concerning the employment of Ottoman subjects as United States consular agents in Egypt have been discussed in some detail above. In 1871 eight such consular agents served Upper Egypt, all in centers of American missionary activity. The use of these agents was in opposition not only to the stated policy of the United States Government but also to that of the Turkish and Egyptian governments, but it greatly assisted the American Mission in protecting the interests of itself and of its adherents. The appointment and retention in office of such persons therefore caused frequent controversy. But until well after 1882, missionary pressure (and the unavailability of resident

[12] *Ibid.*, desp. no. 12 from Thayer, No. 26, 1861; *ibid.*, desp. no. 10 from Charles Hale, Alexandria, Dec. 22, 1864.

[13] *Ibid.*, desp. no. 30 from Thayer, Feb. 17, 1863.

American citizens for the jobs) proved decisive in the Department of State's decision not to abolish the posts.[14]

A more serious question concerned the extent of United States protection to be given American missionaries in Egypt. On the main issues of actual discrimination against and persecution of missionaries, the Department of State took a consistently strong stand, as in the Faris case cited above. Assistance also was rendered in many other ways, both formally and informally.

The American missionaries in Egypt were engaged in difficult and thankless work in an often hostile environment; they can hardly be blamed therefore for seeking as much governmental aid as possible. But it is also true that they stirred up considerable trouble, frequently with diplomatic repercussions, and that at times they made excessive demands upon the Department of State.

The events following the Copt-inspired attacks on the Mission's agents and followers in Upper Egypt in 1867 showed the limits beyond which the United States Government refused to go in furthering the missionaries' cause. Agent and Consul-General Charles Hale refused to serve the Egyptian Government with what he regarded as intemperate demands for retribution originated by the missionaries. He incurred the wrath of the Mission, but the Department of State approved his action in the following words:

. . . The liberal spirit in which the Egyptian Government has complied with your requests is highly appreciated. Neither the Constitution nor the laws of the United States would have justified your demanding or accepting such extreme concessions in these cases as were suggested to you by the missionary friends of the complaining parties.[15]

On this occasion, as on several others, the American Mission felt constrained to appeal to the British Government for stronger

---

[14] *Ibid.*, 6, desp. no. 66 from G. E. Butler, U.S.A.C.G., Cairo, July 17, 1871.

[15] *C.I. B.P.*, 14, inst. no. 48 to Hale, Alexandria, Dec. 24, 1867; see also *C.D., Eg.*, 4, desp. no. 108 from Hale, Alexandria, Nov. 25, 1867.

measures of assistance. In addition to normal interest in the welfare of any Christian mission, the British Government was sympathetic also because Rev. John Hogg of the American Mission was a British subject, and further because the Maharajah, Dhuleep Singh, a benefactor of the Mission, lived in England and exerted considerable influence at court. In any event American missionaries believed that British influence produced results. But, as Hale commented to the Department, the British ambassador at Constantinople had instructed the British agent in Egypt not to act in such cases unless asked by his American colleague and then only jointly.[16]

The vital educational work of the American Mission proceeded simultaneously with the evangelical appeal; wherever the missionaries went, they opened schools. When the Americans arrived in Egypt, they found an inadequate, archaic governmental education system. In spite of Mehmed 'Ali's experiments with Western methods, Egyptian education remained concentrated largely in the *kuttabs* (elementary schools) and in the more advanced theological training of the venerable al-Azhar. Consequently the illiteracy rate remained high all during the period under consideration, although the situation had been somewhat alleviated in the early nineteenth century by the rapid growth of foreign national schools in Egypt, notably French. These institutions attracted numerous Egyptians of all creeds. For the period 1875–1878, for instance, Muslim attendance at foreign schools including those of the American Mission, had increased 111 per cent. In 1880, 52 per cent of all Egyptians were enrolled in Egyptian non-governmental schools of all levels.[17]

---

[16] *Ibid.*, 4, confid. desp. no. 109 from Hale, Alexandria, No. 26, 1867.

[17] Statistics from A. Boktar, *School and Society in the Valley of the Nile* (Cairo, 1936), pp. 133-39 and *passim;* see also J. Heyworth-Dunne, *An Introduction to the History of Education in Modern Egypt* (London, 1938), the most comprehensive treatment of Egyptian education prior to 1882, though it contains very little on American Mission schools; J. Williams, *Education in Egypt before British Control* (Birmingham, Eng., 1939).

To return to the educational activities of the American missionaries, the first school, one for boys, was established in Cairo in 1855. Separate schools for boys and girls in Alexandria and in various towns along the Upper Nile followed in rapid succession. The substantial progress of the educational program of the American Mission can be judged by the statistics for 1881: one Theological Seminary (at Asyut); one training college; 39 boys' and 9 girls' schools. The total number of pupils was reported at 2,410, of whom 896 were in direct Mission schools and the remainder in schools under Mission auspice. The forerunners of Asyut College and Pressley Memorial Institute for Women, both begun by Dr. Hogg at Asyut in 1865, merit special mention. Copts constituted the bulk of the student body, which included also Muslims, Jews and others. In 1880, enrollment figures showed 566 Muslims, or about 18 per cent out of a reported total of 3,070.[18]

An objective evaluation of the educational work of the American Mission presents some difficulty, because the missionaries have written most of the literature on the subject. Of the outside sources available, some take a critical view. Edouard Dor Bey, Swiss Inspector General of Egyptian Education, visited many of the Mission schools in 1871-1872, and formed a poor opinion of them. "Discipline, orderliness, competition and reason —all are lacking," he said drily of those in Cairo.[19] He reported more favorably, however, on the schools in Alexandria, citing especially the girls' school.

Others writers have found more to praise; Boktar has this to say about Asyut College:

> . . . the Protestant American Mission founded its famous schools in upper Egypt. For almost three quarters of a century their

---

[18] 23rd *Ann. Rept., U.P. Ch.* (1883), p. 24; 22nd, *ibid.* (1882), p. 36; A. Watson, *op. cit.,* pp. 72-174. For a brief history of Asyut College, see 46th *Ann. Rept., U.P. Ch.* (1905), pp. 65-73.

[19] Translation mine. V. E. Dor (Bey), *L'Instruction Publique en Egypte* (Paris, 1872), p. 281; cited in Heyworth-Dunne, *op. cit.,* pp. 411-12.

Assiut College has been one of the biggest and most important factors in raising the standard of education in upper Egypt. Thousands of boys from poor peasant homes would not have had the chance of education were it not for the facilities provided by this institution. Attracting the youth from the provinces, particularly from the upper Nile valley, this school has for years provided tuition, residence, and board for five hundred or more students annually.

Many attribute the prosperity of Assiut, its flourishing inhabitants, the relative accuracy and honesty of its artisans to the influence of Assiut College. Its graduates and former students, occupying positions in Government and private concerns, or administering their own business, have long been recognized as relatively honest, straight-forward, thorough and conscientious.[20]

United States consuls-general, while frequently critical of the excessive demands of the American missionaries for protection, applauded their work in education. Consul-General Richard Beardsley reported in 1873 that three-fourths of the employees in the Egyptian telegraph, railway and post offices had been educated in the Mission's schools.[21]

The American Mission schools succeeded because, beyond their relatively high educational standards, the missionaries went to great pains to become expert in Arabic and to know intimately the habits and customs of the country. They were also willing to teach anyone regardless of religion, on the sound theory that widespread, lasting religious reform was impossible until the educational standard of Egypt as a whole had been raised. Also, as pointed out earlier, the missionaries felt they could most effectively reach the Muslims through education. It must be noted here, however, that since the days of Napoleon "enlightened Egypt has been French in language, culture, food and etiquette."[22] Furthermore, the American Mission schools in

---

[20] Boktar, *op. cit.*, p. 136.

[21] *C.D., Eg.*, 8, desp. no. 139 from R. Beardsley, Alexandria, Oct. 7, 1873; Heyworth-Dunne, *op. cit.*, p. 87.

[22] Boktar, *op. cit.*, p. 139; see also *C.D., Eg.*, 3, desp. no. 12 from Thayer, Alexandria, Nov. 26, 1861; Heyworth-Dunne, *op. cit.*, p. 406.

Egypt never equaled in influence the American schools in Syria and Lebanon—especially the American University at Bayrut—where minority groups participated more vigorously and effectively in the social and political life.

EARLY AMERICAN INTEREST IN EGYPTOLOGY

The Americans did not contribute greatly to Egyptology (as archaeology in Egypt is commonly called) in the period prior to the British occupation of 1882. "Only in recent years, largely since 1900," Caroline Williams commented,

> has American scholarship helped in the advancement of the science of Egyptology. The long pioneer work of the nineteenth century was done in Europe, or by Europeans working in Egypt. France, England and Germany were the countries in the lead. . . . A fluctuating interest, however, in Egyptian material may be traced in this country from the first quarter of the century, and even before 1850 Americans began to further Egyptian studies by their financial support.[23]

These early developments, however, should be outlined briefly, for substantial twentieth-century American achievements grew from such small beginnings. United States interest in Egyptology was a logical development from an earlier enthusiasm

_____

[23] The history of early American interest in Egyptology may be found, *inter alia*, in C. R. Williams, "The Place of the New York Historical Society in the Growth of American Interest in Egyptology," *Quarterly Bulletin, New York Historical Society*, IV (1920), 3-20; W. D. Dinsmoor, "Early American Studies in Mediterranean Archaeology," *Proceedings of the American Philosophical Society*, LXXXVII (1943), 70-104; J. D. Cooney, "Acquisition of the Abbott Collection," *Bulletin of the Brooklyn Museum*, X (Spring, 1940), No. 3, 17-23. Although popular in nature, J. A. Wilson, *Signs and Wonders upon Pharaoh: A History of American Egyptology* (Chicago, 1964) esp. chaps. i-iv, is quite useful and rests upon a sound, scholarly base; it also contains a good annotated bibliography and biographical notes. For more extensive biographical data see generally I. Pratt (comp.), *Ancient Egypt: Sources of Information in the New York Public Library* (New York, 1925) and *Ancient Egypt, 1925-41: A Supplement* (New York, 1942).

for biblical archaeology. Considerable initial attention also apparently was centered on Egyptian antiquities, brought to the United States for exhibit. Before the 1830's these were largely mummies, the first of which arrived in Boston in 1823. After establishment of a United States consular agency at Alexandria in 1832, Americans visited the Nile Valley in increasing numbers. The sixty-odd visitors to Egypt between 1823 and 1842 swelled to an annual four thousand by the 1880's. These tourists for the most part engaged in a mad scramble for souvenirs—usually coins, scarabs, mummies and the like—and few of them brought back anything of real value.[24]

According to John Cooney, the first real collection of Egyptian antiquities to arrive in the United States was probably that given to the Peabody Museum of Salem, Massachusetts, by Lieutenant T. Tanner in 1823, and not, as is usually assumed, that brought to Baltimore in 1835 by Colonel M. I. Cohen. A number of other serious collections were also acquired by private American citizens in the 1830's, including that of John W. Hammersley, later given to Columbia University. But none of these compared in size and importance with the Abbott collection. Dr. Henry Abbott, an English physician, made his collection while a resident of Cairo. Not an Egyptologist, he originally brought his Egyptian antiquities to New York in 1852 for commercial exploitation. In the United States it remained unsurpassed until the early twentieth century, and of great influence in the development of American interest in Egyptology.[25]

---

[24] Dinsmoor, *op. cit.*, p. 96; see J. E. Cooley, *The American in Egypt* (New York, 1842), *passim*, for satirical comments on these tourists; cf. G. R. Gliddon, *Appendix to "The American in Egypt"* (Philadelphia, 1942).

[25] The Abbott collection was eventually sold to the American Historical Society of New York in 1860, and in 1948 was acquired by the Brooklyn Museum. See Cooney, *op. cit.*; H. Abbott, *Catalogue of a Collection of Egyptian Antiquities, Property of Henry Abbott, M.D.* (New York, 1853); C. E. Moldenke, "The Language of the Ancient Egyptians and its Monumental Records," *Transactions of the New York Academy of Sciences*, IV (1887), 60-70; cf. L. Poole, "Cohen's First Out of Egypt," *Art News*, XLVII, No. 9 (Jan., 1949), 38-39.

George R. Gliddon's role is also worth mention. Gliddon, though an Englishman, was closely indentified with America and American Egyptology. For a time United States consul at Cairo, he became interested in Egyptology and was able to continue his studies in Paris through the financial assistance of two American citizens. He donated Egyptian antiquities to the National Institute in Washington, and, even more significantly, delivered probably the first lecture in the United States on the subject of Egyptology. His "classes" during the 1840's were extremely popular; and he wrote a number of books on Egypt that were widely read.[26]

Among the many Americans who visited Egypt in search of antiquities, William Prime merits a brief discussion. He actually secured a *firman* from the Egyptian Government permitting him to excavate at Thebes, and hired fifty men to dig in the Valley of the Kings near Luxor. Prime apparently made no significant discoveries, reaching Cairo with only the usual scarabs, coins and mummies (both human and crocodile). The report of his trip follows more the pattern of the countless travel books written in this period by American tourists than what today might be termed a scientific expedition.[27]

The acquisition in 1879 by the city of New York of an Egyptian obelisk, one of "Cleopatra's Needles," constituted a major accomplishment for the United States in the field of Egyptology. Interest in acquiring such a monument was stimulated in the United States by the removal from Alexandria to London in 1877 of an obelisk (companion to the one finally given to New

---

[26] Dinsmoor, *op. cit.*, p. 97; see Gliddon, *An Appeal to Antiquarians* (London, 1841); Gliddon, *Ancient Egypt: Her Monuments, Hieroglyphics, History and Archaeology* (Baltimore, 1847); Gliddon, *Otia Aegyptiaca: Discourses on Egyptian Archaeology and Hieroglyphical Discoveries* (London, 1849); Gliddon, *Handbook of the American Panorama of the Nile* (London, 1849); J. A. Wilson, *Signs and Wonders*, pp. 41-43.

[27] W. C. Prime, *Boat Life in Egypt and Nubia* (New York, 1857), *passim; C. D., Eg.,* 26, desp. no. 26 from E. de Leon, Alexandria, Jan. 18, 1856.

York) bestowed on the British many years before. The French Government had also received an obelisk, moved to Paris in 1833. A campaign to acquire an obelisk for New York City was therefore initiated by Henry B. Stebbins, Commissioner of Public Parks, and by William H. Vanderbilt, who agreed to underwrite the project. In October, 1877, the Department of State instructed its consul-general in Cairo, E. E. Farman, to cooperate with New York City's agent.[28]

Farman was not initially optimistic about the prospects of success, especially since the gift of the obelisk in Alexandria would rob that city of the only one then standing. His fears were soon realized when strong opposition developed, led by certain British and French residents in Egypt. The matter remained quiescent until 1879, when Khedive Isma'il authorized the removal of the Alexandria obelisk to New York City.[29] After Tawfiq became Khedive in June, 1879, the Egyptian Government sought to reverse its decision, but abandoned the effort when it ascertained that the gift had been confirmed by an exchange of official notes.[30]

Lieutenant Commander Henry H. Gorringe, U.S.N., who was commissioned by New Yory City to remove the obelisk, arrived in Alexandria in October, 1879. After many vicissitudes the obelisk was successfully transported to New York and re-erected

------

[28] *C.I.*, *Eg.*, 16, inst. no. 85 to E. E. Farman, Cairo, Oct. 19, 1877; H. H. Gorringe, *Egyptian Obelisks* (New York, 1882); C. E. Moldenke, *The New York Obelisk: Cleopatra's Needle* (New York, 1891); Farman, *Egypt and Its Betrayal*, pp. 142-92; Farman, "Negotiating for the Obelisk," *Century*, XXIV, n.s. II (Oct., 1882), 879-89; J. A. Wilson, *Signs and Wonders*, pp. 58-60.

[29] While unsupported by evidence in the despatches from Cairo, it is quite possible that Isma'il's action was prompted by a desire to draw the U.S. into greater participation in Egyptian affairs; and it is a fact that in Aug. 1879, the U.S. Govt. suddenly requested a seat on Isma'il's proposed Egyptian Debt Liquidation Commission.

[30] *C.D.*, *Eg.*, 15, desp. no. 301 from Farman, May 22, 1879; *ibid.*, desp. no. 343, Nov. 10, 1879; Farman, *Egypt and Its Betrayal*, pp. 142-67.

in Central Park (just behind the Metropolitan Museum of Art) with appropriate ceremonies. The monument still stands there today.[31]

---

[31] The New York obelisk, one of several originally erected at Heliopolis as a part of the Temple of the Sun during the reign of Pharaoh Thatmosis III (1501–1447 b.c.), was removed to Alexandria by the Romans. It is a single shaft of red granite from Assuwan, 86 ft. 10 in. high, and 7 ft. 10 in. by 8 ft. 2 in. at its base, and weighing 220 tons. See Gorringe, *op. cit.*, pp. 68–76. For a copy of a Joint Resolution of Congress thanking Tawfiq for his generous gift, see *C.I., Eg.*, 16, inst. no. 28 to N. D. Comanos, V.C.G., Cairo, Jan. 16, 1882, and Gorringe, *op. cit.*, pp. 57–58.

PART TWO

The British Occupation
Period: 1882 – 1914

PART TWO

The British Occupation Period: 1882–1914

CHAPTER X

Great Britain in Egypt

No event in moden Egypt has cast such a lengthy shadow over its history as the British occupation of 1882. All aspects of the country's life were affected, and though formalities of Ottoman sovereignty and khedivial authority were preserved, the British agent and consul-general possessed the real power in Egypt. United States relations with Egypt will be examined, therefore, in the light of this change.

By mid-September, 1882, British forces had captured 'Arabi Pasha and effectively smashed the military revolt. The first problem facing the occupation authorities was the proper treatment of the leaders of the unsuccessful rebellion. After weeks of indecision in Whitehall, coupled with nervous excitement in Egypt, Lord Dufferin, who had been charged with drafting a rehabilitation program for Egypt, arranged a compromise; 'Arabi and six of his associates pleaded guilty to the charge of rebellion; they were given the death sentence on December 3, but this was immediately commuted to permanent exile in Ceylon.[1]

As befitting a "conquered country," the Khedive was compelled to issue a decree accepting responsibility for losses to foreigners occasioned by the bombardment and subsequent burning and pillage of Alexandria. The six European states most vitally affected (Great Britain, France, Italy, Germany, Austria and Russia) agreed that the Mixed Courts of Egypt should have no jurisdiction over indemnity claims; instead, a special inter-

---

[1] In 1901, 'Arabi was permitted to return to Egypt. See Cromer, op. cit., I, 334-39; cf. Blunt, op. cit., chap. xvii, and A. M. Broadley, *How We Defended Arabi and His Friends* (London, 1884), *passim.*

national commission of indemnities should be formed. The Powers then sought approval from the other governments, including the United States, that had participated in the Mixed Tribunals. The United States at first raised several objections to the proposed plan but in the end agreed so that small claimants would not be harmed by further delay. The indemnities commission held its first meeting on February 17, 1883, with former Agent and Consul-General E. E. Farman as the American representative. The commission had considered 10,000 petitions by September, 1885. American claimants who were paid in full received the small amount of 330,000 francs, or roughly $16,500, out of a total of some $20 million.[2]

Of more vital importance to the Western Powers, the Turkish Sultan and the Khedive of Egypt were the nature and duration of the British occupation. The possibility of turning Egypt into a British colony or protectorate apparently was not seriously considered in Great Britain, and the official government position soon reaffirmed the original character of the occupation as that of a limited "police action." This was done on January 3, 1883, when Lord Granville, British Foreign Secretary, despatched a circular note to the capitals of the important European countries, asserting, *inter alia*, that "Her Majesty's Government are desirous of withdrawing it [the British force in Egypt] as soon as the state of the country, and the organization of proper means for the maintenance of the Khedive's authority will admit it."[3]

Since no time limit was set for the evacuation of Egypt in the declaration of 1883, the British stayed on despite many promises to leave. Indeed, Sir Henry Drummond Wolf, acting for Her Majesty's Government, even signed a convention in 1887

---

[2] *Notes from Br. Leg.*, 108, notes from L. S. Sackville-West, Br. Min., Washington, Sept. 19, Oct. 7 and Dec. 3, 1882; *C.D., Eg.*, 19, desp. no. 121 from N. D. Comanos, V.C.G., Cairo, Oct. 20, 1882; *ibid.*, no. 31, Feb. 20, 1883; *ibid.*, 21, no. 37, Sept. 1, 1885; *C.I., Eg.*, 16, insts. nos. 9 and 13 to G. P. Pomeroy, U.S.A.C.G., Cairo, Nov. 10 and Dec. 28, 1882; *ibid.*, tel., Dec. 28, 1882; Farman, *Egypt and Its Betrayal*, pp. 334-36.

[3] Text in *G.B., A.P.*, cmd. 3462, LXXXIII (1883), 34-36; also in Hurewitz, *op. cit.*, pp. 116-19.

with the Porte, providing, among other things, for the withdrawal of the British troops after three years. However, the agreement was not ratified by the Sultan, primarily because of French and Russian opposition to a clause giving the English the right to re-enter Egypt under certain conditions. Great Britain then refused to renew negotiations. And so matters rested. The outbreak of World War I found the British still in occupation of Egypt.[4]

When the British "took over" Egypt in 1882, they acquired it subject to the liability of the existing capitulatory regime. The British, who, along with thirteen other Western Powers (including the United States), had been enjoying the benefits of this system, were now heard to complain about its abuses, and in particular that it was a hindrance to any real Egyptian progress. Sir Evelyn Baring (later Lord Cromer) expressed the irritation of the British administrators in Egypt in a despatch to Lord Granville, dated January 26, 1885:

> The Capitulations hang like a deadweight around the neck of the Egyptian Government. It is impossible to change in any way the codes administered by the Mixed Tribunals, or to frame the most reasonable Custom-house Regulations to prevent smuggling, or to impose the most equitable taxes on Europeans, or to insure the proper workings of any new municipal or communal institutions without reference in detail to the Powers. . . .[5]

The British claimed that since Egypt was now occupied by a great European Power, the dangers against which the capitulations were supposed to guard, such as the caprices of oriental justice, no longer existed. At the same time they realized that the rights and privileges granted by the system were so lucrative and attractive that other Western Powers would surrender them with reluctance, if at all. The English Government did achieve

---

[4] It has been alleged that between 1883 and 1902 there were 66 British promises to evacuate Egypt. See J. Adam, *L'Angleterre en Egypte* (Paris, 1922), pp. 73-79. See also H. D. Wolff, *Rambling Recollections* (London, 1908), II, chaps. lix-lxii; Cromer, *op. cit.*, Vol II, chap. xlvi; V. Chirol, *The Egyptian Problem* (London, 1920), pp. 53-55.

[5] G.B., A.P., Egypt no. 15, cmd. 4421, LXXXIX (1885), 41.

limited success in curtailing certain specific privileges; these restrictions, primarily connected with the Mixed Courts and taxation, will be considered in some detail later in this chapter.
British efforts to attack the capitulations in a more substantial
manner, however, proved a failure. Foreign governments interested in Egypt were requested in 1904–1905 to transfer to
Great Britain the legislative powers that they collectively possessed under the capitulatory system. The suggested delegation
of authority never won the consent of the other Powers. Indeed,
the capitulatory regime in Egypt was not modified in any basic
way in the period 1882–1914.[6]

'Arabi's trial and the indemnity payments were chiefly mop-
ping-up operations. The British immediately faced the serious
and persistent problem of what to do with Egyptian finances.
Indeed, the race against bankruptcy, to use Lord Milner's oft-
quoted phrase, was not won in Egypt until the late 1880's.[7]

It will be recalled that an Anglo-French dual financial control
had been established in Egypt in 1876 as a result of the economic
chaos. The partnership had never been happy, and when in the
end England acted alone in the occupation of Egypt, she was
determined to free herself from this entanglement. Consequently,
in his circular note of January 3, 1883 (mentioned above), Lord
Granville expressed Great Britain's desire that the control be
ended. To this British proposal the French Government gave
reluctant consent, but, though agreeing to certain minor financial

---

[6] In 1920 a draft convention for the renunciation of the capitulatory
rights in Egypt in favor of Great Britain was submitted to the Powers, but
though it was accepted by some of the small states, it was rejected by the
U.S.; Egypt did not free herself from the capitulations until 1937. H. W.
V. Temperley (ed.), *History of the Peace Conference at Paris* (London,
1924), VI, 96-99, 198-99; Lord Lloyd, *Egypt Since Cromer* (London,
1933), Vol. I, chap. ii; Brinton, *op. cit.*, pp. 340-41; *C.D., Eg.,* 34, confid.
desp. no. 87 from L. M. Iddings, U.S.A.C.G., Cairo, Mar. 31, 1906;
*Abolition of the Capitulations in Egypt, Convention and Protocol between
the U.S.A. and other Powers,* U.S. Treaty Series, No. 939 (1939).

[7] Viscount Milner, *England in Egypt* (13th ed., London, 1926), chap.
viii.

and judicial reforms, in general France used her capitulatory privileges in a highly obstructionist manner until the Anglo-French Entente of 1904. George Young succinctly describes French recalcitrance:

> The French still held two-thirds of the debt. They had, under protest, acquiesced in the abolition of the French controller at the beginning of the British occupation (January 4, 1883). But soon after they adopted the policy they thereafter maintained until 1904, of using the International Debt Commission and its powers under the Law of Liquidation in conjunction with the international Mixed Tribunals, for thwarting whenever possible, by legal proceedings, the British efforts to avoid another bankruptcy with its further development of financial bondage. . . .[8]

Although Germany (also Austria and Italy) subsequently adhered to the Anglo-French Convention of 1904 as it affected Egypt, she replaced France as Britain's chief irritant in Egypt in the following years.[9]

In their effort to reform the Egyptian judicial system, British occupation authorities met with limited success. Again France led the opposition. The Mixed Tribunals of Egypt represented in essence a concession of capitulatory privilege in civil suits. Among the first reforms suggested by the British was a proposal, in 1883, to expand the jurisdiction of these courts to criminal cases involving foreigners. Under the existing system such suits were tried in the consular courts of the defendant's nationality. The recommendation was never adopted, and thereafter the British concentrated on less spectacular reforms, notably those affecting the courts exclusively for Egyptians. "In the diplomatic field," Brinton has stated,

> the Mixed Courts come upon the stage most frequently on the occasions of the several international commissions convened from time to time in Cairo to consider the question of renewal of the

[8] Young, *op. cit.*, p. 155.
[9] Brinton, *op. cit.*, p. 58; Cromer, *op. cit.*, II, 391-93; cf. Lloyd, *op. cit.*, I, 30-31.

life of the courts and the various modifications proposed in the codes and the proposals of reform in the system of the courts themselves. Such commissions were assembled in 1880, 1884, 1890, 1904, and 1910 and the ample folio reports which contain the minutes of these assemblies and the numerous reports and protocols which resulted witness much devoted effort, some small portion of which at least passed into the stage of active realization. . . .[10]

Two British "legislative" reforms, however, demand brief comment. Through Lord Cromer's efforts the Powers consented, in 1889, to a khedivial decree delegating to the General Assembly of the Court of Appeals of the Mixed Courts authority to approve certain "police regulations." Again, in 1906, Cromer urged that the Egyptian Government be permitted to legislate on matters on which the civil codes were silent or obscure, subject to the approval of the Court of Appeals. The project, temporarily shelved, was revived under Cromer's successors, Sir Eldon Gorst and Lord Kitchener, and a modified version was eventually approved. In both instances the Powers retained an effective veto because of their representation on the Court of Appeals.

Lord Cromer attributes the general failure to expand and change the Mixed Courts to the existent relative effectiveness of the tribunals in their limited sphere and to the united refusal of the Powers to permit substantial encroachments on their capitulatory rights and privileges. Indeed, despite increasing British and Egyptian pressure, the Mixed Courts continued in Egypt until 1949.[11]

---

[10] Brinton, *op. cit.*, pp. 58-59.

[11] See generally on this topic, Cromer, *op. cit.*, II, chap. lviii; Lloyd, *op. cit.*, I, 29-32; C.D., Eg., 19, desp. no. 51 from G. P. Pomeroy, Cairo, July 6, 1883; Brinton, *op. cit.*, pp. 52-61, 302, 307-15; Brinton, "The Closing of the Mixed Courts of Egypt," *American Journal of International Law*, XLIV (1950), 303-12.

CHAPTER XI

The United States Reaction

Department of State records apparently contain no official policy statement on British occupation of Egypt for the guidance of American agents and consuls-general at Cairo. Diplomatically the American Government continued to regard the Turkish Sultan as sovereign of Egypt, with the Khedive as his governor, subject to existing *firmans*. In practice, however, the presence of the British further weakened the Khedive's dependence on Constantinople.

In contrast to the Department of State, American consuls-general in Egypt during early occupation days strongly criticized the British administration. Former Agent and Consul-General E. E. Farman, for instance, vigorously condemned British conduct of the 'Arabi trial and the general imperialist character of British "rule" in Egypt.[1] Likewise, Consul-General G. P. Pomeroy (1883–1885) observed:

> After this unfortunate commencement [the 'Arabi trial], a whole series of reforms were drawn up by Lord Dufferin, most commendable ideas, but badly fitted for the present generation of Egyptians. The British reformers omitted to see that the greatest evil is over-taxation and the material impossibility of balancing the budget. . . .[2]

Pomeroy does, however, comment favorably upon the British Government's refusal to give a unilateral guarantee of a loan to Egypt as proof of British determination to abide by the pledge to "limit interference to the restoration of a suitable native gov-

---

[1] Farman, *op. cit.*, pp. 225-27, 337-49.

[2] C.D., Eg., 20, desp. no. 98 from G. P. Pomeroy, Cairo, May 2, 1864.

ernment."[3] "It is an open secret here," complained John Cardwell (1886–1889),

> that Arabi Pasha was led into rebellion that a pretext might be found for English occupation, that the profits of Egyptian industry might likewise be transformed westward. Be this as it may, such has been the result; and moreover still public and private capital has been absorbed through the grossest system of English favoritism. Every hungry Englishman has been provided for and still they come, demanding and receiving public places previously held by competent Egyptians, until both civil and military departments are absolutely in the hands of the Englishmen. The Americans who were here, enjoying as they deserved, the confidence of the Khedivial Government, were all removed excepting one, to give place to less competent and less worthy men. . . .[4]

On the other hand, later United States consuls-general, for example Frederic C. Penfield (1892) and Thomas S. Harrison (1897–1899), expressed favorable opinions regarding the British occupation. Both men were impressed by the benefits of law and order brought to Egypt by the "Cromer regime."[5]

To this latter-day approval must be added the voice of former President Theodore Roosevelt. In characteristic fashion T.R., while visiting the Sudan and Egypt in 1910, gave the Egyptians a sample of his bluff, forceful manner of speaking. In an address at Khartum he had bluntly told Egyptian and Sudanese army officers that they owed a duty of "absolute loyalty" to British rule. Later, in a speech before the National University in Cairo (March 28, 1910), Roosevelt roundly condemned the excesses of Egyptian nationalism—climaxed by a Muslim fanatic's recent assassination of Boutros Pasha Ghali, a Copt, then Prime Minister of Egypt. Such frank talk created a great stir in Egypt— praise from the British occupation authorities, the Copts and the

---

[3] *Ibid.*

[4] *Ibid.*, 110, desp. no. 22 from John Cardwell, Cairo, Sept. 23, 1886.

[5] F. C. Penfield, *Present Day Egypt* (New York, 1899), pp. 140–44; T. S. Harrison, "Egypt under Lord Cromer," *Forum*, XXVII (Aug. 1899), 651–61; Harrison, *The Homely Diary of a Diplomat in the East* (Boston, 1917), *passim*.

American missionaries; angry denunciation from Egyptian nationalists.[6]

Prior to World War I the Department of State never clearly enunciated the United States position regarding British attempts to reform the capitulatory regime in Egypt. But had the question of complete abandonment or serious curtailment of the capitulations been raised, quite probably the American Government would have expressed strong opposition, though, as we shall see, the United States acceded to most of the specific requests for modifying certain privileges regarding taxation and the Mixed Courts. Usually this was done on the express grounds of accommodating the Khedive.

While British occupation authorities sought to limit the scope of capitulations, the United States was considering means for strengthening its consular court system in Egypt and other countries where America enjoyed capitulatory benefits. To this end a bill was introduced in the Forty-seventh Congress for amending existing laws regulating the exercise of extraterritorial judicial relations. The proposed changes, endorsed by the Secretary of State, included delegation of jurisdiction exclusively to consuls, instead of to ministers. Though considered in several sessions of Congress, the bill was never passed. And it appears that no substantial revision of United States statutes on the subject was ever made.[7]

---

[6] Text of Cairo speech in Theodore Roosevelt, *African and European Addresses* (New York, 1910), pp. 15-28; see also J. B. Bishop, *Theodore Roosevelt and His Times: Shown in His Own Letters* (New York, 1920), II, 185-93; for a critical comment by the president of the Constitutional Reform League of Egypt, see A. Yousuff, "Egypt's Reply to Colonel Roosevelt," *North American Review*, CXCI (June, 1910), 729-37.

[7] "Extraterritorial Judicial Rights, Reports and Papers Relative to by the Secretary of State," Apr. 29, 1882, U.S. 47th Cong., 1st Sess., S. Misc. Docs., Vol. 1, No. 89; "Extraterritorial Jurisdiction of the United States, Provision for and Repeal of Secs. 4083 to 4130, Rev. Stats. Inclusive, Relative to, Recommended, March 4, 1886," U.S. 49th Cong., 1st Sess. (H. Bill 333), H. Repts., Vol. 3, p. 864; *U.S. Code Annotated*, Title 22, chap. ii, secs. 141-83.

The British effort to secure reduction of the Egyptian debt by an agreement of the capitulatory Powers only indirectly involved the United States, but the American position is worth discussing. The first post-occupation international conference for considering Egypt's financial status met in London in June–August, 1884. The United States was not represented, despite the recommendation of the American consul-general at Cairo, who felt that the United States might be able to foster an agreement between the British and the French. In 1885 a second conference assembled, again in London; its decisions were embodied in a khedivial decree of July 27, 1888, that altered the Law of Liquidation and added German and Russian representatives to the Debt Commission. As customary in such instances, conference members then sought to obtain adhesion to this decree of all other Powers who had taken part in the establishment of the Mixed Tribunals.[8] The United States, one of the Powers approached, gave a qualified consent, but only after considerable correspondence and with tireless prodding by the British Government. "Our attitude," United States Minister E. J. Phelps in London was instructed, "being one of deference to the Khedive's Government, the communication to that government of our qualified adhesion seems sufficient and preferable to any formal arrangement whereby the signatory powers joined in establishing conditions to bind the Khedive's Government."[9]

The first of many requests to the American Government for approval of specific taxes on foreigners involved the extension, in 1883, of the house tax to American citizens resident in Egypt. The United States consented, provided the decree was nondiscriminatory. In 1888 the Egyptian Government sought American agreement to a proposal raising customs duties in order to establish a municipal council for Alexandria. Inasmuch as solicitations of this nature were arising with increasing regularity,

8 *B.F.S.P.*, LXXV (1883-1884), 189-249; *ibid.*, LXXVII (1885-1886), 480-98; *C.D.*, *Eg.*. 20, desp. no. 114 from G. P. Pomeroy, Cairo, July 14, 1884; *D.D.*, *G.B.*, 52, desp. no. 69 from E. J. Phelps, U.S. Min., London, Aug. 6, 1885.

9 *D.I.*, *G.B.*, 27, inst. no. 153 to Phelps, Dec. 4, 1885.

Consul-General John Cardwell at Cairo asked the Department if he might not be empowered to give United States approval in such cases without reference to Washington.[10] Permission so to act was readily granted by the Department of State, provided the rights of the United States Government and its citizens were not invaded or discriminated against injuriously. Cardwell was instructed that no plenipotentiary credentials were necessary since "our position is rather one of non-dissent, an act of courtesy and comity to the Khedive's Government, than of active participation in an international compact; and a simple exchange of notes suffices to affirm our attitude in each case."[11]

The United States Government was not exclusively altruistic in motive when it claimed deference to the Khedive in Egyptian financial matters. Although not always explicit, a basic factor conditioning American policy in such matters was the relative unimportance of United States investment and commercial interests in Egypt in this period. The view was articulated, for example, in 1907 when, in response to a request that the United States consent to increased taxes on foreigners for perfecting Cairo's drainage system, the Department of State observed: "It is supposed that few American interests will be affected and that but slightly."[12] "So far as I can learn," Consul-General L. M. Iddings replied,

> no Americans in this city would be directly affected by increased tax. The buildings owned in Cairo by Americans, amounting in value to over $600,000 are the property of the American Mission, and pay no taxes at all. Other American residents, dentists, doctors, keepers of hotels and cafes (and worse) so far as I can learn,

---

[10] *Notes from the Br. Leg.,* 110, note from L. S. Sackville-West, Br. Min., Washington, Nov. 2, 1883; *C.D., Eg.,* 23, desp. no. 214 from J. Cardwell, Apr. 4, 1888.

[11] *Insts. to Consuls,* 125, inst. no. 135 to J. Cardwell, Cairo, May 4, 1888. Five months later Cardwell was instructed to "err on the side of reference to the Department in doubtful cases." *Ibid.,* Vol. 127, inst. no. 152, Oct. 13, 1888.

[12] *N.F.,* Vol. 620, No. 8684, inst. no. 98 to John Giffin, Vice and Deputy Con.-Gen., Cairo, Aug. 20, 1907.

have no real estate standing in their own names. But a good system of drainage would be of the greatest benefit to thousands of American tourists, who come to Egypt every winter.[13]

The United States position regarding efforts by the British and Egyptian governments to reform the Mixed Courts of Egypt was basically similar to that taken toward the proposed financial changes noted above. Consent was quickly given in routine matters, such as periodical requests for extension of the life of the courts. Further, the United States generally accepted recommendations of the various international judicial commissions. The advice of her representatives on these commissions—the agent and consul-general and the senior American judge on the Mixed Courts—was followed, though the opinions of other American judges on the courts were also sought.[14] But where the United States Government felt that the reforms contemplated changes that might fundamentally affect American interests, it followed the other Powers in declining to give its approval.

The extent of United States willingness to accept substantial revision of the Mixed Tribunals can be found in the response to the Egyptian Government's proposal in 1883 that jurisdiction of the courts be extended to criminal cases involving foreigners. The Secretary of State set forth the following general principles:

First: that as a general principle the United States is in favor cf the domestic administration of justice, in criminal as well as civil proceedings, whenever satisfied that all the safeguards which attend the administration of justice in the United States are secured to the accused.

Second: that the trial of criminal charges by a Mixed Tribunal in which the United States are represented by a competent judge, would seem to afford such guarantees.

Third: that as our right of extraterritorial jurisdiction flows from our treaty engagements with the Ottoman Government, it

---

[13] *Ibid.*, desp. no. 191 from L. M. Iddings, U.S.A.C.G., Cairo, Sept. 21, 1907.

[14] *C.I., Eg.*, 16, inst. no. 10 to G. P. Pomeroy, Cairo, Dec. 13, 1882; *Insts. to Consuls*, 135, inst. no. 67 to L. B. Grant, U.S.V.C.G., Cairo, Feb. 7, 1891.

being set aside so far as Egypt is concerned, it might require specific negotiation with the Sublime Porte, and would certainly require the assent of Congress to enable the President to accept the criminal jurisdiction of the Mixed Tribunals in like manner as when the civil jurisdiction of those courts was established.

In conclusion it may be stated that any plan submitted by the Khedivial Government or elaborated by the commission of reform, will receive the earnest consideration of this government, but that the United States are not now prepared to commit themselves to an acceptance of the same.[15]

The Secretary's instruction, though worded cooperatively, nonetheless denied the Egyptian Government's request. Furthermore, it highlighted the significance of congressional approval as a practical barrier to any fundamental change in the Mixed Courts.

The United States engaged in a lively dispute with the Egyptian and British governments over the manner of appointing American judges on the Mixed Courts of Egypt. The seeds of the controversy were sown in 1874, when the United States successfully insisted on the right to choose the American judges who were to sit on the Mixed Courts.[16] The first challenge came in 1885, when American Judge G. S. Batcheller resigned. At this time the Egyptian Government requested the United States to nominate Alexander M. Mason Bey, an American who had served in the Egyptian Army and later in civilian posts in the Egyptian Government. A serious conflict was averted when Mason was named head of the Egyptian Cadastre and when the Khedive approved the President's selection of A. M. Keiley.[17]

In addition to objections arising out of national pride, the Egyptians, backed by the British, resented the fact that foreign governments did not always nominate the most suitable candidates. The United States was rarely criticized on this point, though in 1889 the contract of Judge J. B. Kinsman was not

---

[15] *C.I., Eg.*, 16, inst. no. 38 to G. P. Pomeroy, Cairo, Aug. 20, 1883.

[16] See *supra*, pp. 106-7.

[17] *C.D., Eg.*, 21, desp. no. 51 from N. D. Comanos, U.S.V.C.G., Cairo, Dec. 22, 1885; *ibid.*, desp. no. 30 from John Cardwell, U.S.A.C.G., Cairo, Mar. 27, 1885; *ibid.*, desp. no. 61 from Cardwell, June 30, 1886.

renewed because of his alleged inability to speak any of the "judicial" languages (French, Italian and Arabic) used before the Mixed Tribunals. The Egyptian Government again suggested Mason Bey, but did not press the matter, accepting the United States nomination of E. H. Crosby, provided that he could speak either French or Italian.[18]

The issue arose again in 1906, when Lord Cromer unofficially informed the American consul-general at Cairo that "the Egyptian Government sometime ago decided to stand strictly on its rights concerning appointments whenever vacancies should occur in the judgeships of the Mixed Courts as per article 5 of the regulations of judicial organizations of the International Mixed Courts."[19] Two years later, upon the death of Judge Batcheller, who had served on the Court of Appeals, the American Government wanted to replace him by promoting Judge S. Pinkney Tuck, then a judge on the Court of First Instance at Cairo. The Egyptian Government refused initially on the ground that "the regular procedure is that the Khedive nominates the candidate and then the President approves."[20] But in the end Tuck was promoted, though only after the United States had acceded to the Khedive's choice of Walter Berry to replace Tuck as judge of the Court of First Instance. It is significant that the British Embassy in Washington was pushing Berry's appointment.[21]

The diplomatic controversy on this point reached a peak following Judge Berry's resignation in 1911. The Egyptian Government immediately asked United States assent to the appointment of Pierre Crabites of New Orleans. After some hesitation the American Government agreed,[22] but simultaneously it sent

---

[18] *Ibid.*, 24, desp. no. 274 from Cardwell, Mar. 1, 1889; *ibid.*, no. 294, June 16, 1889.

[19] N.F., 3866, desp. no. 116 from L. M. Iddings, U.S.A.C.G., Cairo, June 3, 1906.

[20] *Ibid.*, unnum. desp. from Iddings. Sept. 4, 1908.

[21] *Ibid.*, confid. desp. no. 364, Oct. 19, 1908.

[22] No doubt one reason for this was that Crabites' name had been suggested to the British Embassy in Washington by the Chief Justice of the U.S. Supreme Court. D.F., 883.05/32, desp. no. 112 from P. A. Jay, U.S.A.C.G., Cairo, Feb. 21, 1911.

a sharp note to the Egyptian Minister for Foreign Affairs, which read in part:

It seems expedient moreover to call to your Excellency's attention that in the matter of choosing those persons who shall represent this Government upon the Mixed Tribunals, it would appear the wiser course to follow the procedure which has heretofore been observed and to consult the wishes of this Government as to whom it desires to have appointed, since otherwise this Government might find itself under a constraint to refuse its designation and sanction to one who should be suggested exclusively by the Egyptian Government, to the embarrassment not only of the one who should be suggested and declined, but of the Egyptian Government as well.[23]

The Egyptian Government in reply regretted any misunderstanding but stated that while it had no desire to designate a judge whose selection the United States Government might not sanction, at the same time it wanted to avoid official recommendation of candidates by foreign countries.[24] Further inconclusive correspondence followed, but at the outbreak of World War I neither country had given way on principle. In practice, however, the United States bowed to Egyptian and British pressure in at least two instances.

The British occupation of Egypt did not seriously affect United States–Turkish relations, chiefly because the American Government was careful to acknowledge formally the Ottoman Sultan's sovereignty over Egypt. Exequaturs for United States consuls in Egypt, for example, were requested from the Sublime Porte, as they had been before 1882. The Turkish Government contested every action by American citizens that might suggest that Egypt was not an integral part of the Ottoman Empire. It protested, for example, the failure of masters of American ships bound for Alexandria to have their bills of health visaed by the Turkish consul in New York. It insisted that all visitors to Egypt

---

[23] *Ibid.*, note to Egyptian Minister for Foreign Affairs, Apr. 24, 1911.
[24] *Ibid.*, 883.05/49, unnum. desp. from Jay, May 30, 1911.

should have a Turkish visa. In such matters the Department of State accepted the complaint and promised correction.[25]

For the most part the British occupation of Egypt did not figure in United States–Turkish diplomatic correspondence. An interesting exception was an informal suggestion made by Sir Stephen Lakeman (an Englishman in the service of the Turkish Government) in 1887: Why did not the United States Government propose as a settlement to the "Egyptian Question" that the Turks reoccupy Egypt, except for the Suez Canal, which would be held by an international force, including the United States? Pendleton King, American chargé d'affaires at Constantinople, to whom the plan had been communicated, wrote to the Department that "the United States, according to Sir Stephen, had a great moral influence in the East, which can be made greater. Therefore such a proposition coming from the United States would be listened to with great respect. . . ."[26]

The Department of State, perhaps with the memory of its ill-fated attempt at good offices in 1882, declined Lakeman's invitation, asserting—

> The Egyptian question involves highly important interests, extensive and complicated, pertaining almost wholly to the leading European states which, from the propinquity of their possessions to the Suez Canal or their dependence upon the commercial facilities it affords, are naturally the chief parties interested in its settlement.
>
> The Government of the United States will always be ready to promote amicable arrangements between the other members of the family of nations, but it is not disposed at the present time and in the absence of application to it by the European powers

---

[25] *D.F.* 123AR63/c, tel. to Am. Emb., Constantinople, Sept. 12, 1913; *Notes from Turk. Leg.*, 5, note no. 4597 from Mavroyeni Bey, Washington, May 8, 1884; *Notes to Turk. and Greek Legs.*, I, note to Mavroyeni Bey, Turk. Min., Washington, Mar. 5, 1890.

[26] *D.D., Turk.*, 46, desp. no. 300 from P. King, Chargé, Constantinople, Mar. 12, 1887.

chiefly interested, to make suggestions or tender its intervention in the decision of Egyptian affairs.[27]

The Department of State files contain no further reference to the incident; this leaves unanswered a number of suggestive questions—particularly whether or not Lakeman was acting on his own initiative.

The records reveal only one Turkish attempt to solicit United States aid against the British occupation of Egypt. In the early 1890's, Mavroyeni Bey, Turkish Minister to Washington, left a somewhat confused memorandum with the Department of State. After warning of British antagonism to legitimate American influence in Hawaii, he asked for United States support of Turkish and French opposition to British activity in Egypt.[28] Very probably this document expressed only the private views of the Turkish Minister. In any event, the Department of State did not answer it officially, and certainly it never acted upon the suggestion.

[27] *D.I., Turk.*, 4, inst. no. 6 to Oscar Straus, U.S. Min., Constantinople, Apr. 15, 1887.

[28] *Notes from Turk. Leg.*, 7 (Oct. 1, 1892-June 30, 1895), undated and unum. memo. from Mavroyeni Bey, Turk. Min., Washington.

CHAPTER XII

The United States and the Suez Canal

THE PROBLEM OF NEUTRALIZATION

Hallberg traces the first suggestion for neutralization of the Suez Canal back to Metternich's proposal in 1838. Subsequent developments included a British warning to participants in the Russo-Turkish War of 1877 not to commit belligerent acts in the Canal area. The subject assumes real significance for us only after the British launched their military occupation of Egypt through the Suez Canal. At the time, De Lesseps made strenuous but futile objections, alleging that the Canal concession of 1856 stipulated the principle of neutrality. But as Holland has pointed out, it is obvious that such a bilateral charter could have no binding international significance.[1]

After the occupation of 1882, British concern over the status of the Suez Canal became manifest in Lord Granville's circular note of January 3, 1883, which put forward an eight-point proposal; providing, *inter alia,* for freedom of navigation through the Canal and for absence of fortification. The British overture evoked no immediate response, but in 1887, under French prompting, an Anglo-French draft for neutralizing the Canal was finally agreed upon. The seven European Powers and Turkey formally signed it at Constantinople on October 29, 1888.[2] Ar-

---

[1] T. E. Holland, "The International Position of the Suez Canal," *Fortnightly Review,* o.s. XL, n.s. XXXIV (Dec., 1883), 39-49; see also Hallberg, *op. cit.,* chap. xvii, for an excellent treatment of this whole subject; J. A. Wilson, *Signs and Wonders,* chap. vi.

[2] For text see Hallberg, *op. cit.,* Appendix D; Hurewitz, *op. cit.,* pp. 119-22.

ticle 1 of this Convention provided that the Suez Canal "shall always be free and open, in time of war as in time of peace, to every vessel of commerce or war, without distinction of flag." Other clauses stated that no permanent fortifications were to be erected in the Canal area; no acts of hostility were to be committed within the Canal or three miles from its ports; belligerents were to be allowed twenty-four hours' stay; and by Article 10, the Sultan and the Khedive, acting for the Porte, could take measures "for securing by their own forces the defense of Egypt and the maintenance of public order."[3]

Although the Convention of 1888 was signed by all the important European maritime Powers, the instrument did not become operative for a decade and a half because of a British reservation of 1885—reaffirmed in 1887—to the effect that the United Kingdom would not be bound by its terms for the duration of her occupation of Egypt. We shall see later that as a result of this British action, traditional international-law neutrality rules, not the Convention of 1888, governed United States efforts to stop Admiral Camara's Spanish fleet at the Suez Canal during the Spanish-American War. As a part of the Anglo-French Entente, however, Great Britain specifically withdrew this reservation in 1904.[4]

The United States apparently received no official invitation. Nor did she seek to participate in the diplomatic negotiations involving neutralization of the Suez Canal, either at Paris or at Constantinople. The American Minister to Turkey of course informed the Department of State of the signing of the Convention. But, revealingly, the Department made no comment other than to state that it was filing the report in case the United States should be asked to adhere. Although subsequent actions implied United States acceptance of the terms of this Convention, the

---

[3] *Ibid.*

[4] Hallberg, *op. cit.*, pp. 298-99; W. B. Munro, "The Neutralization of the Suez Canal," *Annals of the American Academy of Political and Social Science*, XVII (May, 1901), 409-30.

Government never formally adopted it.[5] The implications of the neutralization of the Suez Canal for the Panama Canal will be discussed in a separate section.

The Suez Canal Neutralization Convention assumed some significance for the United States at the outset of the Spanish-American War. On June 25, 1898—the day before Admiral Camara's fleet arrived at Port Sa'id—John Hay, American Minister to Great Britain, was telegraphically advised of the Government's desire to send United States warships through the Suez Canal. He was instructed to make prompt and discreet inquiry regarding the British view on this point but to act on the assumption that no objection would be raised. Hay replied on the same day, reporting an interview with Lord Salisbury:

. . . In accordance with your instruction, I assumed no objection would be made to our use of the canal for the passage of our war ships, and merely asked whether there had been any modification of the convention of 1888, which would go to place the nonsignatory powers on any different footing from those signing the convention. He said there had been none, and I gathered from his remarks that he had no idea that any power would make any protest against our use of the canal, nor that any protest would hold if it were made. The attitude of the British Government is that we are unquestionably entitled to the use of the canal for war ships. . . .[6]

On July 14, 1898, the Department of State advised Ambassador Hay, "The object of the Department in telegraphing to you was threefold"—

1. It was desired to avoid even the possibility of objection being made to the use of the canal by our ships of war at a time when the need for such might be immediate and imperative.

---

[5] *D.D., Turk.,* 48, desp. no. 142 from Oscar Straus, U.S. Min., Constantinople, Nov. 20, 1888; *D.I., Turk.,* 5, inst. no. 182 to Straus, Constantinople, Jan. 31, 1889; *United States Treaty Developments* (Washington, current as of May, 1952).

[6] *For. Rels.* (1898), p. 982.

2. The Department, while recognizing the general and unrestricted purpose of the convention of October 29, 1888, was not disposed to rely wholly upon it or formally to appeal to it, since the United States is not one of the signatory powers.

3. The Department was not disposed, by a formal appeal to the convention, to recognize a general right on the part of the signatories to say anything as to the use of the canal in any manner by the United States.

So far as the Department is advised, Great Britain is the only Government that owns any stock or at any rate a considerable amount of stock, in the canal, and therefore the only one in a position to assert any claim of control on that ground.[7]

The instruction did not advert to the British reservation to the Convention of 1888. In any event, convention or no convention, the Department of State showed much sense in sounding out the British, who, as occupying Power in Egypt, would have a decisive voice in the matter. On the other hand, an appeal to the British Government in its capacity as a minority stockholder in the Canal Company would appear to have been rather pointless.

THE SPANISH-AMERICAN WAR AND THE SUEZ CANAL

The refusal to allow Admiral Camara's Spanish fleet to refuel in the Suez Canal while en route to the Far East during the Spanish-American War demonstrated Yankee ingenuity and British good will. Before considering the incident in detail, it is first necessary to sketch its international setting. On February 15, 1898, the U.S.S. *Maine* mysteriously blew up in Havana harbor. The United States formally declared war on Spain on April 24–25, and on May 1, Admiral Dewey destroyed a Spanish fleet at Manila. Both Cuba and Manila were put under sea blockade.[8]

---

[7] *Ibid.*, p. 983.

[8] F. E. Chadwick, *The Relations of the United States and Spain in the Spanish-American War* (New York, 1911), Vol. I, *passim.*

Action on the "Egyptian front" opened on May 21, 1898, with a telegraphic instruction from the Department of State to the American consul at Cairo ordering him "to watch for Spanish vessels passing the Canal."[9] On June 23 the Department amplified the instruction in more concrete, precise terms:

> Should Spanish squadron call at Port Said or Suez, endeavor prevent getting coal and other supplies for belligerent voyage and operations against United States in East. Mail copies this telegram confidentially Aden, Colombo, Singapore, for those consuls take similar action.[10]

The instruction of June 23 is explicable only in the context of developments in the Philippines. Admiral Dewey, who was blockading Manila, had advised Washington on May 27 of his concern over the possible appearance of a Spanish relief squadron. He also requested a battleship or armored cruiser as reinforcement. Dewey was told that General Merritt and part of the American troops assigned to the Philippines land campaign had left the United States on May 25 and that two monitors were also en route to Manila. Apprehension mounted in American quarters as a result of the report from the United States consul at Gibraltar that a Spanish fleet of two armored cruisers, two converted cruisers and four destroyers had been sighted off the coast of Morocco and were believed heading for the Far East.[11]

Upon receiving the Department's instructions of June 23, Ethelbert Watts, acting United States agent and consul-general at Cairo, cleverly secured a lien on all the coal at Suez. He also interviewed Lord Cromer, who advised that he could take no action without instruction from the British Government. This was forthcoming the next day, and Watts was advised to write to the Egyptian Minister for Foreign Affairs requesting that neutrality rules be strictly applied to Spanish war vessels passing through the Canal. Cromer added that he would try to

---

[9] *Insts. to Consuls,* 161, tel. to Am. consul, Cairo, May 21, 1898.
[10] *Ibid.,* 162, June 23, 1898.
[11] Chadwick, *op. cit.,* II, 376-79.

see to it that the Egyptian Government interpreted the spirit of
the neutrality laws, since by the letter of the rules the Spanish
warships might be permitted to get to Aden, whence they could
proceed to the Far East. Watts appealed to the Egyptian Foreign Minister, as the British agent had suggested.[12]

As anticipated, the Spanish fleet under Admiral Camara
steamed into Port Sa'id harbor on June 26. With it came seven
transports and colliers loaded with troops, coal and other sup-
plies. Watts' stratagem appeared successful in denying coal to
Camara, but he was forced to complain that the Spanish
fleet was overstaying the twenty-four-hour period allowed by
international law. The Spanish were ordered to leave immediately. The instruction was apparently not transmitted to the
local Egyptian authorities at Port Sa'id, because Watts was
informed by the United States consular agent there that not only
were Spanish warships still in the harbor on June 30 but coal
was being transferred to them from Spanish transports. The next
morning the coaling was stopped and Camara was again ordered to move. The Egyptian Government informed the Spanish
Admiral that he would be given coal only if his ships did not
have sufficient fuel to get to the nearest Spanish port, and as a
prerequisite, an undertaking to head for such port would have
to be given.[13]

On July 2 the Spanish destroyers returned to Spain, having
received coal specifically for this purpose. Admiral Camara then
despatched two of his colliers into the Canal, withdrawing his
warships from Port Sa'id harbor five miles into the Mediterranean, where his attempt to coal from newly arrived transports
was only partly successful because of heavy seas. On July 5,
Camara entered the Canal, but on his arrival at Suez was re-

---

[12] *Ibid.*, p. 388; *C.D., Eg.*, 30, desp. no. 57 from E. Watts, Acting
U.S.A.C.G., Cairo, June 24, 1898.

[13] *Ibid.*, no. 58, July 1, 1898. Great Britain had followed this practice
with some variations since 1882, though it was not accepted as a general
rule of international law, at least prior to 1914. See Moore, *op. cit.*, VII,
942-49; L. Oppenheim, *International Law: A Treatise*, ed. H. Lauterpacht
(6th ed., London, 1940), II, 566-70.

minded that he could remain only twenty-four hours. Two days later the Spanish Admiral anchored his fleet in the Red Sea, seven miles outside Suez harbor. Here he made another unsuccessful attempt to refuel. As a consequence plans for proceeding to the Philippines were abandoned, and on July 8 the Spanish fleet passed back through the Canal. It began its departure for Spain on July 10.[14]

Authorities differ on whether or not Admiral Camara ever really intended to go to the Philippines. Be this as it may, Watts undoubtedly rendered valuable service to his country in the summer of 1898, and the Department of State was duly appreciative. British assistance also proved invaluable. Apparently blood was thicker than water in Egypt as well as in Manila Bay.[15]

The most revealing aspect of the incident pertains to the backstage diplomatic maneuvering. It had been generally realized that the other European Powers were pro-Spanish in sympathy, but not immediately known was the extent of the active intervention on Spain's behalf by M. Cogordon, French agent and consul-general in Egypt. This was disclosed to American Consul-General Thomas Harrison by Lord Cromer in late October, 1898. In his attempt to secure coal for the Spanish fleet, Cogordon argued that since Port Sa'id was part of the Suez Canal, the Canal Company administration had the power to decide the question of coaling. On this point Cromer ruled that Port Sa'id was an Egyptian, not a Canal, port, and was therefore subject to the regular rules of neutrality. The French agent then contended that after the Spanish ships had refueled, they were to head for the nearest Spanish port, but after proceeding about

---

[14] *C.D., Eg.,* 30, desps. nos. 60 and 61 from Watts, July 8 and 11, 1898; Chadwick, *op. cit.,* II, 378-79, 388.

[15] Chadwick contends that Camara never seriously considered going to challenge Dewey but intended instead to attack the American coast. *Ibid.,* II, 383. Cf. H. W. Wilson, *The Downfall of Spain: Naval History of the Spanish-American War* (Boston, 1900), p. 164, who argues that the payment of £32,000 Suez Canal dues is good evidence a Far Eastern venture was planned. See also *Insts. to Consuls,* 163, inst. no. 61 to E. Watts, July 23, 1898.

fifty miles, there was nothing to prevent the fleet from turning and going in any direction it chose. The British representative at this point, as we have seen, advised the Egyptian Government to issue coal only after a written pledge had been given that the ships would go to some Spanish port. Cromer also told Harrison that during the whole incident he had never seen the Spanish agent and consul-general, conferring instead through the French representative.[16]

THE SUEZ CANAL AND THE PANAMA CANAL

Despite a demonstrated lack of direct concern with Suez Canal affairs, the economic basis of which will be examined later in this section, Americans have been greatly influenced by its history and development because of a parallel interest in constructing an interoceanic canal through Central America. In some ways the two canals possessed almost completely opposite histories. The Suez Canal, for instance, even before the date of its opening in 1869, was encrusted with aspects of the "Eastern Question" and became the object of intricate European rivalries and ambitions. But despite serious difficulties, the European Powers had agreed in 1888 to its neutralization, and it had served as an important waterway for a creditable number of years before the Panama Canal opened. The background of the Panama Canal, on the other hand, involving only British-American competition, was never the subject of a multilateral agreement.[17]

Paradoxically, the records of the two canals show similar approaches to the problem of neutralization. Great Britain and the United States both started from the position that the Suez and Panama canals, respectively, should be neutralized and

---

[16] *C.D., Eg.,* 30, desp. no. 81 from T. S. Harrison, U.S.A.C.G., Cairo, Nov. 4, 1898; Harrison, *Homely Diary of a Diplomat in the East,* pp. 259-73.

[17] A. Siegfried, *Suez and Panama* (New York, 1940), *passim;* Hallberg, *op. cit., passim.*

protected by international guarantees. In the end, however, in order to defend vital national interests, both states resorted to courses of action resulting in their eventual unilateral physical control over the canals themselves.[18]

Great Britain's position regarding the Suez Canal has been outlined in a previous section. In 1904 she finally withdrew her reservation to the Convention of 1888. But despite this belated theoretical acceptance of the principle of neutralization, Britain could effectively determine the destinies of the Canal as long as she was the occupying power in Egypt.

The history of United States policy concerning an American isthmian canal is long and complicated. Two threads run through it: the idea of neutralization and the conflicting desire to exercise unilateral control. Despite the prohibitions of the Monroe Doctrine, Great Britain and the United States engaged in bitter competition for interoceanic canal rights in Central America, a struggle temporarily resolved in the partnership of the Clayton-Bulwer Treaty of 1850.[19] The instrument provided, *inter alia*, that any isthmian canal constructed should be jointly controlled by the two countries; that it should be neutralized; and that the parties were bound to invite other powers to adhere.

As American strength developed after the Civil War, opposition in the United States to cooperation with the British in any proposed interoceanic canal swelled. American opinion was especially aroused when, after De Lesseps' Panama Canal Company began construction in 1880, the French called an international scientific conference to consider drafting neutralization proposals for the new canal. Rumors also circulated that Colombia was seeking a European declaration of neutrality for the Isthmus of Panama. Of interest is the warning given by General Charles P. Stone on May 12, 1881. In a letter to General Sherman, Stone first denounced Anglo-French economic imperialism in Egypt and then added:

---

[18] T. S. Woolsey, "Suez and Panama: A Parallel," *American Historical Association Annual Report for 1902*, I (1903), 305-11.

[19] Text in Malloy, *op. cit.*, I, 659-63.

If the United States allows France and England to make the Panama Canal without the U.S. having entire control, England and France will lend millions to Columbia for the sake of a reason to poke their noses into American politics, and within 20 years the U.S. will need a big army and navy to protect her own prestige and independence of Europe. Little Columbia will find it very jolly for ten years to spend English money; but when the canal shall have been finished and open the same excuse will be made to govern her that was made for putting Egypt under the thumb. . . .[20]

However, despite the Clayton-Bulwer Treaty, the United States Government emphatically reasserted, in a circular to the Powers, dominant political and strategic interest of the United States in the area. "Any attempt," Secretary of State Blaine declared, "to supersede that guaranty [the treaty between Colombia and the United States] by agreement between the European powers . . . whose interest in the canal and its operations can never be so vital and supreme as ours must partake of an alliance against the United States. . . ."[21] This note had the desired effect of quieting talk of European intervention. Great Britain, however, insisted upon rights based on the Clayton-Bulwer Treaty until 1901, when, in the final draft of the Hay-Pauncefote Treaty, she gave up claim to joint control.

The idea of neutralization in the United States, undoubtedly strengthened by the example of the Suez Canal Convention of 1888, persisted in the early drafts of the Hay-Pauncefote treaty, which provided both for neutralization and for an invitation to other Powers to join. The final draft, however, omitted those two clauses. Article III of the signed version of the Hay-Pauncefote treaty, it is true, does provide that "the United States adopts, as the basis of the neutralization of such ship canal, the following rules, substantially as embodied in the Convention of Con-

---

[20] *Gen. Wm. T. Sherman Papers,* Vol. 55, Ltr. from Gen. Charles P. Stone to Sherman, May 12, 1881, Cairo.

[21] Text in *For. Rels.* (1881), pp. 537, 539-40; cited in L. M. Keasbey, "The National Canal Policy," *American Historical Association Annual Report, 1902,* I (1903), 283.

stantinople, for the free navigation of the Suez Canal."[22] But as Padelford has pointed out, the United States need only "treat all nations on terms of entire equality." This replaced the clause "to be free and open in time of war as in time of peace" of the Suez Convention of 1888. The Treaty of 1901 omitted also the prohibition against fortification. Finally the United States incurred treaty liability only to Great Britain. Therefore it seems proper to conclude, as does Padelford, that the Panama Canal was not internationalized. Any remaining theoretical doubts have been resolved by United States practice. Since the opening of the Panama Canal in 1914, ships of all nations have been allowed to pass freely in time of peace, subject to non-discriminatory tolls; but the Canal is heavily fortified by the United States alone and is closed to enemy vessels in time of war.[23]

At the outbreak of World War I the United States and Great Britain controlled the Panama and Suez canals, respectively. America occupied a position somewhat superior to Britain's. Not only did the United States own the Panama Canal zone, but she was not bound by any international neutralization agreement. By contrast the British were restrained, theoretically at least, by the Suez Convention of 1888; in addition, their occupation of Egypt and of the Suez Canal zone could be terminated. Nevertheless, sufficient similarities exist so that activities in one canal regarding policies of control and defense will undoubtedly affect the other. For this reason, if for no other, the United States has watched Suez Canal developments with great attention. Amer-

---

[22] Text in Malloy, *op. cit.*, I, 782-84.

[23] Keasbey, *op. cit.*, pp. 277-88; Woolsey, *op. cit.*, pp. 307-11; Siegfried, *op. cit.*, pp. 370-82; N. J. Padelford, *The Panama Canal in War and Peace* (New York, 1942), chap. ii; J. H. Latané, "The Neutralization Features of the Hay-Pauncefote Treaty," *American Historical Association Annual Report for 1902*, I (1903), 291-303; Hyde, *op. cit.*, I, 626-34. Prior to the opening of the Panama Canal, American military experts differed on the desirability of fortifying it: Adm. Dewey was opposed, opinion cited in Latané, *op. cit.*, pp. 301-2; cf. Adm. Mahan, who wanted fortification plus a big navy: A. T. Mahan, "Fortify the Panama Canal," *North American Review*, CXCIII (Mar., 1911), 331-39.

ican strategic concern for the Suez Canal per se did not develop until World War II and after.

The general United States indifference to Suez Canal political problems in the period prior to World War I is partly due to the practical absence of American shipping in the Canal. This is readily shown by a sampling of transit figures (Table 4).

T A B L E   4

Suez Canal Traffic, 1883–1913
(In Thousand Tons)

Year	U.S.	British	Total
1883	1	4,406	5,776
1887	1	4,517	5,903
1901	45	6,253	10,823
1905	13	8,357	13,134
1910	9	10,424	16,582
1913	7	12,052	20,034

Source: A. T. Wilson, *The Suez Canal* (London, 1939), pp. 135–36.

These statistics show a slight increase in American shipping through the Canal at the turn of the century but a decline thereafter. British shipping, meanwhile, and the over-all figures, increased steadily.[24]

---

[24] Not until 1948 did U. S. traffic through the Suez Canal, largely oil tankers, increase sufficiently to justify the addition of an American member, S. Pinkney Tuck, to the Board of Directors of the Suez Canal Co. See *Le Canal de Suez, Bulletin de la Compagnie Univérselle du Canal Maratime de Suez* (Paris), No. 2,226, June 15, 1948, p. 9226.

CHAPTER XIII

Consular Problems

A CONGRESSIONAL BLUNDER

Perhaps the lowest point in the history of the American agency and consulate-general in Egypt was reached when Congress omitted any appropriation for that post in the Diplomatic and Consular Appropriation Act of July 7, 1884. The Diplomatic and Consular Appropriation bill, as presented to the House of Representatives by the Appropriations Committee, abolished several posts and made salary cuts in many others. The provisions of this bill eliminated the agency and consulate-general at Cairo and established in its place a newly created consulate, with a salary of $2,000.[1]

In the course of heated debate that ensued on many aspects of this bill, Representatives J. F. Follett (Ohio) and R. L. Hitt (Ill.) strongly urged the retention of the Cairo post in its existing form. Otherwise, they argued, the United States would be without diplomatic representation in Egypt, and necessary judicial functions would be unfulfilled.[2]

Representative James N. Burnes (Mo.), who led an economy drive, then launched a savage attack on the agency and consulate-general in Egypt. His remarks are worth quoting in full:

As to this Consulate at Cairo, it should be stated, Mr. Chairman, to the Committee [the House of Representatives was sitting as the Committee of the Whole on the State of the Union] that

---

[1] *Cong. Rec.*, U.S. 48th Cong., 1st Sess., Vol. XV, Pt. 4, p. 4159.
[2] *Ibid.*, pp. 4166, 4197.

Egypt and Cairo are subject to the Ottoman Empire; that the Ottoman Empire in turn is dominated by England, as we all know. Therefore, if we have any diplomatic labors to perform as to that country, in God's name, let us perform them either at Constantinople or London. What diplomatic relations can we have with the inhabitants of Cairo? Have they a government there that amounts to anything, a government that can act upon any international question? None whatever. Then we need no diplomacy there. Let our Minister at Constantinople attend to our business in Egypt, because that country is subject to the domination of the Ottoman Empire.

But, Sir, a Consulate has been maintained at Cairo. And to give character to the consul or consul-general, it is said he is a diplomatic agent, whatever that is. What have we done in the way of supporting that diplomatic agent? First, he has a salary of $5,000 a year; next, we have allowed him for clerk-hire $1,200 a year; then for contingent expenses, G. P. Pomeroy, consul-general, $254.87; contingent expenses, Comanos, vice-consul-general, $129.52; other contingent expenses, $2,505.48; loss by exchanging money in salary in sending his returns home, $161.11; compensation while waiting instructions, $1,657.62; expenses of interpreters, guards, etc., $500; loss by exchange, $4.52.

The business of this consulate for three-quarters of the year —because this diplomatic agent was not able in the press of business to report for the last quarter of the year ending June last— the business for three-quarters of the year was $202.50, while the expenditures were $11,413.12. I ought to say that recently, since it was seen that these matters were to be seriously and soberly looked into, a report has come for the remaining quarter of the year, and it swells the receipts from the diplomatic agent and consul-general at Cairo to the amount of $359.50.

I find from the report of the fifth auditor that that consul-general has afforded no relief whatever to seamen, has collected no wages for seamen. In short, I defy the gentleman to show that he has done anything except to spend this vast amount of money and to protect a few distinguished travellers from America, and perhaps extend hospitalities to Arabs down there on the banks of the Nile. This is the consul-general, the diplomatic agent of this great Government, who is to be maintained at a place dominated by two countries, and which is of no more diplomatic importance than the far-off islands of the Arctic Ocean.[3]

As a sop, Burnes declared that the bill provided for a consul who could handle all the duties of the Cairo post.[4]

Burnes' criticism is valid insofar as it points up the absence of important American commercial relations with Egypt, but for the most part his speech is a mass of inaccuracies and half-truths. Among other things he ignored the trade potential between the two countries, the fact that the Khedive was then empowered to make commercial agreements and the existence of important American missionary activities. In general, he showed astounding ignorance of Egypt's historical and existing international position. However, the appropriation bill passed the House, by a narrow margin. The Senate added a number of amendments, including a specific appropriation for the agent and consul-general at Cairo. A bitter fight followed, primarily over a confidential fund for the Panama Canal. Three Senate-House conferences were required, and somehow, in the give and take of the compromises, the appropriation even for a consul at Cairo was abandoned. This meant no appropriation for any United States representative in Egypt for the fiscal year ending June 30, 1885.[5]

The Department of State informed the incumbent consul-general at Cairo, G. P. Pomeroy, of this congressional action. He was asked to see if he could not persuade Vice Consul-General N. D. Comanos or some other person to act in an unsalaried capacity, since otherwise the office would have to be closed. Comanos agreed to keep the office open, asking only that expenses be paid. This the Department agreed to do. The Egyptian Government and the other consuls-general were informed of Pomeroy's departure but were not told why.[6]

---

3 *Ibid.,* p. 4197.

4 *Ibid.*

5 *Ibid.,* Pt. 5, pp. 4300, 5038, 5094; *ibid.,* Pt. 6, pp. 6074, 6085, 6026 and *passim; U.S. Stats. at Large,* Vol. 23, pp. 227-36 (1884).

6 *C.I., Eg.,* 16, inst. no. 74 to Pomeroy, July 15, 1884; *ibid.,* inst. no. 88 to Comanos. Oct. 2, 1884; *C.D., Eg.,* 20, desp. no. 120 from Comanos, July 24, 1884.

The Department of State, which was preparing a plea to Congress to restore the salary of the American representative in Egypt, asked Comanos to suggest supporting arguments. Comanos in his reply, pointed out that the United States had been considered one of the "great" Powers in Egypt and that the presence of a diplomatic agent strengthened this position. Indeed, he noted, even the smaller Powers, such as Portugal, were so represented. Finally, he urged, a simple consul would not have access to the Khedive. The force of these particular arguments is not known, but Congress in its next session did reinstate the salary of the agent and consul-general at Cairo. The matter produced almost no debate on the floor of the House. In one of the few references to it, Representative Joseph G. Cannon (Ill.), after noting the inclusion of the agency and consulate-general for Egypt in the new appropriation bill, observed sarcastically that this post was just as important last year as now and he could only assume, charitably, that the Appropriations Committee had received new light and further information.[7]

An unfortunate incident marred the restoration of the American representative to his post in Egypt. John Cardwell, the newly appointed consul-general, shortly after arriving in Cairo in 1886, uncovered proof that Comanos, acting in conjunction with a consular clerk, had been systematically extracting money from the American consular agents and dragomans. Comanos was forced to resign, despite his fifteen years of service.[8]

THE ALEXANDRIA CONSULATE, 1908

The United States was represented at Alexandria, Port Sa'id and Suez by unsalaried consular agents who, together with consular agents in Upper Egypt, were under the jurisdiction of the agent and consul-general at Cairo. All were foreigners,

---

[7] *Ibid.*, 21, desp. no. 145; Nov. 17, 1884; *U.S. Stats. at Large*, Vol. 24, pp. 108-9 (1885); *Cong. Rec.*, U.S. 48th Cong., 2nd Sess., Vol. XVI, Pt. 1, p. 814.

[8] *C.D., Eg.*, 21, desp. no. 28 from Cardwell, Mar. 16, 1886; *ibid.*, unnum. desp. from Comanos, June 7, 1886.

though those in the three port cities were generally Europeans, not Ottoman subjects as in Upper Egypt. In 1903, Consul-General John G. Long recommended to the Department of State that it follow the example of the other Western Powers in Egypt and establish consulates at Cairo and Alexandria. He also urged that the United States representatives at Alexandria, Port Sa'id and Suez be American citizens.[9] This recommendation was endorsed by H. H. D. Pierce, third Assistant Secretary of State, who had made an inclusive inspection of American consulates in the Orient in 1904. Commenting on the situation in Egypt, he said:

> Alexandria, Port Said and Suez are all consular agencies under Cairo, and the incumbents are all British subjects, whose regard for American interests in Egypt is of the most perfunctory character. It is hoped that at Alexandria and Port Said Congress may make it possible to appoint salaried consuls. . . .[10]

The criticisms of the consular organization in Egypt cited above were only part of the increasing volume of complaint raised against the United States consular system as a whole. American export trade, which had suffered from the inefficiencies of the system, caused largely by the application of the spoils system in its appointments, played a decisive role in the passage of the Act of April 5, 1906, the first comprehensive reorganization of United States consular service in half a century. The Act provided for entrance examinations, a merit system, classification of consuls and restriction of employment to American citizens.[11]

---

[9] *Ibid.*, 32. desp. no. 373 from Long, June 11, 1903.

[10] "Report of the Inspection of United States Consulates in the Orient," from the Report of H. H. D. Pierce, 3rd Asst. Sec. of State, U.S. 59th Cong., 1st Sess., H. Docs., Vol. 97, No. 665 (Dec. 15, 1904), pp. 5-6.

[11] T. H. Lay, *The Foreign Service of the United States* (New York, 1928), pp. 21-25, and Appendix A, where the Act is set out in full; see also *N.F.*, No. 2108, *passim*, for letters from the National Business League of America, chambers of commerce and various private businessmen approving these reforms.

Following passage of the Act of 1906, Congress, in 1908, authorized the opening of a "class 3" consulate at Alexandria, with a salary of $3,500. An American citizen, David R. Birch, was appointed to this new post. The agent and consul-general at Cairo was informed that he had no supervisory jurisdiction over the new consulate.[12]

Egypt's commerce flowed chiefly through the port of Alexandria, since very early times one of the finest harbors in the Eastern Mediterranean. The establishment of an American consulate there was thus a belated acknowledgment of the port's value for promoting United States–Egyptian trade. The Department of State also took measures to concentrate all commercial functions in the new consulate. In 1919, for instance, the responsibility for preparing commercial reports for Egypt was transferred from Cairo to Alexandria. And supervision of the consular agencies at Suez and Port Sa'id was assigned to Alexandria in 1911.[13]

RELATIONS WITH THE AMERICAN LEGATION IN TURKEY

Even before 1882 the right of the United States consul-general at Cairo to act independently of the American Minister (later Ambassador) at Constantinople was almost fully accepted.[14] The Department's decision recognized the Khedive's autonomous relationship with the Turkish Sultan. After the British occupation the Khedive's position became even stronger; similarly, the independence of the American agent and consul-general would seem to have been fortified.

[12] *U.S. Stats. at Large,* Vol. 35, Pt. I, pp. 100, 101 (1908); *N.F.,* Vol. 379, No. 4189/51A and 95, insts. nos. 179 and 263 to L. M. Iddings, U.S.A.C.G., Cairo, May 18, 1908, and Feb. 19, 1909.

[13] This step may have been taken partly in order to free the consul-general at Cairo for his duties as diplomatic agent. See *D.F.,* 125.2534/153, desp. no. 18 from P. A. Jay, Cairo, June 3, 1910; *ibid.,* 3028/153, inst. no. 80 to D. R. Birch, Am. Con., Alexandria, July 16, 1910; *ibid.,* 125/1318, inst. no. 16 to A. Garrels, Am. Con., Alexandria, Feb. 11, 1913.

[14] See *supra,* pp. 40–42.

An examination of Department of State correspondence with Cairo and Constantinople fails to uncover any instruction covering the problem. Indeed, only on one occasion was it referred to in the despatches, and then only indirectly. In a despatch dated April 6, 1886, S. S. Cox, American Minister to Turkey, discussing the accusations against Vice Consul Comanos, stated: "If I were assured of any authority in the premises, I would forthwith order an investigation."[15] The Department never even acknowledged this suggestion, and the matter was handled exclusively between Washington and Cairo.

The Department of State's ruling of 1882 "emancipating" the consul-general at Cairo carried with it a proviso that the American Minister at Constantinople should be kept advised of significant political developments in Egypt. Undoubtedly, considerable informal correspondence passed between the two posts, but the records do not indicate that the Minister was ever *officially* advised of events in Egypt. As an illustration, Consul-General Peter Jay sent a despatch to the Department from Cairo on April 5, 1911, covering political conditions in Egypt and the Sudan. There is no notation on this despatch of an "information copy" for Constantinople; instead, the Department itself sent the copy to Turkey.[16]

We may conclude, therefore, from the evidence at hand, admittedly largely negative, that the United States agent and consul-general in Egypt was completely free from the jurisdictional control of the American Minister in Turkey in the period 1882–1914.

---

15 *D.D., Turk.*, 45, desp. no. 152 from Cox, Constantinople, Apr. 13, 1886.

16 *D.F.*, 883.00/36, desp. no. 126 from Jay, Cairo, Apr. 5, 1911; *ibid.*, unnum. inst. to John Carter, Acting, Constantinople, Apr. 29, 1911.

CHAPTER XIV

Yankee Traders in Egypt: II

THE COMMERCIAL CONVENTION OF 1884

The Khedive of Egypt, invested with the right to make his own commercial conventions by the *firman* of 1873, began pressing the United States Government to negotiate such an agreement as early as 1881. Consul-General G. P. Pomeroy reported in April 1884, that the Egyptian Government had formally requested the American Government to enter into a commercial treaty similar to one signed between Greece and Egypt on March 3, 1884. The appeal was renewed the following September. In October the Department of State authorized Vice Consul-General N. D. Comanos to sign a commercial agreement with Egypt, but instructed him that the most-favored-nation clause could not be accepted in its unqualified form. The commercial convention between the United States and Egypt was signed November 16, 1884, by Comanos for the United States, and for Egypt by Nubar Pasha, Egyptian Foreign Minister.[1]

The new trade agreement was brief. In substance the United States submitted to the regulations of Egyptian customs attached to the Greco-Egyptian treaty of March 3, 1884. The Egyptian Government promised to grant most-favored-nation treatment to the United States. The convention was to become operative upon consent of the Senate.[2]

---

[1] It was consented to by the Senate on Mar. 18, 1885, and ratified by the President and proclaimed on May 7, 1885. *C.D., Eg.*, 20, desp. no. 95 from G. P. Pomeroy, Cairo, Apr. 14, 1884; *ibid.*, 21, desp. no. 146 from N. D. Comanos, Nov. 17, 1884; *C.I., Eg.*, 16, insts. nos. 95 and 125 to Comanos, Oct. 21, 1884, and June 27, 1885.

[2] Text in Malloy, *op. cit.*, I, 442-65.

The bulk of this instrument is composed of an appendix in the form of the Greco-Egyptian agreement together with the Egyptian customs regulations of April 2, 1884. Article IV of the Greek convention provided that as a general rule, "a fixed duty of 8 per cent *ad valorem* shall be taken as the basis of this tariff, the said duty shall be computed on the price of the goods in the port of discharge." In Article V tobacco, hashish and a few other items were excluded from the terms of the convention. An export duty of 1 per cent ad valorem was provided for by Article IX. According to Article XVI, the agreement was to remain in force for seven years from March 20, 1884, and at the end of that time on a year-to-year basis until notification to the contrary was given.[3]

In a note of February 22, 1890, the Egyptian Minister of Foreign Affairs requested the United States to sign a new commercial treaty similar to that signed by the British in the preceding year. The note did not specifically denounce the Convention of 1884. In September, 1891, the Khedive again asked the United States Government for a new trade agreement, alleging that the agreement of 1884 had terminated on March 20, 1891, the date that the Greek convention expired. He further asserted that the note of February 22nd showed a definite desire for "cessation of the effects of the convention."[4]

The Department of State replied to this Egyptian contention in a long technical instruction dated January 9, 1892. The protocol of November 16, 1884, between the United States and Egypt, it asserted, was in fact a *modus vivendi* based on treaties concluded between Egypt and certain other Powers; it stipulated for most-favored-nation treatment then and thereafter. In the absence of the usual provision for one year's notice of denunciation, the protocol was indeterminate. This fact was not repudiated by anything in the preliminary negotiations of 1884, or in the note of February 22, 1890. Furthermore, the protocol of

---

[3] *Ibid.*

[4] *C.D., Eg.*, 26, desp. no. 22 from J. A. Anderson, Cairo, Sept. 14, 1891; see also *ibid.*, 25, desp. no. 49 from E. Schuyler, Cairo, Mar. 7, 1890.

November 16, 1884, could be separated into two parts: the United States consent to the application of the Greco-Egyptian convention of 1884, and the Egyptian promise of most-favored-nation treatment. The former was terminable, but the latter was permanent and not affected by the terms of the Greek convention. Its independent rights in this regard, the Department pointed out, could not be impaired or concluded by any understanding between Egypt and a third Power to which the United States was not a party.[5]

However, negotiations for a new treaty continued. The Egyptian Government submitted a draft agreement that included a most-favored-nation clause, the right of the United States to enter into reciprocal trade pacts, and a 10 per cent ad valorem import duty. The discussion broke down when the Egyptian Minister for Foreign Affairs refused a suggestion that the 10 per cent tariff be applied to petroleum, one of the most important American exports to Egypt; he insisted that he wanted to use it as a bargaining point with Russia. By November, 1893, all interested Powers except the United States, France and Russia had signed new commercial conventions with Egypt, agreeing to the increase of the Egyptian tariff on imports to 10 per cent. F. C. Penfield, the American agent, complained to the Department that he had not received an instruction on this subject since January, 1892, and that the Egyptian Government was making anxious inquiries because of its need for increased revenues.[6]

Not until May 21, 1894, was Penfield finally instructed that "the present does not appear to be an opportune time for acting upon this question since the indefinite and uncertain state of tariff legislation renders it impossible to proceed with anything like clearness."[7] The consul-general was directed to keep the negotiations open and to advise the Egyptian Government that

---

[5] *Insts. to Consuls*, 138, inst. no. 20 to J. A. Anderson, Cairo, Jan. 9, 1892.

[6] *C.D., Eg.*, 27, desp. no. 111 from L. B. Grant, Acting A.C.G., Cairo, Aug. 22, 1892; *ibid.*, 28, desp. no. 27, from Penfield, Nov. 20, 1893.

[7] *Insts. to Consuls*, 145, inst. no. 44 to Penfield, May 21, 1894.

the matter was receiving careful attention. But despite such assurances, no action was taken by the United States Government until 1930, when a Provisional Commercial Agreement was signed.[8]

The United States–Egyptian commercial convention of 1884 continued for a considerable time on a year-to-year basis. In 1902 a Franco-Egyptian treaty had fixed the Egyptian customs duty at 8 per cent ad valorem, and by most-favored-nation clauses the benefits were extended to the other Western Powers in treaty relation with Egypt. Also, the Khedive was prevented from raising the tariff until 1930, the year when the last of the treaties in force at the time of the Franco-Egyptian agreement had expired. The capitulations forbade the imposition of any new taxes or duties without the consent of all Western Powers who might be affected by the proposed increase.[9]

The custom duties could, of course, be lowered by unilateral action of the Egyptian Government, and for a period around 1906, when times were prosperous in Egypt, the import duty actually was cut from 8 to 4 per cent on coal, timber and several other articles. In 1910 the United States Government replied with a similar expression of good will. Following a finding that Egypt imposed no discriminatory restrictions on American goods, President Taft issued a proclamation, dated January 29, 1910, extending the minimum tariff benefits of the Act of August 5, 1910 to Egypt.[10]

By the terms of the convention of 1884 tobacco was among the products specifically exempted. The Egyptian Government was therefore free to regulate it at will. In an effort to protect the Egyptian cigarette industry, non-governmental domestic cultivation of tobacco was curtailed and finally forbidden, and im-

---

[8] *Most Favored Nation Treatment in Custom Matters, Provisional Commercial Agreement between U.S.A. and Egypt, Effected by Exchange of Notes Signed May 24, 1930*, Ex. Agr. Ser. No. 5.

[9] C.D., Eg., 28, desp. no. 38 from E. C. Little, U.S.A.C.G., Cairo, May 25, 1893; D.F., 611.8331/1, unnum. desp. from Olney Arnold, Cairo, Nov. 21, 1913; Crouchley, *Economic Development of Modern Egypt*, p. 233.

[10] C.D., Eg., 34, desp. no. 29 from L. M. Iddings, Cairo, Jan. 12, 1906; *U.S. Stats. at Large*, Vol. 36, Pt. 2, pp. 2518-19 (1910).

ports of manufactured tobacco products were taxed with increasing severity. This did not, however, seriously affect the United States, as very little tobacco of American manufacture was used in Egypt during this period.[11]

One final problem concerning the United States–Egyptian convention of 1884 should be mentioned. Article II of the Greco-Egyptian agreement, which was incorporated into the American treaty, stipulated that no prohibitory measure should be applied to the commerce of either, except for universal sanitary protective measures. In 1884 the United States Government forbade the import of Egyptian rags into the United States, unless an American Government inspector certified them as disinfected. "These rags," Consul-General E. C. Little explained, "come from the dirt and squalor of Fellah villages, from the decay and filth of Nubian huts of mud and dung, from the noxious and pestilence breeding haunts of Cairenes—where small pox and cholera lie in wait with cheerful assiduity."[12] The regulation was actually instituted before the convention was signed, but its continuance in force thereafter was justified as a necessary sanitary measure. Similarly, an Egyptian quarantine tax on hides being exported from Egypt was accepted as a valid sanitary law, since it did not discriminate against the United States.[13]

AMERICAN INVESTMENT IN EGYPT

In the 1890's foreign capital began pouring into Egypt. Money was invested in banks and other credit institutions, railway development, municipal light and water companies and a variety of private industries. By the outbreak of World War I foreign capitalists controlled most of the industry and commerce of Egypt. England, France and Belgium were the countries primarily concerned; Italy, Germany and Greece participated

[11] C.D., Eg., 25, desp. no. 107 from L. B. Grant, Aug. 5, 1890; ibid., 29, desp. no. 72 from F. C. Penfield, May 3, 1894.

[12] Ibid., 28, desp. no. 6 from E. C. Little, Feb. 9, 1884.

[13] Ibid., 31, desp. no. 97 from J. G. Long, Cairo, Dec. 22, 1900; ibid., desp. no. 145, June 19, 1901.

on a smaller scale. American capital played a minor role.[14]

It is not too difficult to spell out just what United States investments were in Egypt before 1914. Numerous American manufacturers, of course, were represented by local agents in Egypt. But, according to Consul-General Hampson Gary, only three American firms operated in the country under their own names: the Vacuum Oil Company, the Singer Sewing Machine Company and M. Melachrino and Company, cigarette manufacturers of New York and Cairo.[15]

By far the most important of these three American companies was the Vacuum Oil Company.[16] In a letter to Consul-General Gary, C. A. Moser, director of the Vacuum Oil Company in New York City, disclosed that the company's Egyptian branch began operating through agents in about 1898, and in 1907 had established its own installations in that country for the distribution of petroleum products. Moser furnished the following data on Vacuum Oil Company operations in Egypt, based on figures as of November 30, 1917.[17]

Investment in Egypt, plant and other installations	$ 565,625.82
Net sales, Dec. 1, 1915–Nov. 30, 1916	$ 2,986,630.35
Yearly payroll	$ 231,403.76
Total operating expenses, Dec. 1, 1915	$ 397,428.54
No. of stations	90

---

[14] A. E. Crouchley, *The Investment of Foreign Capital in Egyptian Companies* (Cairo, 1936), pp. 42-76 and *passim;* see also *D.F.*, 883.00/73, desp. no. 39 from Hampson Gary, U.S.A.C.G., Cairo, May 9, 1918, pp. 8-10 of a survey report entitled "Relative Importance of Foreign Interests in Egypt."

[15] *Ibid.*

[16] In 1931 the Vacuum Oil Co. was taken over by the Standard Oil Co. of N. Y. and the name changed to Socony-Vacuum Oil Corp.; in 1934 the name became Socony-Vacuum Oil Co., Inc.

[17] The applicability of these statistics to the year 1913-1914 and earlier years is highly questionable in view of the changes brought about by World War I; however, they are presented as the only figures available. See *ibid.*, 883.05/130, copy of ltr. from C. A. Moser, Director of Vacuum Oil Co., New York, to Gary, Cairo, Apr. 8, 1918.

The Singer Manufacturing Company had its Near and Middle Eastern regional headquarters in Cairo. From this center agencies for the sale of sewing machines operated not only in Egypt but also in Eritrea, the Persian Gulf, Mesopotamia and the Sudan. Some 400 persons were employed at salaries amounting to $142,500 anually.[18]

The third American company, M. Melachrino and Company, cigarette manufacturers, reportedly had a capital investment of some $192,500 in Egypt, and employed 75 workmen at an annual salary of $25,000.[19]

No survey of United States investments in Egypt would be complete without mention of American missionary and archaeological activities; while non-commercial, they involved a considerable financial outlay. At the outbreak of World War I the American mission estimated its property in Egypt, largely church buildings and schools, to be worth about $450,000. No figures are available for the expenditures of American Egyptologists. Although they had no permanent installations in Egypt prior to 1914, the various field expeditions must have spent considerable sums on salaries for local workmen, food, housing and the like. The several thousands of American tourists who visited Egypt every winter also must have figured somewhat significantly in the Egyptian economy.[20]

COMMERCIAL RELATIONS

At first glance the increase in United States trade with Egypt from 1883 to 1914 appears impressive. In 1883, Egypt imported American goods valued at $290,782 and exported to the United States goods valued at $320,211, while the 1913 figures for Egyptian trade from and to the United States had reached $1,660,333 and $19,707,828, respectively. In round numbers the United States exported to Egypt about five times as much and imported over nineteen times as much in 1913 as in 1883. However, the

---

[18] *Ibid.*, 883.00/73, desp. no. 39 from Gary, May 9, 1918.
[19] *Ibid.*
[20] *Ibid.*

increases are less spectacular when compared to Egypt's over-all trade statistics. In 1883, Egypt's total imports were approximately $40 million and her exports $61 million, but in 1913 she imported $137 million and exported $156 million.[21]

The picture of United States commerce with Egypt becomes somewhat brighter with the realization that the figures cited above refer only to direct trade between the two countries. In addition, Americans engaged in considerable trade of an indirect character. The absence of direct transportation between the United States and Egypt meant that much American merchandise, carried chiefly in British ships, went to Alexandria via England and Continental Europe. The goods were not credited to the United States, but instead swelled the totals of Great Britain, France and Italy. The extent of indirect trade can be shown in the following figures: Between 1884 and 1903, Egyptian imports from the United States were about $12.4 million, of which only $1 million was officially credited to the United States. This applies also to Egyptian goods shipped to America. But even with the addition of indirect trade, the American share of Egyptian commerce remained relatively small. In 1910, for example, it was estimated that the United States furnished only 3 or 4 per cent of Egypt's total trade. Great Britain, in comparison, supplied, in 1910, about 50 per cent of Egypt's exports and 31 per cent of her imports.[22]

With the notable exception of cotton, the export of which showed rapid growth, the character of Egyptian exports to the United States remained substantially as it was before the British occupation. The main items were of agricultural or animal origin, such as hides, gum arabic, senna, rags, onions and cotton. Sugar assumed some importance, but only for a few years during the

---

[21] Appendix B; *Comm. Rels.* (1885-1886), II, 1536; *Foreign Commerce Year Book, 1933*, p. 28.

[22] *Comm. Rels.* (1885–86), II, 1539; *ibid.* (1904), p. 784; *Con. Repts. Ser. No. 94*, June, 1888, pp. 510-12; *D.C.T.R.*, No. 48, Aug. 29, 1910, p. 629; *ibid.*, No. 267, Nov. 14, 1911, p. 786.

Spanish-American War, when America's normal sources in Cuba were cut off.[23]

Very soon, however, cotton became the primary Egyptian export to the United States. Egyptian cotton was not exported to America in any substantial quantity until 1884. Yet by 1911 the United States was rated as Egypt's second most valuable customer, taking 15 per cent of the total. England remained in first place, receiving 45 per cent.[24] The growing importance of Egyptian cotton to the United States is shown in Table 5.

T A B L E   5

EGYPTIAN COTTON EXPORTS, 1884–1912
(In Egyptian Bales of 700–750 Lb.)

Year	Exports to U.S.	Total Exports
1884–85	4,553	500,000
1890–91	23,790	528,000
1895–96	56,339	684,321
1899–1900	72,196	835,539
1911–12	124,063	965,184

Sources: *Con. Repts. Ser.*, No. 166, July, 1894, p. 422; *ibid.*, No. 256, January, 1902, pp. 43-44; *D.F.*, 883.61321/10, desp. no. 265 from P. A. Jay, Cairo, April 10, 1913.

Cotton constituted about $22 million of the $23.6 million total Egyptian exports to the United States in 1912. It should be observed that Egyptian cotton, a long-staple variety, did not compete with the short-staple cotton grown in America but was put to specialized uses where strength and luster of finish were essential. In this period the United States tried, with little success, to grow Egyptian cotton. The impact of Egyptian cotton on the United States economy was of course very small. But from Egypt's viewpoint it was vitally important. This accounts

---

[23] *Comm. Rels.* (1885-1886), II, 1537; *D.C.T.R.*, No. 267, Nov. 14, 1911, p. 790; *Con. Repts. Ser.*, No. 189, June, 1896, p. 359.

[24] *D.C.T.R.*, No. 185, May 9, 1913, p. 791.

for the suggestion of the Egyptian Minister of Finance just after the outbreak of World War I that American vessels carry coal to Egypt and return with cotton.[25]

Turning now to Egyptian imports from the United States, we find that petroleum and petroleum products, especially kerosene, held first place practically to the outbreak of World War I. Important also were agricultural implements, railway equipment, lumber and wood products, machinery, hardware, spirits, mineral and vegetable oils, and after 1902, coal.[26]

The rising threat of Russian and Roumanian competition to the American monopoly in the sale of petroleum and petroleum products in Egypt has already been noted. Although the Russian oil fields at Baku were in production as early as the 1820's (official records from 1832), they were commercially important only after 1876. Moreover, Russian oil did not begin seriously to compete with American oil in the Near Eastern markets until the early 1880's. The turning point came in 1883, when the Russian companies introduced steamers for carrying petroleum in bulk, thus cutting transportation costs. In 1890, for instance, freight rates on petroleum from Batum to Egypt were reported to be 13.5 cents per case,[27] while the rate from New York to Alexandria was 19.3 cents per case. The difference was even greater when tanker steamers were used. As a result, though inferior in quality to American petroleum, the Russian product soon began to capture the Egyptian market because of its lower price.[28]

[25] *D.C.T.R.*, No. 185, Aug. 9, 1913, p. 795; *Con. Repts. Ser.*, No. 186, July, 1894, p. 422; *ibid., No.* 186, Mar. 1896, pp. 367-70. For the serious consequences of Egypt's becoming a one-crop economy—cotton—see C. Issawi, "Egypt since 1800: A Study in Lopsided Development," *Journal of Economic History*, XXI (Mar., 1961), 1-25.

[26] *Comm. Rels.* (1885-1886), II, 1537; *Con. Repts. Ser.*, No. 262, July, 1902, pp. 451-52; *D.C.T.R.*, No. 198, Aug. 24, 1913, pp. 858-59.

[27] A case was a wooden box enclosing two rectangular cans, each containing four imperial gallons.

[28] *Con. Repts. Ser.*, No. 64, June, 1886, pp. 161-67; *ibid.*, No. 74, Feb., 1887, pp. 400-423; *C.D., Eg.,* 26, desp. no. 127 from L. B. Grant, Cairo, Oct. 6, 1890.

Roumanian oil production centering around Ploesti began in the late 1850's, but did not reach one million barrels until 1899. In 1909 total Roumanian petroleum exports were 460,704 tons; of this amount 79,943 tons was sold to Egypt, which was third on Roumania's list, after England and France. By 1912, Roumania was well on the way to replacing both the United States and Russia in the Egyptian market. Of petroleum and its products, valued at $1,679,972, that were imported into Egypt that year, Roumania supplied 65 per cent, Russia 32 per cent and the United States only 3 per cent.[29]

Table 6 shows the decline of the United States as the chief supplier of Egypt's petroleum needs.

T A B L E   6

VALUE OF EGYPT'S OIL IMPORTS, 1885–1913

Year	United States	All Countries
1885	$ 575,000	$ 770,035
1891	100,000	———
1896	99,498	845,200
1903	23,715	1,057,573
1906	373,265	1,467,180 (for 1907)
1910	352,985	1,345,346
1913	34,920	2,854,625

Sources: Con. Rept. Ser., No. 149, Feb. 1893, p. 320; *ibid.,* No. 217, Oct., 1898, p. 164; *ibid.,* No. 294, Mar., 1905, p. 113; *Com. Rels.* (1906), p. 380; *D.C.T.R.,* No. 267, Nov. 14, 1911, p. 789; *ibid.,* No. 169, July 21, 1914, p. 391.

In the late 1880's, Russia also began contesting the United States previously held monopoly in the Far Eastern kerosene market. By 1893, Russia had sixty to seventy petroleum tank steamers in this trade. What happened in the Far East is beyond the scope of this book, but both Egypt and the United States

---

[29] "World Oil Atlas, 1948," *World Oil,* July 15, 1948, issue, Houston, Tex., p. 27; *M.C.T.R.,* No. 345, June, 1909, p. 149; *D.C.T.R.,* No. 185, Aug. 9, 1913, pp. 789-90.

were drawn into the picture because the Russian oil companies had secured permission from the Suez Canal Company (following the issuance of certain specially devised safety regulations) to ship petroleum in bulk through the Canal. Americn oil companies meanwhile continued to ship oil in cases by sailing vessels via Cape Horn. The Standard Oil Company, which was beginning to feel the pinch of Russian competition, sought assistance from the Department of State. As a result the Turkish and Egyptian government were unofficially advised that the transfer of petroleum in bulk through the Suez Canal constituted not only a threat of fire to other ships using the Canal but also possible injury to the fisheries in the area. Such representations met with no success in Constantinople. The Porte refused to interfere, on the grounds that police regulations of the Canal were a matter for local control. The khedivial government also refused to intervene, and following a decision of the Egyptian Mixed Courts upholding the safety regulations, the United States Government itself declined further diplomatic intercession.[30]

The record of United States participation in Egypt's carrying trade was no better after 1882 than it had been prior to that date. English shipping monopolized United States–Egyptian commerce, both direct and indirect. No American vessels appeared, for instance, in the total listing of 2,312 ships at Alexandria for the year 1892. Similarly, in 1913 no American ships officially entered United States ports from Egypt. Though numerous consular reports stressed the desirability of establishing direct steamship connections between the two countries, such a service never materialized in the years prior to World War I. Nevertheless, German shipping interests somewhat alleviated the situation by instituting direct freight service between New York and Alexandria in 1902. The experiment proved only temporary, since the company eventually routed tis ships via Ham-

---

[30] *C.D., Eg.,* 26, desp. no. 31 from J. A. Anderson, Cairo, Oct. 19, 1891; *ibid.,* desp. no. 32, Nov. 2, 1891; *D.D., Turk.,* 51, desp. no. 401 from S. Hirsch, U.S. Min., Constantinople, Mar. 8, 1892; *D.D., G.B.,* 174, desp. no. 996 from Henry White, Chargé, London, May 17, 1893; *D.I., G.B.,* 30, inst. no. 5 to T. F. Bayard, U.S. Amb., London, June 7, 1893.

burg. In 1909 a steamship line commenced operations between New York and Piraeus, Greece, but apparently abandoned a proposal to make Alexandria a port of call.[31]

THE PAUCITY OF UNITED STATES–EGYPTIAN TRADE: A SECOND LOOK

Clearly the United States paid little attention to Egypt as a potential customer, despite the fact that her foreign trade was greater than any other in the Near East, and that two-thirds of her imports were manufactured goods that could be supplied from American sources. The question naturally arises whether the United Kingdom, as occupying Power, assumed a monopoly of Egypt's trade. Subject to some qualification, the answer is apparently no. It will be recalled that one of Great Britain's reasons for moving into Egypt was a desire to protect her interest in Egyptian cotton. England took most of Egypt's cotton, furnishing in exchange finished textiles and cotton goods. This was a natural combination difficult for other countries to upset regardless of whether the British were or were not in occupation. The British, it is true, discouraged the development of Egypt's textile industry, but this fact alone should, if anything, have assisted American merchants.[32]

It should be borne in mind that the capitulatory system remained substantially intact in Egypt, despite the British occupation. The other interested Powers, especially the French, were careful to insure that their rights were not usurped. United States consular representatives themselves testified to the absence of discrimination against American goods in the Egyptian tariff and other commercial regulations. Although at the start of World War I, Great Britain still retained the largest share of Egyptian trade,

[31] *Comm. Rels.* (1894-95), I, 17; *For. Comm. and Navig.* (1913), p. 871; *Con. Repts. Ser.*, No. 261, June, 1902, pp. 353-54; *D.C.T.R.*, No. 188, Aug. 12, 1911, p. 671; *M.C.T.R.*, No. 348, Sept., 1909, pp. 113-14.

[32] Ralph M. Odell, "Cotton Goods in Egypt," *Spec. Agts. Ser.*, No. 64 (1912), pp. 5, 9; Crouchley, *Economic Development of Modern Egypt*, p. 174.

this in itself was no evidence of monopoly, as total Egyptian exports to Britain fell from 63 per cent in 1885–1889 to 43 per cent in 1913, and Egyptian imports from Britain correspondingly sank from 37.5 per cent to 30 per cent. German competition in particular made considerable inroads. Nevertheless, because of the increased value of Egypt's commerce, Britain's monetary share actually increased by 1914.[33]

Monolopy implications were inherent wherever a European power staked out a sphere of influence in an underdeveloped area. Egypt was no exception, despite the special circumstances of the capitulations. Two examples in the field of Anglo-American commercial competition will illustrate this point. In 1902, when the Egyptian Government purchased several large cargoes of coal from the United States, British coal merchants raised an immediate outcry, asserting that cheaper and better coal could be procured from Great Britain.[34] More significant was Lord Cromer's statement in 1907:

> A certain amount of special plant has been received from America, and this, though excellent in design, has been in every single instance of inferior quality structurally. For example, some well-boring plant of the American oil-well type, though admirably designed, was of the worst description, with faulty casings and bearings and unfinished machine work. . . .[35]

United States Consular Agent E. Alexander Powell at Alexandria denied this sweeping indictment. "The railways, irrigation works, and, in fact, pretty much every public work of importance are," he asserted, "in the hands or under the supervision of the British, and perhaps it is too much to expect them to give an American-built engine preference over one made by their own countrymen, even if the American is obviously the best machine. . . ."[36]

Since the lack of United States–Egyptian trade cannot be

---

[33] *Comm. Rels.* (1904), p. 792; Crouchley, *Economic Development of Egypt.*
[34] *Con. Repts. Ser.,* No. 262, July, 1902, pp. 451-52.
[35] *M.C.T.R.,* No. 362, Nov., 1907, p. 55.
[36] *Ibid.,* p. 56.

accounted for in any widespread exclusion policy by the British occupation authorities, we must seek the answer elsewhere. The fact that commerce between the two countries remained in such a poor state cannot be attributed to a want of interest on the part of the American Government. The published *Consular Reports Series*, begun on a monthly basis in 1880, appeared on a daily basis in 1909. Regular Department of State consular reporting was supplemented in 1905 by reports of special agents of the Department of Commerce and Labor (later Department of Commerce).[37] Nor did American representatives in Egypt lack energy. Their despatches were filled with suggestions of trade opportunities. Typical of these was a special consular report in 1911 pointing out that the $1 million worth of rope annually imported into Egypt, chiefly from Germany and Italy, would provide a good market for American manufacturers who could meet Italian and German prices. In 1906, George Wissa, United States consular agent at Asyut, offered to open a depot for the exclusive sale of American goods in Egypt. He agreed to absorb the risk by putting up a guarantee of one or two million dollars. The project was presented to the National Association of Manufacturers of the United States. But that group, while showing some initial interest, refused to undertake the responsibility. A proposal in 1911 to open a showroom for the display of American merchandise apparently met a similar fate.[38]

United States consular representatives in Egypt during this period were convinced that a flourishing trade between the United States and Egypt was entirely possible, if only American businessmen would exert the necessary enterprise and initiative.

---

[37] There is indeed evidence of some jealousy on the part of consular officers in Egypt because of the prominence given to reports of these special agents. See *N.F.*, Vol. 538, No. 6900, pvt. ltr. from L. M. Iddings, U.S.A.C.G. at Cairo, New York, May 25, 1907.

[38] *Spec. Con. Repts.*, No. 45 (1911), p. 40; *Comm. Rels.* (1906), p. 382; *N.F.*, 11643, desp. no. 218A from Iddings, Dec. 22, 1907; *D.C.T.R.*, No. 226, Sept. 27, 1911, p. 1456; *D.F.*, 116.131/2 and 9, ltr. from Ewer Sales Co., Detroit, Sept. 28, 1911, and unnum. desp. from D. R. Birch, U.S. Con. at Alexandria, Philadelphia, Oct. 10, 1911.

They criticized American business for its failure to establish direct transportation between the two countries, for faulty packing of merchandise, for refusal to extend credit, for the absence of a United States bank in Egypt, for neglecting to analyze and cater to local needs and desires and for other inept commercial practices.[39]

The above criticisms, however just, seem to be symptoms rather than basic explanations for the lack of American trade. But these consular reports do contain several thought-provoking suggestions that, while not providing a completely satisfactory answer, hint at the possible roots of the question. In 1886, Consul-General John Cardwell, after stating that more than one cause for the small amount of United States–Egyptian commerce existed, asserted:

> Its [America's trade] decline began with that of American shipping, and has kept pace with diminishing American bottomry and a misdirected excessive system of taxation acting as an embargo on American trade with foreigners. As a natural consequence of the damage arising from these causes, the manufacturers of the United States have failed to make the merits of their goods known in foreign countries. . . .[40]

United States Minister to Turkey John Leishman advanced the theory that America's unfavorable trade position in the Near East could be explained by her concentration on the Far East.[41] Special Agent of the Department of Commerce Ralph Odell offered a final explanation: "apparently manufacturers in the United States have assumed that competition in Egypt is not open or that trade is secured to England because of her in-

---

[39] *Comm. Rels.* (1903), I, 236; *ibid.* (1904), pp. 783-90; *ibid.* (1909), pp. 978-84; *D.C.T.R.*, No. 108, May 9, 1911, pp. 593-97. It should be noted that similar complaints were being made by U.S. consuls in other countries during this period.

[40] *Con. Repts. Ser.*, No. 67, Sept., 1886, p. 481.

[41] *N.F.*, Vol. 279, No. 2866, desp. no. 102 from Leishman, Nov. 16, 1906.

fluence in that country, and they have little interest in trying to obtain business."[42]

Mention should be made of a domestic development within the United States that has a bearing on this problem. During the years of "the great American boom" (1870's–1890's), American businessmen showed little interest in competing for Egyptian or other foreign markets for their manufactured goods. Consistent attention, however, was directed to the disposal abroad of surplus cotton, tobacco, wheat and other primary products.

[42] Odell, *op. cit.*, p. 16.

CHAPTER XV

American Pioneers in Egyptian Oil Fields

The development of Egypt's oil fields is discussed separately because of the role played by American citizens in its early history. This history also provides a necessary background for more important later operations of United States oil companies—the Standard Oil Company (New Jersey) and the Socony-Vacuum Oil Company.

Although the existence of petroleum had been known since ancient times, and although a specific report of its presence at Gemsah appeared in 1868, the Egyptian Government took no action until the spring of 1884. At that time M. de Bay (sometimes referred to as "Debay"), a Belgian engineer, was employed to make a petroleum survey of the Egyptian Red Sea coast. Following his favorable report, De Bay was commissioned to supervise extraction operations. Work began in 1885, and on February 28, 1886, oil was struck at 115 feet at Gemsah, located on the Egyptian Red Sea coast about 180 miles south of Suez. Although only a relatively small amount of petroleum was obtained, the Egyptian Government showed great interest in the discovery.[1]

L. H. Mitchell, an American mining engineer, was engaged to make a new survey of the Red Sea coast region. This he accomplished in the summer of 1886. His report in 1887, citing the

---

[1] *D.D., Turk.*, 45, desp. no. 159 from S. S. Cox, U.S. Min., Constantinople, May, 4, 1886; London *Times*, Apr. 24, 1886; T. S. Bowman, *Report on Boring for Oil in Egypt* (Cairo, 1925-1931), pp. 17-44. Bowman gives the most comprehensive and accurate report of oil developments in Egypt during this period. See also S. H. Longrigg, *Oil in the Middle East* (London, 1954), pp. 15, 22-24.

presence of extensive evidences of oil on the surface, convinced the Egyptian Government that it possessed substantial deposits of petroleum. Simultaneously with the employment of Mitchell, De Bay was discharged, and Herbert Tweddle, an American experienced in Pennsylvania oil fields, was given a year's contract as adviser to the Egyptian Government and as supervisor of operations. About $150,000 was allocated to Tweddle to buy boring and prospecting equipment in England. De Bay's well having petered out, Tweddle drilled five new wells at Gemsah and one at Jabal Zeit, nearby. These wells, also unproductive, were eventually abandoned.[2]

The Egyptian Government, restive at mounting expenses and at the failure to find oil in any quantity, accordingly sent Colonel C. E. Stewart (accompanied by Mitchell) to re-examine the situation and report whether operations should be continued. After an extensive survey Stewart recommended three new drillings, including one on the eastern side of the Gulf of Suez. However, despite this favorable advocacy, the Egyptian Government temporarily suspended operations. The Government reportedly had spent about $500,000 between 1885 and 1888 in its search for petroleum.[3]

Thus ended American participation in the early development of Egyptian oil fields. For the remainder of the period prior to World War I, British interests dominated the picture. By 1910 four British oil companies operated concessions along the Egyptian shore of the Red Sea and two on the Sinai side.

[2] L. H. Mitchell, *Ras Gemsah and Gebel Zeit* (Cairo, 1887), *passim;* C.D., *Eg.,* 22, desp. no. 94 from John Cardwell, Cairo, Sept. 3, 1886; G. Schweinfurth, "The Petroleum Wells of the Red Sea Coast of Egypt," *Athenaeum,* No. 3087 (Dec. 25, 1886), p. 865; Bowman, *op. cit.; Comm. Rels.* (1885-1886), II, 1515.

[3] C. E. Stewart, *Report on the Petroleum Districts Situated on the Red Sea Coasts* (Cairo, 1888), *passim; Con. Repts. Ser.,* No. 92, Apr., 1888, p. 62. Con.-Gen. Cardwell blamed this debacle on Mitchell's lack of knowledge. See *C.D., Eg.,* 23, desp. no. 223 from J. Cardwell, Cairo, May 29, 1888; cf. Bowman, *op. cit.,* who, while admitting Mitchell made errors, asserted that Mitchell was sound considering the then stage of development of petroleum geology.

Numerous wells were sunk, but oil was not found until 1911, again at Gemsah. The first shipment of petroleum, some 3,000 tons in a tank steamer, was made from this area in 1912. However, in the opinion of British and American oil experts who examined the area, oil was not present in sufficient quantity at Gemsah to justify large financial outlay. Anglo-Egyptian Oil Fields, Ltd., which was to become the most important company in Egyptian oil production, won a concession from the Egyptian Government in 1913. This concession provided that the company be given leases in specified areas for thirty years (renewable under certain conditions for fifteen years); operations were to be commenced within a year; a refinery, then under construction at Suez, was to be completed; and while there was no provision for royalties, preference was to be given to Egyptian oil, with maximum prices being set for its sale. Anglo-Egyptian Oil Fields' most succeful operations were at Hurghada, on the Egyptian Red Sea coast south of Gemsah, where oil was discovered in 1913. This field remained the source of nearly all Egyptian petroleum up to 1930. The refinery at Suez began operations in 1913.[4]

Egyptian crude-oil production has never been very high, particularly when contrasted with rich finds in Iran, Iraq and elsewhere in the Middle East. In 1911, the first year Egyptian figures were listed, only 21,000 barrels were extracted. By 1914 total Egyptian oil production had been raised to 753,000 barrels.[5]

---

[4] Bowman, *op. cit.*, *passim; D.C.T.R.*, No. 104, Nov. 3, 1910, pp. 450–51; *ibid.*, No. 65, Mar. 18, 1912, p. 1117; *ibid.*, No. 10, Jan. 13, 1914, p. 151; *ibid.*, No. 169, July 21, 1914, p. 395; for text of Anglo-Egyptian Oil Fields, Ltd., concession in full, see *Journal Officiel de l'Egypte*, Dec. 10, 1913, suplement.

[5] Egypt's crude-oil production was listed on Jan. 1, 1951, as 16,299,000 bbl., or 0.39 per cent of the world output; her estimated reserves as of Jan. 1, 1952, were 164,000,000 bbl., or 0.16 per cent of the world's estimated reserves. "World Oil Atlas, 1952," *World Oil*, July 15, 1952, issue, Houston, Tex., p. 71.

CHAPTER XVI

The Cultural Impact: II

MATURING OF THE AMERICAN MISSION

After 1882, American missionaries in Egypt still retained the avowed goal of proselytizing the Muslims, despite an alleged lack of cooperation from British occupation authorities. In the 1900's a vigorous evangelical campaign was launched in the Delta, but with largely negative results. The membership of the Evangelical Church of Egypt remained primarily ex-Coptic, though larger and more self-sufficient.

A maturing of the Mission's institutions represented perhaps the most important development of the period 1882–1914. This was especially noticeable in the field of education and in the newly developed medical branch; there the most effective work continued to be accomplished. The trend toward centralization and toward a concentration of interest in churches, schools and hospitals *qua* institutions became even more pronounced.

Rev. Andrew Watson was one of the first American missionaries to return to Cairo after the fateful days of the bombardment of Alexandria and the British occupation. He arrived in Cairo on September 28, 1882, to find that though the Mission and its adherents had suffered no harm, "it was the universal belief among native Christians that unless the British had reached Cairo before Friday, September 15, on that day there would have been a general massacre of them, and a division of their property among the 'believers.' "[1]

Shortly after the British occupation of 1882, the American Mission, which had hitherto enjoyed a practical monopoly of Protestant missionary work in Egypt, found itself faced with

[1] A. Watson, *op. cit.*, p. 351.

serious competition from other foreign mission groups. The British Church Missionary Society, first of the new arrivals, appeared in 1883. This group, which had operated in Egypt in the 1820's with the purpose of reforming the Coptic Church from within, returned now to focus primarily on the conversion of Muslims. The other new foreign misssions included the North African Mission (British, 1894), Egypt General Mission (British, 1898), Seventh-Day Adventist (United States, 1899) and a number of smaller sects. Although a survey of all Protestant missions in Egypt for the year 1906 showed that as of that date, the American Mission's predominance was not seriously threatened, the Americans did feel some resentment over what was referred to as a "breach of mission comity."[2]

Despite the difficulties mentioned above, evangelical work continued with renewed energy. Comparative Table 7 shows the Mission's success.

T A B L E 7

GROWTH OF EVANGELICAL CHURCH OF EGYPT, 1883–1914

Year	No. of Stations	American Missionaries	Church Members	Organized Congregs.	Avg. Sunday Attendance
1883	55	27	1,516	19	2,863
1890	151	30	3,155	29	6,132
1895	190	42	5,004	37	8,886
1900	213	51	6,526	50	13,029
1905	191	95	8,639	59	17,205
1910	273	115	11,200	72	21,986
1914	291	122	12,412	85	23,614

Sources: 25th, 32nd, 37th, 42nd, 47th, 52nd and 56th *Ann. Repts., U.P.Ch.,* (1884, 1891, 1896, 1901, 1906, 1911 and 1915), pp. 88-89, 74-77, 81-84, 153-54, 252-56, 145-50 and 145-50, resp.

In 1903 the American missionaries, stirred by a vision of the

---

[2] *Ibid.,* p. 407; C. R. Watson, *Egypt and the Christian Crusade,* pp. 199-204, 274-75; J. I. Parker (ed.), *Interpretative Statistical Survey of the World Mission of the Christian Church* (London, 1938), p. 102; "The Egypt General Mission, 1898–1905," *Blessed Be Egypt,* VI, No. 22 (Jan. 1905), p. 7.

actual and total evangelization of Egypt, appealed to the parent church in the United States for 290 new missionaries. The General Assembly of the church endorsed the appeal as an expression of the need and ultimate purpose of the Mission; but obviously church finances did not allow for the expense of additional missionaries. Indeed, the American Mission in Egypt was able to maintain its expanded activities only because the Evangelical Church became gradually more and more self-sufficient.[3]

In addition to purely evangelical work, great expansion took place in two closely related departments—hareem, or Zanana, work, and religious-book distribution. The hareem work was an effort to reach the great mass of Egyptian women, largely illiterate. Systematic work among them commenced in 1868, when an American woman missionary arrived in Asyut specifically for this purpose. Visits to the home, teaching of elementary reading and writing, and prayer meetings were stressed.[4]

Religious-book distribution also increased greatly, from 30,000 books sold in 1883 to more than 86,000 in 1914. An important administrative change was made in this department in 1902. The American Bible Society, and the British and Foreign Bible Society, which formerly had assisted the American Mission by grants and discounts, called for a clear delimitation of territory in Egypt in order to begin their own Bible distribution. This resulted in a great expansion in the sale of Bibles, but a falling off in the sale of other religious literature, since many of the colporteurs were employed solely to sell Bibles.[5]

[3] C. R. Watson, *Egypt and the Christian Crusade*, pp. 198-99; 36th, 42nd and 50th *Ann. Repts., U.P. Ch.* (1895, 1901 and 1909), pp. 62, 105 and 53, resp. In 1900 the U.P. Ch. established a separate Mission to the Sudan; the Mission to Egypt provided initial assistance and maintained close ties with the sister Mission to the south. See generally J. K. Giffen, *The Egyptian Sudan* (New York, 1905); C. R. Watson, *The Sorrow and the Hope of the Egyptian Sudan* (Philadelphia, 1913); and Jamison, *op. cit.*, pp. 179-87.

[4] A. Watson, *op. cit.*, pp. 435-41; 56th *Ann. Rept., U.P. Ch.* (1915), p. 104, gives statistics showing progress made.

[5] 25th, 44th and 56th *Ann. Repts., U.P. Ch.* (1884, 1903 and 1915), pp. 14, 188-90 and 127-30, resp.

By 1890 the American Mission had given up its press in Cairo and had to rely largely on the missionary press in Bayrut for the printing of religious literature. The founding in Alexandria of the Nile Mission Press in 1905, however, improved matters considerably; thereafter it served all Protestant interests in the Nile Valley.[6]

One of the effects of the great over-all expansion in the American Mission's work was a drift toward centralization and compartmentalization. The missionaries found themselves increasingly tied down by administrative work to the main stations. No longer was it possible for them to travel personally among the towns and villages. Similarly, the single Presbytery of Egypt became too cumbersome to handle properly; consequently, on February 22, 1899, with the consent of the parent church in America, Egypt was divided into four presbyteries—Delta, Middle Egypt, Asyut and Thebes. On May 11 of the same year a Synod of Egypt was formed.[7]

The American Mission now enjoyed better relations with the Coptic Church than in the preceding period. Coptic opposition still persisted, accompanied by occasional outbursts, as in the Fayyum in 1906 when threats and excommunications were used against Protestant converts, but without the violence of the 1860's. In fact, Coptic propaganda developed an increasing subtlety. In 1904, for instance, Coptic priests reportedly attempted, with some success, to prevent their members from

---

6 *A Record of the Nile Mission Press: Silver Jubilee, March 12, 1930* (Cairo, 1930); A. T. Upson (pseud. Abdul-Fady), *Highlights in the Near East* (London, 1932 [?]); *Blessed Be Egypt*, VI, No. 22 (Jan., 1905), 30-31; *ibid.*, No. 23 (Apr., 1905), pp. 77-78; *ibid.*, No. 25 (Oct., 1905), pp. 129-33; J. R. Menzies, "The Nile Mission Press," *Moslem World*, XXVI, No. 2 (Apr., 1936), 161-69; A. Van Sommer, "The Work of the Nile Mission Press," *Missionary Review of the World*, o.s. XXIX, n.s. XIX (1906), 928-29.

7 C. R. Watson, *Egypt and the Christian Crusade*, pp. 185-99.

deserting by claiming that no difference existed between the two churches.[8]

The American missionaries reported with pleasure evidence of reforms within the Coptic Church, such as a partial cessation of picture worship, use of Arabic vernacular instead of archaic Coptic in church services, training of preachers, increase in the number of schools and wider use of the Bible. This development was attributed partly to the example of the Protestant Church and partly to an effort by the Copts to check their loss of members. In 1892 the Coptic Church at Asyut appointed an American Mission–trained licentiate to conduct religious services. This employment lasted only one year, but such a thing would have been impossible in the early days. Further, in 1892 a progressive group within the Coptic clergy succeeded temporarily in ousting the Patriarch, who had refused to initiate any changes. Although this effort ultimately failed, it did represent healthy opposition within the Coptic Church to dictatorial, archaic policies.[9]

The British occupation of 1882 had raised the expectations of the American Mission. The missionaries believed that a new era for the advancement of their cause had arrived and that Egyptian Muslims themselves, anticipating a definite Chrstian orientation, were prepared to act accordingly. A test of the English occupation attitude took place in 1883, when an educated Muslim became converted to Christianity. He was seized by an angry mob, beaten, and finally imprisoned. His goods were seized, his wife was forced to leave him, and he himself was committed as insane. He was eventually released, but the British, giving way to Muslim pressure, deported him to Cyprus for his own safety.[10]

---

[8] 30th, 46th, 48th and 51st *Ann. Repts.*, *U.P. Ch.* (1889, 1905, 1907 and 1910), pp. 41, 52, 52-53 and 130-32, resp.

[9] Cromer, *op. cit.*, II, 211-13; 33rd and 34th *Ann. Repts.*, *U.P. Ch.* (1892 and 1893), pp. 24-26 and 54-56, resp.

[10] A. Watson, *op. cit.*, pp. 360-61; 25th *Ann. Rept.*, *UP. Ch.* (1884), pp. 24-27.

British failure in this instance to take a strong stand in behalf of Christianity indicated their general *laissez faire* policy toward Muslim religious and social institutions in Egypt—a sore point with the missionaries throughout the occupation. The Mission complained, for example, about the Egyptian Government's refusal to close government schools on Sunday, about the general preference for Muslims in the Army and the civil service and about other alleged discriminations. Rev. D. M. Thornton put the case for the missionaries rather sarcastically as follows:

> The missionaries of the Gospel in the pursuance of purely spiritual work have little to gain from official support; but surely they might expect, when laboring within a sphere of British influence, to be placed in a position at least as advantageous as the followers of the False Prophet.[11]

American missionaries were not deterred by this setback. Instead they embarked boldly on a program oriented primarily toward the conversion of Muslims. This meant concentrating attention primarily in the Delta region, rather than in Upper Egypt, where the strong Coptic communities were located. "We give place to none," asserted the Mission's annual report for 1903, "in our endeavor to reach Moslems. Among our Evangelical Church members are more Moslem converts that all other missions in Egypt can show."[12] A survey of the American Mission's work among the Muslims does reveal certain clear signs of progress. More Muslims were reading the Scriptures and studying in Mission schools; colporteurs were better received; and many Muslim women responded to the hareem work. In 1902 it was reported that a former Muslim, now an Evangelical Church member, was permitted to preach to his former co-religionists within the precincts of the Al Azhar Mosque in Cairo. And in 1911 the first conference of converts from Islam (thirty-five men

---

[11] *Missionary Review of the World,* o.s. XXIX, n.s. XIX (1906), p. 873; see also C. R. Watson, *Egypt and the Christian Crusade,* pp. 185-99.
[12] 45th *Ann. Rept., U.P. Ch.* (1904), p. 40.

from all Near East countries) to be held in North Africa took place near Cairo.[13]

Despite this evidence of substantial growth of tolerance in Egypt, the new program can be termed only moderately successful. For example, as of 1904, approximately fifty years after the founding of the American Mission in Egypt, only one hundred Muslims had been baptized. The difficult situation notwithstanding, this is not an impressive figure. Also, though there were fewer reports of Muslim violence against Christians, even the missionaries realized the persistent, if latent, anti-Christian feeling. It came to the surface especially in such times of nationalist unrest and anti-foreignism as the Turko-Italian War of 1911–1912.[14]

When Lord Cromer retired as British agent and consul-general in 1907, the American Mission thanked him for his services, though at the time specifically disapproving English policy in the "promotion of the Moslem religion." The British, it is true, found it politically expedient not to interfere with Islam. However, if they did not "promote" Christianity in Egypt, they did give that country a period of law and order unique in its modern history. Thus, as a by-product of Great Britain's political policy the path was smoother for American missionaries and their converts in Egypt than for Christians in Turkey proper, where plunderings, killings and forced conversions to Islam were not uncommon.[15]

The two issues of friction between the Mission and the United States Government—consular agents, and the amount of diplomatic assistance to be furnished to the missionaries—were more

[13] C. R. Watson, *Egypt and the Christian Crusade*, p. 190; 44th, 51st and 54th *Ann. Repts., U.P. Ch.* (1903, 1910 and 1913), pp. 139, 132-34 and 53-54, resp.

[14] 46th and 53rd *Ann. Repts., U.P. Ch.* (1905 and 1912), pp. 52-55 and 16, resp.; *D.F.*, 6120/24, desp. no. 651 from L. M. Iddings, Cairo, Apr. 11, 1910.

[15] 48th *Ann. Rept., U.P. Ch.* (1907), p. 17; *D.D., Turk.*, 62, desp. no. 796 from A. W. Terrell, U.S. Min., Constantinople, Feb. 4, 1896.

definitively answered after 1882. The American Mission continued to insist that only through the consular agents could it receive necessary and immediate protection for its personnel and for its extensive interests in Egypt. It argued that these agents should be retained even though only Egyptians were available to fill the posts. In 1904 the Department of State, after years of argument and concessions, finally ordered the closing of all consular agencies in Upper Egypt, except the one at Asyut. This decision merely reasserted the Department's general policy against employment of Ottoman subjects in this capacity. The strong protests of the missionaries were of no avail.[16]

As if to justify the Department's strict adherence to its rule, Wissa Bey, the remaining consular agent at Asyut, was the subject of a strong note from the Egyptian Government in 1911. Wissa, despite a warning from the American consul-general, had taken a leading part in the Coptic Congress of 1911, which met at Asyut and passed vigorous resolutions condemning the Egyptian Government's treatment of the Copts. Sir Eldon Gorst, the British agent and consul-general, complained that Wissa's action constituted not only a breach of etiquette but also an unwarranted intervention in the internal affairs of Egypt by a foreign consular officer. The Department of State ordered Wissa's immediate dismissal, but later suspended his sentence on good behavior.[17]

On the question of the extent of diplomatic protection to the missionaries, the Department of State became more and more reluctant to grant this group special treatment. Although unexpressed in official correspondence, this policy probably originated in the feeling that the presence of the British in Egypt insured proper safeguards for the American Mission's rights

---

16 *Insts. to Consuls*, 157, inst. no. 17 to E. Watts, U.S.V.C.G., Cairo, Sept. 27, 1897; *ibid.*, 177, inst. no. 67 to J. G. Long, U.S.A.C.G., Cairo, May 2, 1901; *ibid.*, 180, no. 92, Oct. 12, 1901; *ibid.*, 185, no. 150, Mar. 17, 1903; *ibid.*, 192, no. 15 to J. W. Riddle, July 11, 1904; *N.F.*, Vol. 294, No. 3078, inst. no. 62 to L. M. Iddings, Cairo, Dec. 17, 1906.

17 *D.F.*, 883.00/35, desp. no. 120a from P. A. Jay, Cairo, Apr. 25, 1911; *ibid.*, 125381/8-9, inst. no. 82 to Jay, Apr. 27, 1911; *ibid.*, desp. no. 143 from Jay, May 18, 1911; *ibid.*, inst. no. 100 to Jay, July 26, 1911.

through domestic channels of justice. Two cases will illustrate the Department's position. In 1887, Consul-General John Cardwell advised that the American Mission was involved in a dispute with local authorities in Upper Egypt over land ownership, and that he was planning to bring the matter to the attention of the Egyptian Government in Cairo. The Department replied that Cardwell might use his good offices, but should not take formal diplomatic action unless the missionaries were denied the customary resort to justice. In 1904, using a similar line of reasoning, the Department refused to act on a request of the missionaries that cases involving their property should be withdrawn from the Mixed Courts of Egypt and put under the jurisdiction of the United States consular courts.[18]

The instance of the suspension of the religious newspaper published by the Mission deserves special mention. After several attempts, permission to publish a weekly newspaper in Arabic had been granted to the American Mission. In 1910 this paper reprinted portions of a book violently attacking Islam, which caused a great outburst of resentment throughout Egypt. Instead of fighting the issue on capitulatory rights, a compromise was reached whereby the paper was suppressed for two months, but after that period a license to publish a new paper would be granted without a fee.[19]

This new shift in emphasis did not mean, however, that the American missionaries were left without any protection or assistance. In 1890, for instance, when two missionaries were falsely accused of desecrating an ancient Egyptian tomb, the American agent and consul-general insisted upon, and secured, an apology from the Egyptian Minister of Public Works.[20]

The establishment of a medical department was one of the

---

[18] *C.D. Eg.*, 22, desp. no. 177 from Cardwell, Aug. 18, 1887; *Insts. to Consuls*, 122, inst. no. 114 to Cardwell, Sept. 20, 1887; *ibid.*, 191, inst. no. 13, to J. W. Riddle, June 6, 1904.

[19] *D.F.*, 383.116 P92/12-13, desp. from E. Bell, U.S.V.C.G., Cairo, Aug. 27, 1910; *ibid.*, inst. no. 13 to P. A. Jay, Oct. 13, 1910; A. Watson, *op. cit.*, pp. 392-94.

[20] *C.D., Eg.*, 25, desp. no. 59 from E. Schuyler, Cairo, Mar. 31, 1890; *Insts. to Consuls*, 133, inst. no. 34 to Schuyler, Apr. 28, 1890.

most significant developments of the American missionary work in Egypt after 1882. Actually the first steps were taken on December 23, 1868, when Dr. D. R. Johnstone arrived at Asyut to start his medical work. The small beginnings included the opening of a daily clinic, after initial but futile opposition from the Coptic clergy. However, Johnstone returned to the United States in 1874, and except for a few months during 1882, there was no medical missionary in Egypt until the arrival of Dr. Elmer Lansing in 1884. When Lansing left in 1889, the Mission was again unrepresented in the medical field until 1891.[21]

The arrival in Egypt of Dr. L. M. Henry in 1891 opened an era of permanent and rapid development of American medical missionary work. Henry, whose work centering in Asyut made him beloved and respected by everyone, was retired in 1927, but continued to work in Egypt until 1939. He was responsible for the first Mission hospital—a makeshift affair at Asyut in 1894— and for most subsequent improvements. The statistics for the year 1914 indicate the remarkable strides made in the medical field. In that year 7 doctors, 15 nurses and 3 hospitals were listed. Clinical patients numbered 56,043, and hospital patients, 4,601.[22]

The years from 1882 to 1914 saw rapid growth in all types of educational institutions in Egypt. Foreign-controlled schools shared in this expansion, as did the Egyptian Government to a limited extent. Most critics agree, however, that, in contrast to their excellent work in the financial and developmental fields, British educational efforts in Egypt were a failure. This criticism can be documented by examining the amounts expended for public education: 1.02 per cent of the total budget in 1882, 0.87 per cent in 1890 and 1.03 per cent in 1910.[23]

---

21 46th *Ann. Rept., U.P. Ch.* (1905), pp. 106-7.

22 56th *Ann. Rept., U.P. Ch.* (1915), p. 150; A. A. Milligan and F. C. McLanahan, *Dr. Henry of Asiut* (Philadelphia, 1945), *passim.*

23 On education in Egypt in general, see Boktar, *op. cit.,* pp. 116-18, 133-38; R. D. Matthews and M. Akrawi, *Education in Arab Countries of the Near East* (Washington, 1949), pp. 16, 90, 111-18; Issawi, *Egypt: An Economic and Social Analysis,* pp. 40-42; Young, *op. cit.,* pp. 165-66. See

As with other foreign schools, the American Mission's educational endeavors prospered under the British-enforced regime of law and order. Betwen 1883 and 1914 the number of schools directly under Mission control increased from 10 to 27, but an even greater expansion took place over the same period in schools operated by the Evangelical Church, from 53 to 196. At the same time the total number of students of all kinds jumped from 4,552 to 15,727.[24]

Despite this creditable showing, American missionaries complained of growing competition both from the Egyptian Government and from the Copts. Beginning about 1900, as a part of its program of internal reform, the Coptic Church initiated a campaign to expand its educational facilities. Many of these new schools were opened close beside the Mission's schools and successfully drew away the latter's pupils. The Mission's complaint against the Egyptian Government was more serious. It alleged that government schools, appearing now in increasing number, were both unfair and antagonistic to Christianity because of compulsory teaching of the Koran, school sessions on Sundays and other discriminations.[25]

As one result of this increased educational competition, the American Mission decided, in 1912, not to create any more new schools for the present but to concentrate on raising the quality of those in existence. To this end a system of school inspection and teacher training was recommended. It should not be assumed, however, that the appearance of strong rivals in the educational field discouraged the attendance of Coptic and Muslim students at the Mission schools. On the contrary, the

---

Bibliog. Abu Al-Futouh Ahmad Radwan, *Old and New Forces in Egyptian Education* (New York, 1951), contends that the British had a definite policy of restricting Egyptian education. Cf. Cromer, *Modern Egypt*, II, pp. 424-42, and R. Galt, *The Conflict of French and English Educational Philosophies in Egypt* (Cairo, 1933), pp. 6-11.

[24] 25th and 56th *Ann. Repts.*, U.P. *Ch.* (1884 and 1915), pp. 30 and 88 and 148-49, resp.

[25] 36th, 43rd and 53rd *Ann. Repts.*, U.P. *Ch.* (1895, 1902 and 1912), pp. 77-78, 39 and 85-90, resp.

enrollment of such students remained relatively stable. In 1900, out of a total of 14,181 students in schools directly and indirectly controlled by the American Mission, 7,290 were Copts and 3,077 Muslims. The corresponding figures for 1914 were: out of a total of 15,727, 8,497 Copts and 2,175 Muslims.[26]

The American missionaries faced several problems in their educational program. In 1913 the Egyptian Government, in an effort to raise the standard of education, issued regulations specifying the type of playground, classroom and general equipment to be used in all schools except those under direct foreign control or protection. Had these regulations been applied to the Evangelical schools, most of them would have been forced to close. The American Mission, therefore, at the request of the Synod of Egypt, agreed to take these schools under its protection, thereby exempting them from the new law. The Mission stated, however, that it would try to bring the schools up to the new standards.[27]

The Mission was also concerned at this time with the expansion of its curriculum. As early as 1902 the desirability of establishing a commercial school to train clerks and assistants in modern business methods, and an industrial school to teach modern mechanical agricultural methods, was discussed. The agricultural branch had to wait until the interwar years, but in 1910 a commercial department was added to the Mission's Men's and Boys' School in Alexandria.[28]

The proposal to found a Christian university in Egypt created a final problem. In 1912 the American Mission recommended the establishment of such an institution to the Board of Foreign Missions of the United Presbyterian Church in the United States. Dr. Samuel M. Zwemer, who had been active in missionary work in Arabia, arrived in Egypt in 1912 to work actively on the project. The next year the General Assembly of the parent church

---

26 42nd, 54th and 56th *Ann. Repts., U.P. Ch.* (1901, 1913 and 1915), pp. 129, 57-60 and 148-49, resp.

27 55th *Ann. Rept., U.P. Ch.* (1914), pp. 96-98.

28 44th, 52nd and 53rd *Ann. Repts., U.P. Ch.* (1903, 1911 and 1912), pp. 160-62, 89 and 90, resp.

approved the recommendation. A board of trustees, selected on an inter-denominational basis, assumed control, holding its first meeting on November 30, 1914. The various Protestant churches interested in Egypt expected to make their influence felt in the selection of the trustees. In June, 1914, Lord Kitchener, the British agent and consul-general, suggested that in view of Muslim opposition, the inauguration of the new institution should be postponed a year and opened in Alexandria rather than in Cairo. Actually the new university was not established until 1920, but it was located in Cairo.[29]

The American Mission schools continued to attract favorable comment. Lord Cromer voiced high praise for the Mission's educational work, especially for the college at Asyut. In 1907, John D. Rockefeller made a $100,000 gift to the United Presbyterian Church for use toward permanent property needs in Egypt and the Egyptian Sudan, with the largest part going to the erection of buildings at Asyut College.[30] Further favorable comments on the educational and medical work of the American missionaries came from Consul-General Lewis Iddings. "For intellectual and spiritual purposes," he wrote in 1907,

> Americans occupy Egypt as fully as does England for material purposes. Our missionaries there have the best existing schools and the most of them, and hospitals. . . . America is doing more for Egypt in a certain way than England, because our schools are educating the native to be a better citizen while England is only looking after the material possibilities of the country.[31]

Not all of the reports, however, even by American observers, were so complimentary. Edward Mead Earle, for instance, after

---

[29] 54th, 55th and 56th *Ann. Repts., U.P. Ch.* (1913, 1914 and 1915), pp. 18 and 59, 31-34 and 31-32, resp.; *D.F.*, 383.116 AM31, unnum. confid. desp. from Olney Arnold, U.S.A.C.G., Cairo, June 5, 1914; Matthews and Akrawi, *op. cit.*, 115.

[30] C. R. Watson, *Egypt and the Christian Crusade*, pp. 53-54; *Missionary Review of the World*, o.s. XXX, n.s. XX (1907), p. 149.

[31] N.F., Vol. 496, no. 6120/10, confid. desp. from L. N. Iddings, May 16, 1907.

praising the missionaries for courage and devotion to duty, makes the following criticism of their work in the Middle East, including Egypt:

> . . . For almost a century American public opinion concerning the Near East was formed by the missionaries. If American opinion has been uninformed, misinformed and prejudiced, the missionaries are largely to blame. Interpreting history in terms of the advance of Christianity, they have given an inadequate, distorted, and occasionally a grotesque picture of Moslems and Islam. . . . In portraying conditions in the old Ottoman Empire, for example, they failed to point out that many of the sufferings of the Christian minorities were shared *in toto* by their Turkish compatriots. . . . In order to raise funds, missionaries, and more recently relief organizations, have often exploited half-truths, with the result that the American mind became closed to the patent fact that all peoples of the Near East, regardless of nationality or religion, have been common victims of common misfortunes.[32]

AMERICAN EGYPTOLOGY COMES OF AGE

American interest in Egyptology continued at a quickened tempo during the last decades of the nineteenth century. The United States assisted the cause of Egyptology at this time primarily through substantial contributions to the Egypt Exploration Fund (E.E.F.) and the Egyptian Research Account (known after 1906 as the British School of Archaeology). The E.E.F., founded in England in 1882, sent out to Egypt a number of prominent archaeologists whose achievements were outstanding both in discoveries and in published works. Rev. W. C. Winslow of Boston established an American branch of this organization in 1883; by 1903, some eighty local secretaries of this branch were scattered throughout the United States. Active direction of the E.E.F. remained in British hands, although in

---

[32] Edward M. Earle, "American Missions in the Near East," *Foreign Affairs*, 7: 398-417 (1928-1929) at p. 417.

1911 an American professor, Thomas Whittemore, was made a member of the executive committee in London, and also was named as American representative on the staff of explorers in Egypt. Between 1883 and 1902 approximately $126,000 was donated to the E.E.F. from American sources. At the same time, American museums benefited by the acquisition of important objects of Egyptian antiquity. This was made possible because of a rule of the E.E.F. that all discoveries (after one-half had been given to the Egyptian Government as required by law) be distributed to museums designated by donors, on the basis of the amounts contributed. In 1889 a five-month lecture tour of the United States by Amelia B. Edwards did much to stimulate interest in the work of the E.E.F.[33]

The Egyptian Research Account was formed in England in 1895, with Flinders Petrie as field director. This organization, although chiefly concerned with the recording of data from the monuments of Egypt and the training of students, also distributed a limited number of antiquities among its patrons. Museums in the United States received a share of the finds as a consequence of American donations. According to John A. Wilson, Petrie, through the care and control of his field techniques, "made Egyptology a science instead of a pastime."[34]

The United States had not yet reached the stage of undertaking active, sustained archaeological operations in Egypt. How-

---

[33] *The Work of the Egyptian Exploration Fund, 1882-1918* (London, 1918); W. C. Winslow, "Egyptian Antiquities in Our Museums," *Biblia: A Magazine of Oriental Research and Discoveries*, VII (1900), 1-8; W. C. Winslow, "The Queen of Egyptology, Amelia B. Edwards," *American Antiquarian Magazine*, XIV (1892), 305-15; Winslow, *The Truth about the Egyptian Exploration Fund* (Boston, 1903); C. H. S. Davis, "Dr. Winslow and the Egyptian Exploration Fund," *Records of the Past*, II (1903), 309-13; "Egypt Exploration Fund," *Brooklyn Museum Quarterly*, I (1915), 153, 216.

[34] Wilson, *Signs and Wonders upon Pharaoh*, p. 98; "Mr. Petrie's Egyptian Research Account," *American Journal of Archaeology*, X (1895), 67-68; W. C. Winslow, "The Egyptian Research Account" (Ltr. to Editor), *Nation*, LXXXII (Feb. 8, 1906), 117.

ever, in addition to the usual large number of tourists primarily interested in souvenirs, Americans did complete a few scattered worthwhile projects. At the top of this list stands Charles E. Wilbour (1833–1896), an Egyptologist and collector of considerable distinction, although not a "publisher." Charles Latimer was given a *firman* in 1884 to examine the Great Pyramids at Gizeh. Latimer, president of the International Institute of Weights and Measures, was interested in securing data to discredit the French metric system. In 1897 the American Exploration Society received permission to explore for antiquities in the district of Tanis. F. Cope Whitesouse's rediscovery of ancient Lake Maeria in the Wadi Rayian in Fayyum in 1887 was more spectacular. He recommended the revival of its use as a reservoir for surplus Nile water. The Egyptian Government did not follow this suggestion, and as late as 1911 Whitehouse vainly pursued a claim for compensation and for a land concession in the area.[35]

The most vital development of the 1880's and 1890's was the gradual emergence in the United States of a corps of expert Egyptologists. The group, under instruction or serving apprenticeships at this time, included James Henry Breasted, George Reisner, Herbert E. Winlock, A. M. Lythgoe and many others. One of the best-known of the Americans was Breasted, destined to enjoy a distinguished reputation not only in the United States but throughout the world. After studying at Chicago (1888–1890), Yale (A. M., 1892) and Berlin (Ph.D., 1894), Breasted was named instructor (later professor) at the University of Chi-

---

[35] Wilson, *Signs and Wonders*, pp. 101-9; *C.D., Eg.*, 21, desp. no. 2 from N. D. Comanos, U.S.V.C.G., Cairo, Jan. 5, 1885; *ibid.*, 23, desp. no. 221 from J. Cardwell, U.S.A.C.G., May 22, 1888; *ibid.*, 29, desp. no. 6 from T. S. Harrison, Nov. 23, 1897; *D.F.*, 383.115 W 58/48, ltr. from F. C. Whitehouse, New York, May 22, 1911; "Claims to Certain Desert Lands in Egypt" (Frederic Cope Whitehouse), U.S. 59th Cong., 1st Sess., S. Docs., Vol. 3, No. 104, Dec. 30, 1905; W. R. Dawson (ed.), *Who Was Who in Egyptology* (London, 1951), p. 167; Harrison, *Homely Diary of a Diplomat in the East*, pp. 148 ff.: C. Latimer, *The French Metric System* (Cleveland, 1879).

cago. In the course of a career of writing, teaching and excavating, he found time in 1911 to organize the Oriental Institute in Chicago and was its first director.[36]

The year 1899 marks the inauguration of an outstanding American era in Egyptian archaeology. Between 1899 and 1914 the big American universities and museums sent large-scale scientific expeditions to Egypt. The first of these was sponsored by the University of California and financed by Mrs. Phoebe Hearst. This group, led by George A. Reisner, formerly of Harvard University, arrived at Alexandria in 1899. Its major work was concentrated in the eighteenth-century dynasty cemeteries at Koptos, Der-al-Ballas and Naja-ed-Der. From 1903 to 1905 the Hearst expedition excavated in the northern third of the great cemetery of the first pyramid at Gizeh. The University of California expedition was followed by that of the Harvard University–Boston Museum of Fine Arts in 1903. Under the directorship of G. A. Reisner and C. S. Fisher it made extensive diggings around the Great Pyramids; later the work was divided between the Great Pyramid cemetery and the Sudan.[37]

---

[36] Dawson, *op. cit.*, p. 21; *Encyclopaedia Britannica* (14th ed., Chicago, 1947), IV, 80-81; Ludlow Bull and others, "James Henry Breasted, 1856-1935," *Journal of the American Oriental Society*, LVI, No. 2 (June, 1936), 113-20; W. F. Albright, "James Henry Breasted: In Memoriam," *"Bulletin, American Schools of Oriental Research*, No. 61 (Feb., 1936), pp. 2-4; G. E. Hale, "The Work of an American Orientalist," *Scribner's Magazine*, LXXIV (1923), 392-404; C. Breasted, *Pioneer to the Past: The Story of James Henry Breasted, Archaeologist* (New York, 1943), *passim*: Wilson, *Signs and Wonders*, chap. vii.

[37] J. L. Dobbins, "Egyptian Excavations of the University of California as Conducted by George A. Reisner, Ph.D.," *Overland Monthly*, XLII (Aug., 1902), 2nd ser., 99-104; G. A. Reisner, "Recent Explorations in Egypt," *Independent*, LXVIII (1) (Feb. 10, 1910), 302-6; "American Explorations," *American Journal of Archaeology*, III (1899). 2nd ser., 511; Dawson, *op. cit.*, pp. 132-33; G. A. Reisner, "Harvard University–Museum of Fine Arts Egyptian Expedition," *Museum of Fine Arts Bulletin*, IX, No. 50 (Apr., 1911), 13-20; *ibid.*, various reports by Reisner and C. S. Fisher, 1913-1915, *passim*. For a sympathetic sketch of Reisner, see Wilson, *Signs and Wonders*, pp. 144-50.

In 1905, James H. Breasted headed the University of Chicago expedition for three seasons' work in Nubia. He was assisted by Norman de Garris Davies, a British Egyptologist. Chiefly interested in making a comprehensive above-the-ground survey, largely photographic, of existing monuments, they engaged in very little excavation.[38]

The year 1905 was important also for the publication of Breasted's *History of Egypt.*[39] This scholarly work has had a world-wide circulation, and has been a significant factor in stimulating interest in Egyptology. "When it was issued in 1905," L. S. Bull commented,

> it was hailed at once as a monument of sound economy and as an extraordinarily clear and logical presentation of the story of an ancient civilization. It was in this latter quality particularly that the book excelled. The works of one or two other great historians of Egypt show equally sound scholarship, but their chronicles have not the wisdom and enthusiasm of Breasted's. *The History* has held its own unchallenged. . . .[40]

A Frenchman, Henri de Morgan, was selected by the Brooklyn Museum to head its expedition to Egypt in 1906. De Morgan worked chiefly among the tombs in the vicinity of Esuch and Mohamerich. He forwarded a certain number of antiquities to the Museum, but when he died in 1908, the expedition fell apart, and it was never revived.[41]

In 1907 the University of Pennsylvania sent a field expedi-

---

[38] *American Journal of Archaeology*, XIII, 2nd ser. (1909), 72-73; J. H. Breasted, *The Oriental Institute* (Chicago, 1933), pp. 129-68; C. Breasted, *op. cit.*, pp. 140-60.

[39] J. H. Breasted, *A History of Egypt from the Earliest Times to the Persian Conquest* (1st ed., New York, 1905); there was a 2nd ed. in 1909, and there have been numerous reprints.

[40] L. S. Bull and others, *op. cit.*, p. 115.

[41] *N.F.*, Vol. 166, No.. 1491, inst. no. 54 to L. M. Iddings, Cairo, Oct. 10, 1906; *Brooklyn Museum News*, II (1907), 130; H. de Morgan, "Report on Excavations Made in Upper Egypt during the Winter of 1907-08," *Service des Antiquités de l'Egypte, Annales*, XII (1912), 25-50.

tion to Nubia, led by D. Randal MacIver and Leonard Wooley. Diggings were made in and around Wadi Halfa and Anibeh until 1910. The Museum's second expedition, headed by C. S. Fisher, arrived in Egypt in 1914. The group selected a number of sites for excavation, but its operations were interrupted by the outbreak of World War I.[42]

The Metropolitan Museum of Art of New York City established a department of Egyptian art in 1906, with A. M. Lythgoe as curator. Its first Egyptian expedition went into the field in 1907. Lythgoe, H. E. Winlock, A. C. Mace and N. de G. Davies were prominent in the excavations at the Pyramids of Lisht and at Thebes. This museum achieved notable successes in Egypt for approximately thirty years.[43]

In addition to the work of the American museums and universities, mention must also be made of the contributions of a private American citizen, Theodore M. Davis. Active in Egyptology since the 1880's, Davis advanced substantial funds for excavations actually undertaken by officials of the Egyptian Service des Antiquités. The American's disinterested generosity was evident in his agreement with the Egyptian Government that all discoveries become the property of the Egyptian Museum at Cairo. Most of the Davis-financed digging was done in the Valley of the Kings near Luxor; between 1902 and 1912 some astonishing finds were made, such as the discovery of the tomb of Queen Hatshepsut. Toward the end of this intensive period of excavation, Davis stated that the Valley of the Kings was "exhausted." And so it appeared, until Howard Carter and Lord

[42] *American Journal of Archaeology*, XIII, 2nd ser. (1909), 71; *ibid.*, XIV, 2nd ser. (1910), 99-100; *ibid.*, XV, 2nd ser. (1911), 82-83, 406; *Museum Journal*, VI, No. 2 (Philadelphia, June, 1915), 63; *D.F.*, 883.927/1-3, correspondence regarding Univ. of Pennsylvania expedition to Egypt, Nov. 2, Nov. 7 and Dec. 2, 1914; Winlock's field work is described in Wilson, *Signs and Wonders*, pp. 184-92.

[43] L. S. Bull, "The Work of the Metropolitan Museum in Egypt, 1907-1923," *Art and Archaeology*, XVI, No. 6 (Dec. 1923), 211-24; *ibid.*, XVII, Nos. 1, 2 (Feb., 1924), 19-42; Dawson, *op. cit.*, pp. 99, 170.

Carnarvon astounded the world with their discovery of Tutankhamen's fabulous tomb in 1924.[44]

It should be apparent from this brief survey that the United States achievement in the field of Egyptology, especially after 1899, was very great indeed. James Henry Breasted stands out among American Egyptologists. His versatility was shown in scholarship, teaching, writing and administration. In all fairness it should be noted that the United States produced a number of other less well known but highly qualified Egyptologists. Such men as George Reisner and A. M. Lythgoe, to name only two, were the backbone of the great field expeditions sent to Egypt by the large American universities and museums. These archaeologists not only advanced the science of Egyptology but secured many important acquisitions for American museums. The expeditions, financed by wealthy philanthropists, who also assisted the E.E.F. and the British School of Archaeology, were well equipped, and their work was characterized by a scientific methodology and thoroughness. John A. Wilson, director of the Oriental Institute of Chicago, surveying the progress of Egyptology since 1908, has succinctly summarized the American achievements:

> The last thirty years have seen excavation recognized as a profession with high standards of technique. Detailed examination of objects *in situ*, thoroughgoing methods of recording, and ingenious devices to rescue perishing evidence are giving the world a noteworthy documentation of past days. The same period has been characterized by refinement of facts and theories which result from archaelogy. Several names stand honorably in this period. To mention only one, the American Egyptologist George Reisner has had a very wide influence by his insistence upon a careful control of materials found.[45]

---

[44] James Baikis, *A Century of Excavation in the Land of the Pharaohs* (New York, 1924), pp. 167-76; "American Discoveries in Egypt," *National Geographic Magazine*, XLIII, No. 5 (May, 1923), 461-508; Dawson, *op. cit.*, p. 45; Wilson, *Signs and Wonders*, pp. 115-23.

[45] J. A. Wilson, "The Present State of Egyptian Studies," *The Haverford Symposium on Archaeology and the Bible*, ed. Elihu Grant (New Haven, 1938), p. 208.

The United States contribution to Egyptology was recognized
by the invitation of prominent American Egyptologists to the
International Archaeological Congress held at Cairo in April,
1909.[46]

The high caliber and non-political nature of American archaeological work in Egypt created additional good will for the
United States. Undoubtedly the American Egyptologists differed
with the Egyptian Government over allocation of digging concessions and division of finds (division of finds became an increasingly serious problem after World War I), but apparently
nothing was serious enough to require the intervention of the
United States agents and consuls-general.[47]

---

[46] Those invited from the U.S. included J. S. Hoppin, Walter Den-
nison, J. H. Breasted, G. A. Reisner, A. M. Lythgoe, Paul Baur and Theodore M. Davis. *N.F.*, Vol. 790, No. 11977, unnum. desp. from L. M.
Iddings, Cairo, Feb. 18, 1908; *ibid.*, insts. nos. 159, 194 and 221 to Iddings,
Apr. 7, June 29 and Nov. 6, 1908; *ibid.*, tel. to Iddings, Apr. 2, 1909.

[47] This statement is based on the negative evidence of the absence of
any mention of these matters in the Dept. of State correspondence.

Conclusion

Were United States relations with Egypt plotted on a graph, political activities would show up somewhat as follows: 1832–1848, an almost flat line indicating practically no developments of consequence during the Alexandria consulate; 1848–1861, a short sharp rise for the early consulate-general period; 1861–1865, an equally definite decline during the Civil War; 1865–1882, a gradually ascending curve reaching a peak in the twelve years after 1870; and 1882–1914, a gradual dip to a plateau reflecting a final stabilized relationship with the British occupation. Economic relations would be indicated: 1832–1861, a jagged, very gradual rise indicating the uneven, slow development of early United States–Egyptian trade; 1861–1865, a sharp decline resulting from the absence of trade during the Civil War; 1865–1914, a slowly ascending line reflecting the healthy, steady increase in commerce after stabilization in 1873. A chart for missionaries' activities would depict constant growth and expansion during the entire period from their arrival in 1856 to 1914. The graph of the work of American Egyptologists would show a slowly rising curve from the 1830's to reflect the gradual development of interest in Egyptology in the United States; after 1900 the line would suddenly shoot almost straight up to represent the spectacular achievements of the following fourteen years.

This brings us to the most interesting and crucial question raised by this paper. Why were United States political and economic relations with Egypt so negligible, particularly in view of the comparatively greater development of cultural relations between the two countries? The matter is worth exploring, even though it is very complicated and a definitive explanation may not be forthcoming.

The easiest approach to this problem is from the cultural side.

In assessing the contribution of the American missionaries in Egypt, one is immediately faced with the difficulty of making qualitative evaluation of spiritual matters. Nevertheless, certain data are available. The missionaries had virtually no success in proselytizing Muslims, though this was their purpose in coming to Egypt and though it remained their officially avowed goal. Instead, the American Presbyterians gained converts largely from the ranks of the Copts, a minority group in Egypt. The American missionaries, undisturbed by the fact that the Coptic Church was an ancient Eastern Christian church, regarded the Copts as ignorant followers of heretical doctrines. Matters of faith are involved here; and while not questioning the sincerity of the missionaries, one cannot but feel a certain sympathy for the Coptic Patriarch, who in a moment of exasperation raised the question of just who it was that had the "Holy Gospel."

The American Mission was on surer ground when employing the traditional instrumentalities of doctors and teachers, both for spreading Christianity and for performing good works per se. From all reports, American doctors and hospitals did excellent work with the available facilities. On the whole the Mission schools were praiseworthy; there is some suggestion, however, that the quality, particularly of the Evangelical schools, needed improvement. The Mission realized this and just before the outbreak of World War I took remedial steps. Educational work was confined mainly to the Copts, although a fair percentage of Muslims and others also attended. French and other foreign schools provided competition for the Mission's schools, and after 1900 the quality of the Egyptian government schools improved. In the over-all picture it is well to remember that while American missionary schools did laudable work, enlightened Egypt retained its French cultural orientation throughout the entire period under consideration.

American interest in Egyptology was slow in developing. Prior to 1900 it emphasized building collections of Egyptian antiquities, in training competent personnel and in assisting British archaeological organizations in Egypt with substantial donations. The flowering of American Egyptology came after 1900, when a series of large-scale expeditions, sponsored by the great universities and museums, was sent to Egypt. Such expert archaeological leaders as Breasted, Reisner and Lythgoe achieved substantial results, characterized by the most advanced scientific methodology. Their contributions equaled the best European efforts.

The work of American missionaries and Egyptologists stood somewhat apart from other United States activities in Egypt. It did not exist in a vacuum, of course; but the political and economic implications flowing from their action were relatively small. Such difficulties as the Egyptologists must have encountered in securing suitable digging sites and in dividing the finds were not severe enough to require official United States diplomatic assistance. The missionaries had their troubles, demanding in some instances excessive attention from the Department of State. But for a variety of reasons—primarily their concentration on the Copts, a docile minority—their relations with the Egyptian Government were relatively serene. Both missionaries and Egyptologists benefited from the absence of United States imperialistic designs on Egypt.

A Johnny-come-lately, the United States reached Egypt only in 1832, via the Sublime Porte. With no background of previous commercial relations with Egypt, Americans found European merchants already well established. To a centuries-old trade rivalry the British and French added—after Napoleon's brief campaign in Egypt—political and strategic competition. Furthermore, shortly after the establishment of the United States consulate at Alexandria, the European Powers dictated the settlement of 1841, by the terms of which Mehmed 'Ali, the Egyptian Pasha, though confined to Egypt, was granted considerable autonomy under the suzerainty of the Turkish Sultan. This arrangement, though modified to expand the powers of the Egyptian rulers, governed Egypt's existence until 1914. The salient fact in all this was the highly complicated background of European Power competition in United States political and economic relations with Egypt.

Both the Turkish Sultan and the Egyptian Viceroy welcomed

the arrival of the United States, seeking a counterpoise to the two powerful rivals for control of Egypt—Great Britain and France. But America responded slowly. Trade, the initial attraction, did not amount to much before the Civil War. Participation in the capitulatory regime (and later in the Mixed Courts of Egypt)—privileges acquired by the Turkish Treaty of 1830—compelled at least a steady minimal attention by the Department of State and gave the early American consuls-general a chance to perform their duties with a zeal far in excess of America's power position and interest in Egypt at that time. The truth is, however, that the United States Government did not intervene actively in Egyptian affairs despite the urgings of American consuls-general and, on occasions, of the Egyptian and Turkish governments. Congressional apathy toward Egypt was epitomized in the failure in 1884 to make an appropriation for an American representative of any sort at Cairo. In the 1870's some evidence suggested that the United States might be abandoning its non-interventionist policy: the "American military mission" to the Khedive, application for membership on the Khedive's Debt Liquidation Commission and Minister to Turkey Lewis Wallace's (unsuccessful) attempt at good offices between the British and the Sultan on the eve of the bombardment of Alexandria. Such as they were, however, American intentions coincided with a determined Anglo-French political and financial assault on Egypt, culminating in Great Britain's occupation of Egypt in 1882.

Even before 1882, American consuls-general at Cairo had shown considerable Anglophobia and suspicion of Britain's intentions toward Egypt. Such sentiments were also not lacking among United States congressmen. Indeed, some of these suspicions appear to be documented in Lewis Wallace's abortive attempt at good offices. After the British military occupation of 1882, American consuls of the early 1880's retained their hostility. Later United States representatives, however, held more favorable views. The position of the United States Government was officially correct. It agreed to certain minor British reforms in Egypt but emphatically refused to accept any substantial modifications of the capitulations, and fought very hard on the question of appointment of judges for the Mixed Courts of Egypt. Most British requests were accepted as an accommodation to the Khedive. It is well to remember that the United States and England were not allies until World War I.

And so we come again to the question of why there was not greater United States intervention in the political and economic affairs of Egypt. The logical place to look for the answer would seem to be the instructions from the Department of State. But the Department, though it threw out a few hints from time to time, never made a really definitive statement on the subject. In declining intervention in 1868, for instance, the phrase "remoteness from Egypt" was used.[1] Again in 1876 mention was made of "our comparatively small political and unfortunately small commercial relations with Egypt."[2] More significantly, although speaking unofficially to the press, Second Assistant Secretary of State William Hunter in 1879, after referring to the folly of meddling with the Egyptian debt, stated that "our policy is to let the affairs of the old world alone."[3] The Department made another valuable statement in 1887 when it declared: "The Egyptian Question involves highly important interests, extensive and complicated pertaining almost wholly to the leading European states which, from the propinquity of their possessions to the Suez Canal or their dependence upon the commercial facilities it affords, are naturally the chief parties interested in its settlement."[4]

Hunter's statement and the reference in the instruction of 1887 to the fact that the Egyptian Question involved almost wholly European interests gives us real clues. The Egyptian Question was but one aspect of the so-called Eastern Question, with its many ramifications involving the integrity of the Otto-

---

[1] *C. I., B.P.*, 14, inst. No. 49 to Charles Hale, U.S.A.C.G., Alexandria, Jan. 13, 1868.

[2] *C.I., Eg.*, 16, inst. No. 27 to E. E. Farman, Cairo, Nov. 25, 1876.

[3] New York *Times*, Sept. 3, 1879.

[4] *D.I., Turk.*, 4, inst. No. 6 to Oscar Straus, U.S. Min., Constantinople, Apr. 15, 1887.

man Empire, the defense of India and so on. This meant that even apart from their commercial importance per se, the fates of Egypt and the Suez Canal were intimately tied to Europe. President Washington in his farewell address in 1796 gave his now famous advice that the United States should not become involved in European entanglements. Whatever its original ambiguities and subsequent interpretations, the concept had remained basic in American political thought, and its application to Europe, at least, was never seriously questioned prior to 1914. The application of Washington's "Great Rule" to Turkey in Europe (the Balkans) and the Straits seems clear. And although never so stated by the Department of State, the extension of the doctrine to Egypt appears a logically inevitable step, not only on the grounds of the Europeanized political and economic climate of the Nile Valley but also because of Egypt's propinquity to Europe and her inclusion within the Ottoman Empire. This would account for America's refusal to intervene in the complicated politico-financial maneuvers in Egypt prior to the British occupation. Even after 1882, Egypt still should be considered basically a European problem. Although England was in sole occupation, her position was not clearly defined. France was definitely hostile, at least until 1904; after that Germany was an irritant. Washington's interdiction would seem still applicable, therefore, to deter United States political meddling in Egypt on the ground of either a possible clash with Great Britain or possible involvement in the pre–World War I system of alliances and alignments.

There were undoubtedly other factors that prevented serious American political involvement in Egypt. For one, Egypt was technically under Turkish sovereignty through 1914. The Porte consistently pointed this out to the Department of State. It was a moral argument that may have had some influence. Great emphasis, however, should not be placed on this as a deterrent. Certainly it never stopped the European Powers.

Two queries can be raised to the above explanation. For one thing, it does not account for the paucity of United States–Egyptian trade. There is nothing in Washington's dictum forbidding commercial relations in any part of the world. Department of State instructions again are of little assistance. But American consular officials in Egypt did offer many suggestions for remedying the situation. For the most part their recommendations—involving improving business methods, shipping facilities and credit facilities—failed to reach the heart of the problem. Before attempting an answer, perhaps we might instructively look at yet another criticism. How is it that United States trade flourished in the Far East, notably in China and Japan, during this same period? American clipper ships were in the China trade at a very early date, and in ingenuity and enterprise Yankee merchants were second only to the British. Furthermore, the United States Government was an active participant in opening China and Japan for American traders and at a later date in trying to secure the open-door principle in the face of European spheres of influence in China.

The following is suggested as an answer to both queries: Whatever President Washington's original intention (and there is considerable ambiguity in his language), his Great Rule was never in fact applied to American relations in the Far East as it was in Europe. America's westward continental expansion quite possibly helped to produce a sort of *Drang nach Westen*. (If the United States had done the naming, the Orient might well have been called the Far West.) Further considerations were involved. American merchants were active in the China trade since the last decades of the eighteenth century, competing with the British, French and Portuguese almost from the beginning. Therefore, when in 1842 the British for the first time used force to secure privileges from the Chinese, the United States Government soon secured most-favored-nation benefits for American merchants. This wedding of politics and economics continued in the Far East during the remainder of the nineteenth century and beyond.

The Egyptian situation was decidedly different. There, as was mentioned above, American merchants upon their arrival in Alexandria found that European traders had preceded them by several centuries and naturally resented the prospect of competition. Add to this an original discouragement of identity of basic agricultural products of the two countries. These difficulties might have been overcome had it not been for an even more crucial matter. Although technically free from the restraints of Washington's interdiction, American merchants contemplating trade prospects with Egypt must have been oppressed by the Europeanized atmosphere in a country where commerce, politics and strategy were so tightly interwoven. What is more, Yankee traders in Egypt could not expect the assistance from their government that they received in the Far East. Other factors may well have been involved, but this analysis appears to account for the actual initial apathy of American traders and shippers. Later the Civil War was a destructive force in United States–Egyptian trade; with it came the cotton boom in Egypt and the inevitable tightening of the British financial grip on the Egyptian economy. By the time the United States had completed her continental expansion and become partly industrialized, looking now for new markets, the Anglo-French dual financial control had been established, to be followed by the British occupation of 1882. Somewhat contrary to expectation the largest increase in United States–Egyptian trade occurred between 1882 and 1914. But in 1910 the United States had only 3 or 4 per cent of Egypt's total trade.

The above comments make apparent the limited character of United States participation in Egyptian affairs on political and economic levels (especially when compared to that of Great Britain and France) but relatively more extensive participation in cultural matters. This peculiar combination built for the United States a great reservoir of good will. Numerous quotations from both Turkish and Egyptian sources have been cited in this study praising the position of the United States—unique among the Great Powers—as free from the desire to take political or economic advantage of Egypt. The refusal of the United States Government to make political capital out of the presence of an "unofficial military mission" in Egypt typified this attitude. In like manner America refuted the old imperialist maxim that missionaries are the precursors of political and commercial exploitation. Of course, after 1882 the presence in Egypt of the British occupying forces considerably lessened opportunities, had they been sought, for American penetration. Similar conduct elsewhere in the Near and Middle East during this period was building a like measure of friendly feeling toward the United States.

One result of the United States' disinterested activity in Egypt and in other parts of the Near East was that the Turkish Sultans, the Viceroys and Khedives of Egypt, and others frequently tried to draw her into more active political participation. Undoubtedly the motive was to set up the United States as a counterfoil to the more predatory European states. Various approaches were employed. There was, for example, Khedive Tawfiq's earnest expression of hope in 1879 that America would play a more active role in Egyptian affairs. A more notable example was the previously mentioned attempt by the United States at good offices between the British and the Turkish Sultan, at the Sultan's request. A failure here cooled American enthusiasm for this type of intervention, and in 1888 the United States declined a suggestion by Sir Stephen Lakeman, an Englishman employed in the Turkish Government, that it propose a settlement of the Egyptian Question. The United States also received several offers, or at least suggestions of offers, of naval bases in Mediterranean and Near Eastern waters. One such overture was made by the Greek Government in 1854 as a consequence of Consul-General de Leon's assistance to Greek residents in Egypt. Other instances, not previously recorded in this book but mentioned in despatches from Constantinople, included a report in 1836 of Turkish offers to sell to the United States various islands, including Cyprus and several islands near Negropont (Eubosa) Island (near Greece), and a Turkish proposal in 1874 to lease strategic Bab-el-Mandeb (at the Aden end of the Red Sea) to the United States as a coaling and fitting station. None of the offers and suggestions tempted the United States to play a more active role in Turkish and Egyptian affairs. Indeed, this non-interventionist attitude was characteristic of pre–World War I American approach to world affairs generally. One detects in this aloofness an occasional holier-than-thou attitude. However this may be, the United States retained her great popularity with the Egyptian and other Near Eastern governments up to and after World War I.

Appendices

APPENDIX A

CONSULAR OFFICERS BY POST: EGYPT, 1835–1914

Name	Office	Appointed From	Appointment Date
	Alexandria, Egypt		
Gliddon, John[1]	Con.	– –	Mar. 3, 1835
Tod, Alexander	Con.	– –	Aug. 14, 1844 —recess
			Jan. 13, 1845 —cnfd.
Humphrey, Henry B.	Con.	Mass.	Apr. 2, 1845 —never served
Macauley, Daniel S.	Con.-Gen.	Pa.	Aug. 14, 1848
Jones, Richard B.	Con.-Gen.	Pa.	Dec. 28, 1852
De Leon, Edwin	Con.-Gen.	S.C	May. 24, 1853 —recess
			Apr. 18, 1854 —cnfd.
Thayer, William S.	Con.-Gen.	N.Y.	Mar. 20, 1861
Hale, Charles[2]	Con.-Gen.	Mass.	May 18, 1864
Butler, George H.[2]	Con.-Gen.	Cal.	Mar. 15, 1870
Beardsley, Richard	Agt. & Con.-Gen.	Ind.	July 23, 1872 —recess
			Dec. 11, 1872 —cnfd.

---

[1] Served as U.S. consular agent, Alexandria, from Jan. 13, 1832, to Mar. 3, 1835.

[2] Post of Agt. and Con.-Gen. at Alexandria created by Act of Congress, June 20, 1864; in 1876, Dept. of State admitted clerical error in failing to designate Hale and Butler in this capacity.

Name	Office	Appointed From	Appointment Date
		Cairo, Egypt	
Morley, Frederick	Agt. & Con.-Gen.	Mich.	Feb. 14, 1876 —declined
Farman, Elbert E.	Agt. & Con.-Gen.	N.Y.	Mar. 27, 1876
Wolf, Simon	Agt. & Con.-Gen.	D.C.	June 20, 1881 —recess Oct. 29, 1881 —cnfd.
Pomeroy, George P.	Agt. & Con.-Gen.	N.Y.	July 1, 1882
Cardwell, John	Agt. & Con.-Gen.	Tex.	Oct. 2, 1885
Schuyler, Eugene	Agt. & Con.-Gen.	N.Y.	June 26, 1889
Anderson, John A.	Agt. & Con.-Gen.	Kans.	Feb. 27, 1891
Little, Edward C.	Agt. & Con.-Gen.	Kans.	Nov. 15, 1892 Dec. 8, 1892
Penfield, Frederic C.	Agt. & Con.-Gen.	Conn.	May. 18, 1893 —recess Aug. 25, 1893
Harrison, Thomas S.	Agt. & Con.-Gen.	Pa.	Apr. 2, 1897
Long, John G.	Agt. & Con.-Gen.	Fla.	Oct. 30, 1899 Dec. 13, 1899
Biddle, John W.	Agt. & Con.-Gen.	Minn.	Sept. 8, 1899 Nov. 24, 1903
Iddings, Lewis M.	Agt. & Con.-Gen.	N.Y.	Dec. 15, 1905
Jay, Peter Augustus	Agt. & Con.-Gen.	R.I.	Dec. 21, 1909
Arnold, Olney	Agt. & Con.-Gen.	R.I.	Sept. 2, 1913

Source: Records of the Dept. of State, National Archives, Washington.

APPENDIX B

U.S.–EGYPTIAN TRADE, 1835–1914[3]
(in U.S. dollars)

Year	Egyptian Imports From U.S.	Egyptian Exports to U.S.
1835[4]	1,700	3,933
1844	......	30,048
1845	......	12,399
1855	......	43,592
1856	......	54,979
1857	28,163	106,158
1858	108,197	93,083
1859	13,880	105,399
1860	36,420	71,709
1861	60,420	26,329
1862	3,080	146
1863	......	......
1864	27,531	89,383
1865	......	47,632
1866	......	12,222
1867	39,624	......
1868[5]	41,527	760
1873	225,406	263,318
1874	332,421	270,631
1875	316,735	190,432
1876	287,297	43,819
1877	477,649	146,421
1878	395,962	127,104
1879	365,170	113,316
1880	305,893	187,457
1881	509,058	423,478

---

[3] Despite use of official U.S. sources all figures should be treated with caution particularly prior to 1865.

[4] First year any figures available.

[5] No separate listing for Egypt, 1869-1872.

Year	Egyptian Imports From U.S.	Egyptian Exports to U.S.
1882	756,090	408,968
1883	290,782	320,211
1884	357,808	257,992
1885	549,442	236,470
1886	183,311	264,931
1887	303,257	255,696
1888	268,027	341,997
1889	117,426	648,205
1890	131,531	759,122
1891	200,776	1,595,867
1892	136,274	2,250,484
1893	128,687	3,354,825
1894	181,252	2,165,485
1895	137,694	3,628,462
1896	215,540	8,043,797
1897	323,761	7,027,005
1898	816,915	5,017,707
1899	494,196	7,489,929
1900	1,095,613	8,278,022
1901	1,216,773	7,212,279
1902	1,264,449	11,368,301
1903	692,580	10,714,205
1904	564,957	7,868,244
1905	752,489	8,580,751
1906	3,012,253	8,810,434
1907	2,829,157	16,927,432
1908	1,081,770	5,632,500
1909	901,285	15,165,440
1910	1,200,451	16,623,591
1911	9,944,040	7,216,420
1912	1,994,639	20,369,584
1913	1,660,833	19,907,828
1914	1,930,016	12,311,233

Sources:

1835	*C. D., Cyprus, Alexandria, Stancho*, Vol I, from John Gliddon, U.S. Con., Alex., Jan. 1, 1836.
1844	*Ibid.*, unnum. desp. from Alexander Tod, U.S. Con., Alex., Dec. 26, 1844.

1845   *Ibid.*, unnum. desp., Feb. 20, 1846.
1855-1864 *For. Comm. and Navig.*, 1855-1864, *passim.*
1865-1905 *The Commercial Orient in 1905*, p. 59.
1906-1912 *Comm. Rels.* (1906–1912), *passim.*
1913-1914 *For. Comm. and Navig.*, 1914, p. xiii.

SELECTED BIBLIOGRAPHY

No attempt has been made to present an exhaustive list of titles. Only that material which had a direct bearing on the preparation of the text has been included. Emphasis has been put on sources dealing with American activities in Egypt, as these titles are scattered and difficult to find. Readers seeking additional references to the voluminous literature on Anglo-Egyptian relations should consult the general background references at the end of this list.

UNPUBLISHED MATERIAL IN THE NATIONAL ARCHIVES, WASHINGTON, D.C.

United States, Department of State

Consular Despatches, Egypt, 1835–1906.
Consular Despatches, Great Britain (London, Leeds, Liverpool and Manchester), 1860–1866.
Consular Instructions, Egypt, 1835–1906.
Decimal File, 1910–1914.
Diplomatic Despatches, France, 1830–1906.
Diplomatic Despatches, Great Britain, 1830–1906.
Diplomatic Despatches, Turkey, 1830–1906.
Diplomatic Instructions, France, 1830–1906.
Diplomatic Instructions, Great Britain, 1830–1906.
Diplomatic Instructions, Turkey, 1825–1906.
Notes from France, 1826–1899.
Notes from Great Britain, 1830–1906.
Notes from Turkey, 1867–1906.
Notes to France, 1826–1884.
Notes to Great Britain, 1830–1906.
Notes to Turkey, 1834–1906.
Numerical File, 1906–1910.
Post Records, Cairo (also Alexandria).
Reports of Bureau Officers (Consular Bureau), Vol. II.
Special Missions, Instructions, Vol I.

United States, Navy Department

European Squadron, Letters from Rear Adm. J. W. A. Nicholson, U.S.N., 1882.

Letter Book of U.S.S. *Constitution*, Cruising in Mediterranean, Mar. 3. 1833, to Mar. 1, 1837, Commod. I. D. Elliott, U.S.N.

Letters to Flag Officers Commanding Stations, Vol. 8 (Dec. 7, 1876– May 29, 1886).

United States, War Department

Adjutant General's Office, Letter Book (Letters From), Nov., 1868– Mar, 1884.

Office of Secretary of War, Letters Sent, 1868–1883.

Records of Adjutant General's Office, Letters Received, 1869–1881.

War Office, Register of Letters Received, 1870–1883.

UNPUBLISHED LETTERS—GENERAL

Letter from Assistant Director General, Compagnie Universelle du Canal Maritime de Suez, July 30, 1952.

Papers of Gen. William T. Sherman, Vols. 31-60 (1871–1883), Manuscripts Division, Library of Congress, Washington.

PUBLIC DOCUMENTS

Egypt

General Staff. *General Report on the Province of Kordofan. Submitted to General C. P. Stone, Chief of the General Staff, Egyptian Army, by Major H. G. Prout.* Cairo: Printing Office of the General Staff, 1877.

Journal Officiel de l'Egypte, Dec. 10, 1913, supplement.

Great Britain

Accounts and Papers, 1830–1914.

Bowring, John. "Report on Egypt and Candia in 1832," *Accounts and Papers.* Cmd. 277. XXI (1840).

British Foreign and State Papers, 1830–1914.

Hansard. Parliamentary Debates (3rd ser.). Vol. 272 (July 12-27, 1882). Pp. 253 ff. London: Hansard, 1882.

United States

Congress. "Army Officers who have Signified their Intention of Entering Foreign Service, Letter from the Secretary of War, January 15, 1876, in Compliance with Resolution of the House of Representatives of 6 January, 1876." 44th Cong., 1st Sess., H. Ex. Docs., Vol. 10, No. 78.

——. "Claims to Certain Desert Lands in Egypt" (Frederic Cope Whitehouse). New York City, May 22, 1911. 59th Cong., 1st Sess., S. Docs., Vol. 3, No. 104, December 30, 1905.

——. "Extraterritorial Jurisdiction of the United States, Provision for the Repeal of Sections 4083 to 4130 Revised Statutes, Inclusive, Relative to, Recommended (March 4, 1886)." House Bill 333, 49th Cong., 1st Sess., H. Repts., Vol. 3, No. 864.

——. "Extraterritorial Juridical Rights, Reports and Papers Relative to by the Secretary of State (April 29, 1882)." 47th Cong., 1st Sess., S. Misc. Docs., Vol. I, No. 89.

——. "Letter from the Secretary of State, December 14, 1846, Transmitting a Report upon the Consular System of the United States, in Compliance with a Resolution of the House of Representatives of 10 August, 1846." 29th Cong., 2nd Sess., H. Ex. Docs., Vol. 3, No. 12.

——. Nourse, J. E. "The Maritime Canal of Suez from its Inauguration, November 17, 1869, to the Year 1884. Prepared under Orders of the Bureau of Navigation, Navy Department." 48th Cong., 1st Sess., S. Ex. Docs., Vol. 7, No. 198.

——. Pierce, H. H. D. "Report on Inspection of United States Consulates in the Orient." 59th Cong., 1st Sess., H. Docs., Vol. 97, No. 665, Dec. 15, 1904.

——. "Proceedings at Alexandria, Egypt. Letter from the Secretary of Navy, July 28, 1882, in Response to a Resolution of the House of Representatives of 17 July, 1882." 47th Cong., 1st Sess., H. Misc. Docs., Vol. 12, No. 46.

——. Ravndal, Gabriel Bie. "The Origins of the Capitulations and the Consular Institution." 67th Cong., 1st Sess., S. Docs., Vol. 9, No. 34.

——. Van Dyck, Edward A. "Capitulations of the Ottoman Empire." In two parts: 46th Cong., Spec. Sess., S. Ex. Docs., Vol. 3. No. 3; and 47th Cong., 1st Sess., S. Ex. Docs., Vol. 4, No. 87.

Congressional Globe.

Congressional Record.

GALES and SEATON. *Register of Debates in Congress.* 22nd Cong., 1st Sess., House, Mar. 16, 1832, Vol. 8 (2). P. 2190.

Court Cases. Dainese v. Hale, 8 D.C. 86; 1 MacArthur 86 (1873).

——. Dainese v. Hale, 91 U.S. 13 (1875).

Department of Commerce. *Commercial Relations of the United States with Foreign Countries, 1911–1914.*

——. *Daily Consular and Trade Reports, 1913–1914.*

——. *Foreign Commerce and Navigation of the United States, 1913–1914.*

——. *Foreign Commerce Year Book, 1933.* Washington: Government Printing Office, 1934.

——. *Special Agents Series, 1913–1914.*

——. *Special Consular Reports, 1913–1914.*

Department of Commerce and Labor. *The Commercial Orient in 1905.* Washington: Government Printing Office, 1906.

——. *Commercial Relations of the United States with Foreign Countries, 1903–1910.*

——. *Daily Consular and Trade Reports, 1910–1913.*

——. *Foreign Commerce and Navigation of the United States, 1904–1912.*

——. *Monthly Consular Reports, 1904–1905.*

——. *Monthly Consular and Trade Reports, 1905–1910.*

——. *Special Agents Series, 1905–1912.*

——. *Special Consular Reports, 1905–1912.*

Department of the Interior, Bureau of Education. *An Account of the Systems of Public Instruction in Belgium, Russia, Turkey, Servia and Egypt.* Circular of Information No. 3. Washington: Government Printing Office, 1875. Pp. 261-294.

Department of State. *Abolition of the Capitulations in Egypt. Convention and Protocol between the United States of America and Other Powers. Signed at Montreux, May 8, 1937. And Related Papers.* Treaty Series No. 939. Washington: Government Printing Office, 1939.

——. *Agreement between the United States of America and Egypt regarding Commercial and Customs Regulations, November 16, 1884.* Proc. May 7, 1885; 244 S.L., 1004 Treat. and Con. p. 272. S. Ex. Doc. 48-2, Vol. 1, Pt. 2, No. 47, pp. 272-95. Washington: Government Printing Office, 1884.

——. *Commercial Relations of the United States with Foreign Countries, 1856–1902.*

------. *Consular Regulations.* 3rd ed. rev. and enl. Washington: French and Richardson, 1868.

------. *Consular Reports, 1880–1903.*

------. *Most Favored Nation Treatment in Custom Matters. Provisional Commercial Agreement between the United States of America and Egypt. Effected by Exchange of Notes Signed May 24, 1930.* Executive Agreement Series No. 5. Washington: Government Printing Office, 1930.

------. *Papers Relating to the Foreign Relations of the United States, 1861–1914.*

------. *Special Consular Reports, 1890–1903.*

------. *Treaty Developments.* 2 vols. Washington: Department of State, current as of May, 1952.

Opinions of the Attorney General. Vol. 9, p. 296. Washington: W. H. and O. H. Morrison, 1869.

The Statutes at Large of the United States of America, 1830–1914.

Treasury Department. *Foreign Commerce and Navigation of the United States, 1830–1903.*

REPORTS: MISSIONARY

American Bible Society. *Annual Reports.* New York. 1857–1883.

Board of Foreign Missions of the United Presbyterian Church of North America. *Annual Reports.* Philadelphia. 1866–1914.

General Assembly of the United Presbyterian Church of North America. *Minutes.* Various Places. 1860–1863.

Missionary Review of the World. Various Places. 1878–1914.

BOOKS

ADAM, MADAME JULIETTE (Juliette Lamber). *L'Angleterre en Egypte.* Paris: Imprimerie du Centre, 1922.

ADAMS, CHARLES FRANCIS. "The Confederate Cotton Campaign: Lancashire, 1861–1862," *Trans-Atlantic Historical Solidarity.* Oxford: Clarendon Press, 1913.

BAIKIS, JAMES. *A Century of Excavation in the Land of the Pharaohs.* New York: F. H. Revell Co., 1924.

BAILEY, THOMAS A. *A Diplomatic History of the American People.* 3rd ed. New York: F. S. Crofts and Co., 1946.

BIGELOW, JOHN. *Retrospections of an Active Life.* 5 vols. New York: Doubleday, Page and Co., 1909-1913.

BISHOP, JOSEPH B. *Theodore Roosevelt and His Times: Shown in His Own Letters.* 2 vols. New York: Scribner's Sons, 1920.

BLUNT, WILFRID SCAWEN. *Secret History of the English Occupation of Egypt: Being a Personal Narrative of Events.* London: T. Fischer Unwin, 1907.

BOKTAR, AMIR. *School and Society in the Valley of the Nile.* Cairo: Elias' Modern Press, 1936.

BOWMAN, THOMAS SUTTON. *Report on Boring for Oil in Egypt.* Cairo: Government Press, 1925-1931.

BREASTED, CHARLES. *Pioneer to the Past: The Story of James Henry Breasted, Archaeologist.* New York: Scribner's, 1943.

BREASTED, JAMES HENRY. *A History of Egypt from the Earliest Times to the Persian Conquest.* 2nd ed. New York: Scribner's Sons, 1909.

———. *The Oriental Institute.* Chicago: University of Chicago Press, 1933.

BRINTON, JASPER YEATES. *The Mixed Courts of Egypt.* New Haven: Yale University Press, 1930.

BROADLEY, A. M. *How We Defended Arabi and His Friends: A Story of Egypt and the Egyptians.* London: Chapman and Hall, 1884.

BROWN, J. H. (ed.). *Lamb's Biographical Dictionary of the United States.* Vol. II. Boston: J. H. Lamb and Co., 1900.

BROWN, PHILIP MARSHAL. *Foreigners in Turkey: Their Judicial Status.* Princeton: Princeton University Press, 1914.

CAPART, JEAN (ed.). *Travels in Egypt: Letters of Charles Edwin Wibour.* Brooklyn: Brooklyn Museum, 1936.

CHADWICK, FRENCH E. *The Relations of the United States and Spain in the Spanish-American War.* 2 vols. New York: Scribner's, 1911.

CHAILLÉ-LONG, CHARLES. (Long, Charles C.). *The Burning of Alexandria: American Marines at the Historical Egyptian Massacre.* (Originally in *Evening Star*, Washington, D.C., Pt. III, pp. 7-8, Sunday Mag. Sec., June 2, 1907.) Washington, D.C., 1907.

———. *Central Africa: Naked Truths of Naked People, An Account of Expeditions to the Lake Victoria Nyanza and Makraka Niam-Niam, West of the Bahr-el-Ab'ad (White Nile).* New York: Harper Bros., 1877.

———. *My Life in Four Continents.* 2 vols. London: Hutchinson and Co., 1912.

———. *Three Prophets: Chinese Gordon, Mohammed Ahmed (the Maahdi), Arabi Pasha—Events before and after the Bombardment of Alexandria.* New York: D. Appleton and Co., 1884.

CHARLES-ROUX, FRANÇOIS. *Le Coton en Egypte*. Paris: Librairie Armand Colin, 1908.

CHARLES-ROUX, JULES. *L'Isthme et le Canal de Suez—Historique—Etat Actuel*. 2 vols. Paris: Librairie Hachette et Cie., 1901.

CHIROL, SIR VALENTINE. *The Egyptian Problem*. London: Macmillan and Co., Ltd., 1920.

COLLUM, RICHARD S. *History of the United States Marine Corps*. Philadelphia: L. R. Mamersly and Co., 1890.

COOLEY, JAMES EWING. *The American in Egypt, with Rambles through Arabia Petra and the Holy Land during the Years 1839–1840*. New York: D. Appleton and Co., 1842.

CRABITES, PIERRE. *Americans in the Egyptian Army*. London: Geo. Routledge, 1938.

———. *Ismail: Maligned Khedive*. London: Geo. Routledge, 1933.

———. *The Spoliation of Suez*. London: Geo. Routledge, 1940.

———. *The Winning of the Sudan*. London: Geo. Routledge, 1934.

CROMER, EVELYN BARING, 1st Earl of. *Modern Egypt*. New York: Macmillan Co., 1908.

CROUCHLEY, ARTHUR EDWIN. *The Economic Development of Modern Egypt*. London: Longmans, Green and Co., 1938.

———. *The Investment of Foreign Capital in Egyptian Companies and Public Debt*. Cairo: Government Press, 1936.

CULLUM, BVT. MAJ. GEN. G. W. *Biographical Register of Officers and Graduates of the United States Military Academy at West Point, New York, from its Establishment in 1802*. 8 vols. 3rd ed. red. and ext. Boston: Houghton, Mifflin and Co., 1891, and supplements.

DAWSON, WARREN R. (ed). *Who Was Who in Egyptology: A Biographical Index of Egyptologists; of Travellers; Explorers and Excavators in Egypt; of Collectors and Dealers in Egyptian Antiquities; of Consuls, Officials, Authors and Others whose Names occur in the Literature of Egyptology from the Year 1700 to the Present Days, but Excluding Persons now Living*. London: Egyptian Exploration Society, 1951.

DE LEON, EDWIN. *The Khedive's Egypt, or the Old House of Bondage under New Masters*. London: Sampson, Low, Marston, Searle and Rivington, 1879.

———. *Thirty Years of My Life on Three Continents*. 2 vols. London: Ward and Downey, 1890.

DODWELL, HENRY HERBERT. *The Founder of Modern Egypt: A Study of Muhammad 'Ali.* Cambridge, Eng.: Cambridge University Press, 1931.

DOR, V. EDOUARD (Bey.). *L'Instruction Publique en Egypte.* Paris: Lacroix, Verboeckhoven et Cie., 1872.

DYE, WILLIAM MCENTYRE. *Moslem Egypt and Christian Abyssinia; or Military Service under the Khedive, in his Provinces and beyond their Borders, as Experienced by the American Staff.* New York: Atkin and Prout, 1880.

ELLISON, THOMAS. *The Cotton Trade of Great Britain.* London: Effingham, Wilson, Royal Exchange, 1886.

ELLSWORTH, CAPT. HARRY A., U.S.M.C. *One Hundred Eighty Landings of the United States Marines, 1800–1934: A Brief History.* In two parts; Part One. Mimeographed. No place given, 1934.

FARMAN, ELBERT ELI. *Egypt and Its Betrayal: An Account of the Country during the Periods of Ismail and Tewfiq Pashas, and of how England Acquired a New Empire.* New York: Grafton Press, 1908.

FELLER, A. H., and HUDSON, MANLEY O. *A Collection of the Diplomatic and Consular Regulations of Various Countries.* 2 vols. Washington: Carnegie Endowment for International Peace, 1933.

FINNEY, DAVIDA. *Tomorrow's Egypt.* Pittsburgh: Woman's General Missionary Society, 1939.

FITZGERALD, PERCY. *The Great Canal at Suez: Its Politics, Engineering and Financial History, with an Account of the Struggles of its Projector, Ferdinand de Lesseps.* 2 vols. London: Tinsley Bros., 1876.

GHORBAL, SHAFIK. *The Beginnings of the Egyptian Question and the Rise of Mehmed Ali.* London: Geo. Routledge, 1928.

GIFFEN, J. KELLY. *The Egyptian Sudan.* New York: F. H. Revell and Co., 1905.

GLIDDON, GEORGE R. *An Appeal to the Antiquarians of Europe on the Destruction of Monuments of Egypt.* London: J. Madden and Co., 1841.

——. *Appendix to "The American in Egypt."* Philadelphia: Merrihew and Thompson, 1842.

——. *Ancient Egypt: Her Monuments, Hieroglyphics, History and Archaeology, and other Subjects connected with Hieroglyphical Literature.* Baltimore: W. Taylor and Co., 1847.

——. *Handbook of the American Panorama of the Nile: Being the*

Original Transparent Lecture Exhibited in London. London: J. Madden and Co., 1849.

——. *A Memoir on the Cotton of Egypt.* London: J. Madden and Co., 1841.

——. *Otia Aegyptiaca: Discourses on Egyptian Archaeology and Hieroglyphical Discoveries.* London: J. Madden and Co., 1849.

GOODRICH, LT. COMM. CASPER FREDERICH. *Report on the British Naval and Military Operations in Egypt, 1882.* War Series No. 3. U.S. Office of Naval Intelligence, Bureau of Navigation, Navy Department. Washington: Government Printing Office, 1883.

GORDON, LELAND JAMES. *American Relations with Turkey, 1830–1930: An Economic Interpretation.* Philadelphia: University of Pennsylvania Press, 1932.

GORRINGE, HENRY H., Lt. Comm., U.S.N. *Egyptian Obelisks.* New York: Privately printed, 1882.

HACKWORTH, GREEN H. *Digest of International Law.* 8 vols. Washington: Government Printing Office, 1940.

HALLBERG, CHARLES W. *The Suez Canal: Its History and Diplomatic Importance.* New York: Columbia University Press, 1831.

HARRISON, THOMAS SKELTON. *The Homely Diary of a Diplomat in the East, 1897–1899.* Boston: Houghton, Mifflin Co., 1917.

HEITMAN, FRANCIS B. *Historical Register and Dictionary of the United States Army from its Organization, September 29, 1789, to March 2, 1903.* 2 vols. Washington, 1903.

HESSELTINE, WILLIAM B., and WOLF, HAZEL B. *The Blue and the Gray on the Nile.* Chicago: University of Chicago Press, 1961.

HEYWORTH-DUNNE, J. *An Introduction to the History of Education in Modern Egypt.* London: Luzac and Co., 1938.

HINCKLEY, FRANK E. *American Consular Jurisdiction in the Orient.* Washington: W. H. Lowdermilk and Co., 1906.

HOGG, RENA L. *A Master Builder on the Nile: Being a Record of the Life and Work of John Hogg, D.D., Christian Missionary.* New York: F. H. Revell Co., 1914.

HOSKINS, HALFORD LANCASTER. *British Routes to India.* London: Longmans, Green and Co., 1928.

HUME, W. F. *Report on the Oilfields Region of Egypt.* Cairo: Government Press, 1916.

HUREWITZ, J. C. (ed.). *Documents of Near East Diplomatic History.* Mimeographed. New York: Columbia University Press, 1950.

HYDE, CHARLES CHENEY. *International Law Chiefly as Interpreted by the United States.* 3 vols. 2nd ed. Boston: Little, Brown and Co., 1945.

ISSAWI, CHARLES PHILIP. *Egypt: An Economic and Social Analysis.* London: Oxford University Press, 1947.

JAMISON, WALLACE N. *The United Presbyterian Story: A Centennial Study, 1858–1958.* Pittsburgh: Geneva Press, 1958.

LANSING, REV. GULIAN. *Egypt's Princes: A Narrative of Missionary Labor in the Valley of the Nile.* New York: Robert Carter and Bros., 1865.

LATIMER, CHARLES. *The French Metric System, or the Battle of the Standards: A Discussion of the Comparative Merits of the Metric System and the Standards of the Great Pyramid.* Cleveland: J. B. Savage, 1879.

LAY, TRACY H. *The Foreign Service of the United States.* New York: Prentice-Hall, Inc., 1928.

LESSEPS, FERDINAND, VISCOUNT DE. *Lettres, Journal et Documents pour Servir à l'Histoire du Canal de Suez, 1875–81.* 8 vols. Paris: Didier et Cie., 1875-1885.

———. *Recollections of Forty Years.* English trans. by C. B. Pitman. 2 vols. London: Chapman and Hall, 1887.

LLOYD, GEORGE AMBROSE LLOYD, BARON. *Egypt Since Cromer.* 2 vols. London: Macmillan and Co., 1933-1934.

LONGRIGG, STEPHEN H. *Oil in the Middle East: Its Discovery and Development.* London: Oxford University Press, 1954.

LORING, WILLIAM WING. *A Confederate Soldier in Egypt.* New York: Dodd, Mead and Co., 1884.

McKEE, IRVING. *"Ben Hur" Wallace: The Life of General Lew Wallace.* Los Angeles: University of California Press, 1947.

MALLOY, WILLIAM M. (ed.). *Treaties, Conventions, International Acts, Protocols and Agreements between the United States and Other Powers, 1776–1909.* 3 vols. Washington: Government Printing Office, 1910.

MALONE, DUMAS (ed.). *Dictionary of American Biography,* Vol. XVIII. New York: Scribner's Sons, 1936.

MARRIOT, J. A. R. *The Eastern Question: An Historical Study in European Diplomacy.* 3rd ed. London: Oxford University Press, 1924.

MATTHEWS, RODERIC D., and AKRAWI, MATTA. *Education in Arab Countries of the Near East.* Washington: American Council on Education, 1949.

MILLER, DAVID HUNTER. *Treaties and other International Acts of the United States.* 5 vols. Washington: Government Printing Office, 1933.

MILLIGAN, ANNA A., and McLANAHAN, FRANK C. *Dr. Henry of Asiut: Pioneer Medical Missionary in Egypt.* Philadelphia: United Presbyterian Board of Foreign Missions, 1945.

MILNER, ALFRED MILNER, 1ST VISCOUNT. *England in Egypt.* 13th ed. London: Edward Arnold, 1926.

MITCHELL, L. H. *Ras Gemsah and Gebel Zeit: Report on their Geology and Petroleum.* Cairo: National Printing Office, 1887.

MOLDENKE, CHARLES E. *The New York Obelisk: Cleopatra's Needle, with a Preliminary Sketch of the History, Erection, Uses and Significance of Obelisks.* New York: A. D. F. Randolph and Co., 1891.

MOORE, JAMES BASSETT. *A Digest of International Law.* 8 vols. Washington: James T. White and Co., 1901.

NUSSBAUM, ARTHUR. *A Concise History of the Law of Nations.* New York: Macmillan and Co., 1947.

OPPENHEIM, L. *International Law: A Treatise.* 2 vols. Ed. by H. Lauterpacht. 8th ed. London: Longmans, Green and Co., 1940.

OWSLEY, FRANK LAWRENCE. *King Cotton Diplomacy: Foreign Relations of the Confederate States of America.* 2nd ed., rev. by H. C. Owsley. Chicago: University of Chicago Press, 1959.

PADELFORD, NORMAN J. *The Panama Canal in Peace and War.* New York: Macmillan and Co., 1942.

PARKER, JOSEPH I. (ed.). *Interpretative Statistical Survey of the World Mission of the Christian Church.* London: International Missionary Council, 1938.

PAULLIN, CHARLES OSCAR. *Diplomatic Negotiations of American Naval Officers, 1778–1883.* Baltimore: Johns Hopkins Press, 1912.

PENFIELD, FREDERIC COURTLAND. *Present Day Egypt.* New York: Century Co., 1899.

PRIESTLY, HERBERT INGRAM. *The Mexican Nation: A History.* New York: Macmillan and Co., 1935.

PRIME, WILLIAM COWPER. *Boat Life in Egypt and Nubia.* New York: Harper and Bros., 1857.

RADWAN, ABU AL-FUTOUH AHMED. *Old and New Forces in Egyptian Education: Proposals for the Reconstruction of the Program of Egyptian Education in the Light of Recent Cultural Trends.* New York: Teachers College, Columbia University, 1951.

RICHARDSON, J. D. (comp.). *A Compilation of Messages and Papers of the Presidents, 1789-1908.* 7 vols. New York: Bureau of National Literature and Art, 1909.

RIPPY, JAMES FRED. *The United States and Mexico.* New York: F. S. Crofts and Co., 1926.

RIVLIN, HELEN A. B. *The Agricultural Policy of Muhammad 'Ali in Egypt.* Cambridge, Mass.: Harvard University Press, 1961.

ROOSEVELT, THEODORE. *African and European Addresses.* New York: G. P. Putnam and Co., 1910.

SATOW, SIR ERNEST. *A Guide to Diplomatic Practice.* 2 vols. 2nd rev. ed. London: Longmans, Green and Co., 1922.

SCHERER, JAMES A. B. *Cotton as a World Power.* New York: F. A. Stokes and Co., 1916.

SCHUYLER, EUGENE. *American Diplomacy and the Furtherance of Commerce.* New York: Scribner's, 1886.

———. *Selected Essays, with a Memoir by Evelyn Schuyler Schaeffer.* New York: Scribner's, 1901.

SCOTT, JAMES HENRY. *The Law Affecting Foreigners in Egypt.* Edinburgh: William Green and Co., 1907.

SIEGFRIED, ANDRÉ. *Suez and Panama.* New York: Harcourt, Brace and Co., 1940.

SOUSA, NASIM. *The Capitulatory Régime in Turkey: Its History, Origin and Nature.* Baltimore: Johns Hopkins Press, 1933.

STEWART, COL. C. E. *Report on the Petroleum Districts Situated on the Red Sea Coasts.* Cairo: National Printing Office, 1888.

TEMPERLEY, H. W. V. (ed.). *A History of the Peace Conference of Paris.* 6 vols. London: Frowde and Hodder and Stoughton, 1920-1924.

UPSON, ARTHUR T. (pseud. Abdul-Fady). *Highlights in the Near East: Reminiscences of Nearly 40 Years' Service.* London: Marshall, Morgan and Scott, 1932(?).

The United States Code Annotated. Title 22, Chap. 2, Secs. 141-182. St. Paul: West Publishing Co., 1952.

WALLACE, LEWIS. *Lew Wallace: An Autobiography.* 2 vols. New York: Harper and Bros., 1906.

WARREN, EDWARD. *A Doctor's Experiences in Three Continents.* Baltimore: Cushings and Bailey, 1885.

WATSON, ANDREW. *The American Mission in Egypt, 1854-1896.* 2nd ed. Pittsburgh: United Presbyterian Church Board of Publications, 1904.

Watson, Charles Roger. *Egypt and the Christian Crusade.* Philadelphia: Board of Foreign Missions of the United Presbyterian Church, 1907.

———. *In the Valley of the Nile: A Survey of the Missionary Movement in Egypt.* New York: F. H. Revell and Co., 1908.

———. *The Sorrow and the Hope of the Egyptian Sudan: A Survey of Missionary Conditions and Methods of Work in the Egyptian Sudan.* Philadelphia: Board of Foreign Missions of the United Presbyterian Church. 1913.

Williams, James. *Education in Egypt before British Control.* Birmingham, Eng.: no publisher given, 1939.

Wilson, Sir Arnold T. *The Suez Canal: Its Past, Present and Future.* 2nd ed. London: Oxford University Press, 1939.

Wilson, Herbert Wrigley. *The Downfall of Spain: Naval History of the Spanish-American War.* Boston: Little, Brown and Co., 1900.

Wilson, John A. *Signs and Wonders upon Pharaoh: A History of American Egyptology.* Chicago: University of Chicago Press, 1964.

Winslow, William C. *The Truth about the Egyptian Exploration Fund.* Boston: Privately printed, 1903.

Wolf, Simon. *Some of the Personal Reminiscences at Home and Abroad of Simon Wolf.* Washington: no publisher given, 1914.

Wolff, Sir Henry Drummond. *Rambling Recollections.* 2 vols. London: Macmillan and Co., 1908.

Young, George. *Egypt.* London: E. Benn, Ltd., 1927.

ARTICLES AND MONOGRAPHS

Abbott, Henry. *Catalogue of a Collection of Egyptian Antiquities, the Property of Henry Abbott, M.D., now Exhibiting at Stuyvesant Institute, New York.* New York: J. W. Watson and Co., 1853.

Albright, W. F. *James Breasted: In Memoriam.* Bulletin, American Schools of Oriental Research, No. 61 (Feb., 1936), pp. 2-4.

"American Discoveries in Egypt," *National Geographic Magazine,* XVIII (Dec. 6, 1907), 801-6.

"American Explorations," *American Journal of Archaeology,* III, Ser. 2 (1899), 511.

"American Influence in Egypt," *Nation,* XXXII (Feb. 3, 1881), 77.

American Journal of Archaeology, XIII, 2nd Ser. (1909), 71, 72-73;

XIV, 2nd Ser. (1910), 72-73; XIV, 2nd Ser. (1910), 99-100; XV, 2nd Ser. (1912), 82-83, 406.

Blessed Be Egypt, VI (Jan., 1905), No. 22, 7, 30-31; VI (Apr., 1905), No. 23, 77-78; VI (Oct., 1905), No. 25, 129-33.

BERNSTEIN, SAMUEL. "The Opposition of French Labor to American Slavery," *Science and Society*, 17 (1952), No. 2, 136-54.

"James Henry Breasted," *Encyclopaedia Britannica* (14th ed.), IV, 80-81.

BRINTON, JASPER Y. "The Closing of the Mixed Courts of Egypt," *American Journal of International Law*, XLIV (1950), 303-12.

Brooklyn Museum News, II (1907), 130.

BULL, LUDLOW, and others. "James Henry Breasted, 1865–1935," *Journal of the American Oriental Society*, LVI (June, 1936), No. 2, 113-20.

BULL, LUDLOW S. "The Work of the Metropolitan Museum in Egypt, 1907-23," *Art and Archaelogy*, XVI, No. 6 (Dec., 1923), 211-40; XVII, Nos. 1, 2 (Feb., 1924), 19-42.

Le Canal de Suez. Bulletin de la Compagnie Universelle du Canal Maritime de Suez, No. 2, 226 (June 15, 1948), p. 9226.

CHAILLÉ-LONG, CHARLES. "La Découverture des Sources du Nil," *Bulletin, Société Khédiviale de Géographie*, III (Cairo, 1891), Ser. no. 7, 539-45.

COONEY, JOHN D. "Acquisition of the Abbott Collection." *Bulletin of the Brooklyn Museum*, X (Spring, 1949), No. 3, 17-23.

COX, FREDERICK J. "The American Naval Mission in Egypt," *Journal of Modern History*, 26 (1954), 173-78.

——. "Arabi and Stone: Egypt's First Military Rebellion, 1882," *Cahiers d'Histoire Egyptienne*, VIII (Apr. 1956), 155-75.

——. "The Suez Canal Incident of 1874," *Cahiers d'Histoire Egyptienne*, IV (Oct., 1952), 194-204.

CROMER, EVELYN BARING, 1st Earl of. "The Capitulation in Egypt," *Nineteenth Century and After*, LXXIV (June, 1913), 1-10.

DAINESE, FRANCIS. *The History of Mr. Seward's Pet in Egypt—his Acts Denounced, and his Usurpations Condemned by the Courts: Memorial to United States Congress in Regard to Charles Hale, Consul to Egypt, December 26, 1866*. Washington, 1867(?).

DAVIS, CHARLES H. S. "Dr. Winslow and the Egyptian Exploration Fund," *Records of the Past*, II (1903), 309-11.

DE LEON, EDWIN. "Ferdinand de Lesseps and the Suez Canal," *Putnam's Magazine*, n.s. III (1869), 647-63.

DINSMOOR, WILLIAM B. "Early American Studies in Mediterranean Archaeology," *Proceedings of the American Philosophical Society,* LXXXIX (1943), No. 1, 70-104.

DOBBINS, J. L. "Egyptian Excavations of the University of California as Conducted by George A. Reisner, Ph.D.," *Overland Monthly,* XLII (Aug., 1902), 2nd ser., 99-104.

EARLE, EDWARD MEADE. "American Missions in the Near East," *Foreign Affairs,* 7:398-417 (1928-29).

———. "Egyptian Cotton and the American Civil War," *Political Science Quarterly,* XLI, No. 4 (Dec., 1926), 520-45.

"Egypt Exploration Fund," *Brooklyn Museum Quarterly,* I (1915), 153, 216.

"The Egypt General Mission, 1898–1905," *Blessed Be Egypt,* VI (Jan., 1905), No. 22, 7.

"Egypt," *Service des Antiquités de l'Egypte, Annales,* XII (1912), 25-50.

FARMAN, ELBERT ELI. "Negotiating for the Obelisk," *Century,* o.s. XXIV; n.s. II (Oct., 1882), 879-89.

GALT, RUSSELL. *The Conflict of French and English Educational Philosophies in Egypt.* Cairo: American University at Cairo, Mar., 1933.

GILBERT, FELIX. "The 'New Diplomacy' of the Eighteenth Century," *World Politics,* X, No. 1 (Oct., 1951), 1-38.

HALE, GEORGE E. "The Work of an American Orientalist," *Scribner's Magazine,* LXXIV (1923), 392-404.

HARRISON, THOMAS S. "Egypt under Lord Cromer," *Forum,* XXVII (Aug., 1899), 651-61.

HOLLAND, T. E. "The International Position of the Suez Canal," *Fortnightly Review,* o.s. XL; n.s. XXXIV (Dec., 1883), 39-49.

ISSAWI, CHARLES. "Egypt since 1800: A Study in Lopsided Development," *Journal of Economic History,* XXI (Mar., 1961), 1-25.

KEASBEY, LINDLEY M. "The National Canal Policy," *American Historical Association, Annual Report 1902,* I (1903), 277-88.

LATANÉ, JOHN H. "The Neutralization Features of the Hay-Pauncefote Treaty," *American Historical Association Annual Report for 1902,* I (1903), 291-303.

LOCKETT, SAMUEL H. "Arabi and his Army," *Nation,* 35 (Sept. 28, 1882), 257-58.

LOGAN, F. A. "India: Britain's Substitute for American Cotton, 1861–1865," *Journal of Southern History,* 24 (Nov., 1958), 472-86.

MAHAN, REAR ADM. A. T., U.S.N. "Fortify the Panama Canal," *North American Review*, CXCIII (Mar., 1911), 331-39.

MENZIES, J. R. "The Nile Mission Press," *Moslem World*, XXVI, No. 2 (Apr., 1936), 161-69.

"Mr. Petrie's Egyptian Research Account," *American Journal of Archaeology*, X (1895), 67-68.

MOLDENKE, CHARLES E. "The Language of the Ancient Egyptians and its Monumental Records," *Transactions of the New York Academy of Sciences*, IV (1887), 60-74.

MORGAN, HENRI DE. "Report on Excavations Made in Upper Egypt during the Winter of 1907–08," *Service des Antiquités de l'Egypte, Annales*, XII (1912), 25-50.

MUNRO, WILLIAM BENNETT. "The Neutralization of the Suez Canal," *Annals of the American Academy of Political and Social Science*, XVII, No. 3 (May, 1901), 409-430.

Museum Journal, VI, No. 2 (Philadelphia, June, 1915), 63.

National Geographic Magazine, XLIII, No. 5 (May, 1923), 461-508.

POOLE, LYNN. "Cohen's First out of Egypt," *Art News*, XLVII, No. 9 (Jan., 1949), 38-39.

A Record of the Nile Mission Press, Silver Jubilee, Cairo, Mar. 12, 1930.

REISNER, GEORGE A. "Harvard University–Museum of Fine Arts Egyptian Expedition," *Museum of Fine Arts Bulletin*, IX, No. 50 (Apr., 1911), 13-20.

———. "Recent Explorations in Egypt," *Independent*, LXVIII (1) (Feb. 10, 1919), 302-6.

SCHMIDT, L. B. "The Influence of Wheat and Cotton on Anglo-American Relations during the Civil War," *Iowa Journal of History and Politics*, XVI (1918), 400-439.

SCHWEINFURTH, G. "The Petroleum Wells of the Red Sea Coast of Egypt," *Athenaeum*, No. 3087 (Dec. 25, 1886), p. 865.

SERPELL, DAVID R. "American Consular Activities in Egypt, 1849–1863," *Journal of Modern History*, X, No. 3 (Sept., 1939), 344-63.

STONE, LT. GEN. CHARLES P. "Military Affairs in Egypt," *Journal of the Military Service Institution of the United States*, V, No. 18 (June, 1884), 154-83.

———. "Stone Pasha and the Secret Despatch" (Ltr. from Lt. Gen. Charles P. Stone, Flushing, L. I., N. Y., Oct. 8, 1886), *Journal*

of the Military Service Institution of the United States, VIII,
No. 29 (Mar., 1887), 94-95.

STONE, FANNY. "Diary of an American Girl in Cairo during the War
of 1882," *Century*, o.s. XVIII; n.s. VI (1884), 288-302.

*United States Army and Navy Journal and Gazette of the Regular
and Volunteer Forces*, XII (Nov. 28, 1874, and Jan. 23, 1875),
215 and 374, resp.; XVI (Aug. 17, 1878), 27; XIX (July 15,
1882), 1164, 1168-69.

VAN SOMMER, ANNIE. "The Work of the Nile Mission Press," *Missionary Review of the World*, o.s. XXIX; n.s. XIX, No. 12 (Dec.,
1906), 928-29.

TIGNOR, ROBERT L. "Some Materials for a History of the Arabi
Revolt: A Biographical Survey," *Middle East Journal*, 16 (Spring,
1962), 239-48.

"The Wilbour Catalogue," *Brooklyn Museum Quarterly*, XI (1924),
169-70.

WILLIAMS, CAROLINE RANSOM. "The Place of the New York Historical Society in the Growth of American Interest in Egyptology,"
Quarterly Bulletin, New York Historical Society, IV (1920), 3-20.

WILSON, JOHN A. "The Present State of Egyptian Studies," *The
Haverford Symposium on Archaeology and the Bible*, ed. Elihu
Grant. New Haven, American Schools of Oriental Research, 1938.

WINSLOW, WILLIAM C. "Egyptian Antiquities in Our Museums,"
Biblia: A Magazine for Oriental Research and Discoveries, VII
(1900), 1-8.

——. "The Egyptian Research Account" (Ltr. to the Editor), *Nation*,
LXXXII (Feb. 8, 1906), 117.

——. "The Queen of Egyptology, Amelia B. Edwards," *American
Antiquarian Magazine*, XIV (1882), 305-15.

WOOLSEY, THEODORE S. "Suez and Panama: A Parallel," *American
Historical Association Annual Report for 1902*, I (1903), 305-11.

The Work of the Egypt Exploration Fund, 1882–1918. London:
Egypt Exploration Fund, 1918.

"World Oil Atlas, 1948," *World Oil*, July 15, 1948, issue, Houston,
Texas, p. 27.

——, 1952, *World Oil*, July 15, 1952, issue, Houston, Texas, p. 71.

WRIGHT, MARCUS J. "Some Bold Diplomacy in the United States in
1861," *American Historical Association Annual Report for 1895*
(1896), pp. 405-10.

Yousuff, Sheikh Ali. "Egypt's Reply to Colonel Roosevelt," *North American Review*, CXCI (June, 1910), 729-37.

NEWSPAPERS

New York *Commercial Advertiser*, Jan. 21 and 23, 1847.
New York *Herald*, 1882.
New York *Times*, 1830–1914.
North American Review (Philadelphia), Feb. 10, 1847.
The Times (London), July 13, 1882, and Apr. 24, 1886.

BIBLIOGRAPHICAL REFERENCES

Ettinghausen, Richard (comp.). *A Selected and Annotated Bibliography of Books and Periodicals in Western Languages Dealing with the Near and Middle East, with Special Emphasis on Mediaeval and Modern Times.* Washington: Middle East Institute, 1952.

Library of Congress, European Affairs Division. *Egypt and the Anglo-Egyptian Sudan: A Selective Guide to Background Reading.* Washington: University Press of Washington, D.C., 1952; same material in Library of Congress, European Affairs Division. *Introduction to Africa.* Washington: University Press of Washington, D.C., 1952, pp. 98-119.

Pratt, Ida (comp.). *Ancient Egypt: Sources of Information in the New York Public Library.* New York: New York Public Library, 1925.

——. *Ancient Egypt, 1925–1941: A Supplement to "Ancient Egypt: Sources of Information in the New York Public Library," 1925.* New York: New York Public Library, 1942.

——. *Modern Egypt: A list of References in the New York Public Library.* New York: New York Public Library, 1929.